QUEEN MERYL

QUEEN MERYL

The Iconic Roles, Heroic Deeds,
and Legendary Life of Meryl Streep

ERIN CARLSON

Illustrations by Justin Teodoro

hachette
BOOKS

NEW YORK   BOSTON

Hachette Books
Hachette Book Group
1290 Avenue of the Americas
New York, NY 10104

hachettebookgroup.com

twitter.com/hachettebooks

First Edition: September 2019

Hachette Books is a division of Hachette Book Group, Inc.
The Hachette Books name and logo are trademarks of Hachette Book Group, Inc.

The publisher is not responsible for websites (or their content) that are not owned by the publisher.

The Hachette Speakers Bureau provides a wide range of authors for speaking events. To find out more, go to www.hachettespeakersbureau.com or call (866) 376-6591.

Illustrations copyright © 2019 by Justin Teodoro

Photo Credits: p. 34: Photo © Jack Mitchell / Getty. p. 39: Photo © Columbia Pictures / Courtesy Everett Collection. p. 64: Photo © Christian Simonpiétri / Getty. p. 71: Photo © ABC Photo Archives / Getty. p. 87: Photo © Barry King / Getty. p. 130: Photo © Time & Life Pictures / Getty. p. 155: Photo © Universal Pictures / Handout / Getty. p. 169: Photo © Archive Photos / Stringer / Getty. p. 240: Photo © Marc Ausset-Lacroix / Getty.

Library of Congress Cataloging-in-Publication Data has been applied for.

ISBNs: 978-0-316-48527-2 (paper over board), 978-0-316-48528-9 (ebook)

Printed in the United States of America

LSC-W

10 9 8 7 6 5 4 3 2 1

To Jennifer Atchison, Caroline Olinger, and Kerry Olinger

Take your heart to work, and ask the most and best of everybody else too. Don't let your special character and values, the secret that you know and no one else does, the truth—don't let that get swallowed up by the great chewing complacency.

> —Meryl Streep's commencement speech to
> the Vassar College Class of 1983

I am a pain in the ass! How can I hide it?

> —Streep to NPR's Terry Gross on
> February 6, 2012

CONTENTS

QUEEN MERYL

Gird Your Loins!

This is a true story verging on legend, and I would be remiss not to tell it again:

A young actress auditions for producer Dino De Laurentiis's 1976 remake of *King Kong*. Virtually unknown outside New York theater circles, she has zero experience working in film. Her long, blonde hair, porcelain skin, high cheekbones, and aquiline nose combine to form otherworldly beauty: the equivalent of the mysterious muse in a Renaissance painting, a Mona Lisa for the '70s. People who witnessed the actress's extraordinary performances onstage could vouch for her talent. But all De Laurentiis sees is her face.

"This is so ugly. Why do you bring me this?" he complains in Italian to son Federico.

Well, *this* had a name: Meryl Streep. And, unfortunately for De Laurentiis, she studied Italian at Vassar College and understands what he's saying.

"I'm very sorry that I'm not as beautiful as I should be but, you know, this is it. This is what you get," she retorts in his native tongue, showing herself the door.

It's pretty safe to assume that De Laurentiis thought twice before repeating the faux pas in an audition room again. He was hardly the last critic to underestimate Meryl, but the moment serves to underline just a few of her character strengths: deep intelligence, grace under pressure, and, when insulted, a steely refusal to humor another Hollywood misogynist. Through ups, downs, more than sixty feature films, dozens of accents, one husband, and four children, Meryl has defied ageism to become the most celebrated actress of the past four decades and counting. She immerses herself in each role, from learning Polish for *Sophie's Choice* to bringing Julia Child back to joyous life in *Julie & Julia*. She never tackles the same character twice. Instead, she leverages her rarified platform to channel a range of unusual, complicated women—Margaret Thatcher, Karen Silkwood, Florence Foster Jenkins—rather than accept the unfulfilling parts for which other actresses must settle: Supportive Wife. Supportive Mother. Supportive (and Mostly Nonspeaking) Love Interest to the Leading Man.

Meryl will have none of that.

Born and raised in New Jersey, she came of age during the second-wave feminist movement and has worn her activism on her sleeve even when it was unfashionable. For instance, in an episode that caused Meryl to be briefly labeled "difficult" and "angry," she skewered *Pretty Woman* and other popular films of the time while delivering a speech at the Screen Actors Guild's first National Women's Conference in 1990: "There's very little work for women," she protested. "And when we do work, we get paid much less than our male counterparts. And what work there is lately is odd."

Given the options available, she joked, one might assume "the chief occupation of women on Earth was hooking, and I don't mean rugs."

That remark likely did not endear her to *Pretty Woman* fans. But Meryl, more interested in humanizing "unlikable" characters that revealed truths about women than in conforming to two-dimensional stereotypes that appealed to men, had been seriously alarmed: As studios devoted more resources to male stars, pushing them front and center, would she have a harder time finding work that mattered to her? Since turning forty in 1989, a time when leading ladies transitioned to Supportive Mother (see Sally Field in *Forrest Gump*), were her days numbered as a movie star? At one point,

Meryl fielded offers for three different witch roles in the same year. "It was almost like the world was saying or the studios were saying, *We don't know what to do with you,*" she said.

Rather than go quietly into the next phase of her career, the Yale Drama grad—for whom acting was a higher calling, not a hobby—plunged forward, choosing material that interested her and winning a pile of awards along the way. She's earned a record number of Oscar nominations, winning Best Actress twice for *Sophie's Choice* and *The Iron Lady* and Best Supporting Actress for *Kramer vs. Kramer.*

Remarkably, Meryl's box-office clout managed to grow with age. *The Devil Wears Prada,* starring the fifty-six-year-old as an indomitable magazine editor, earned $326 million worldwide. Her wildly popular *Mamma Mia!* movies nearly tripled that. The irony, of course, is that Meryl risked a lot by refusing to compromise her artistic ideals, and now—at seventy—she's as bankable as Jennifer Lawrence.

Unlike many artists who lose inspiration over time, Meryl has retained a childlike delight in assuming new identities; she approaches each film as though it were her first. From a distance, she's imperious and queenly, an untouchable—unknowable—stateswoman. Move in closer, and you'll discover the mischievous personality that Streepers love to love and haters love to lament: her refined, aristocratic presence hinting at the playful, fun-loving troublemaker underneath; her creative ambition and risk-taking; her moral authority as a vocal critic of Donald Trump, who called her "one of the most overrated actresses in Hollywood" in an apparent 4 a.m. toilet tweet.

Like the bully in the Oval Office, she courts controversy—and seems to revel in politicizing her pulpit and making her opinions known. Meryl, however, advocates for empathy and equality where Trump emboldens bigots to follow in his path of division and hatred. In these coarsening times, she's embodied an uptown, twenty-first-century equivalent of Rosie the Riveter, increasingly compelled to roll up her sleeves and fight the good fight. Though Meryl speaks her mind, she often prefers to let her movies do the talking. She blazed the trail for younger thespians, including her daughters, to land the kinds of wide-ranging roles that Robert De Niro got to play. Most of all, she represents a meaningful goal for women: the courage to shed fear and inhibition and live a big, bold, authentic life.

This is the story of a shrewd and opinionated girl who first honed her craft in high school, manifesting a dramatic transformation to homecoming queen; a leading lady who outlasted male costars like Jack Nicholson, Dustin Hoffman, and the Roberts (De Niro, Redford) with no sign of slowing down; a mother who conquered the entertainment industry while living in small-town Connecticut. It's the story of the world's greatest living actor. She's known for morphing seamlessly into characters sharply divergent from each other, and from her public persona. But each character represents a key part of her, from Joanna Kramer's independent streak to Miranda Priestly's exceptional competence.

Before you turn the page, dear reader (or shall I say Streeper?), allow me to quote Stanley "the Tooch" Tucci announcing Miranda's arrival in *Prada:* "GIRD YOUR LOINS."

Mary Louise Streep

CHAPTER 1

From Geek to Streep

I wanted to learn how to be appealing. So I studied the character
I imagined I wanted to be, that of the generically pretty high
school girl.

Meryl Streep was six years old when she discovered a talent for getting into character. Her role: the Virgin Mary. The scene: the Streep family living room, standing in for the nativity. Meryl's younger brothers, Harry the Third and Dana, whom she tended to boss around, were cast as Joseph and a barnyard animal, respectively. When Meryl wrapped her mother's half slip around her head and held baby Jesus (her Betsy Wetsy doll), she fell under a trance of quiet holiness that spread like gospel to her siblings, following their sister's solemn lead. While the kids' father, Harry the Second, shot footage on Super 8, Meryl learned an important lesson: she didn't have to yell at her costars to get them to do what she wanted.

Flash-forward a few years: Meryl wanted to experience what it felt like to be her beloved grandmother, so she put on a sweater, took her mother Mary's eyebrow pencil, and drew wrinkle lines all over her face to transform into an older version of herself. To complete the metamorphosis, she stooped as an elderly woman would and channeled her grandmother's cheerfulness, feeling old age weigh down her body but not her spirits. Mary photographed the moment per her daughter's request. As Meryl later observed, "We are who we're going to be when we're very old, and when we're very old we are who we were when we were 8."

Young Meryl had glasses and brown, permed hair, and her mature appearance and outspoken personality alienated classmates, who viewed her as no different from their teachers. "The kids would chase me up into a tree and hit my legs with sticks until they bled," she told *Time* in 1979. At home in leafy, suburban New Jersey, Meryl directed home movies, dressing her brothers in costumes and getting them to dance for the camera. Harry had once described her as a "ghastly" little girl, and Meryl seemed to agree, remembering "an ugly little kid with a big mouth, an obnoxious showoff."

She was born Mary Louise Streep on June 22, 1949, to parents Harry, a pharmaceutical company executive, and Mary, who worked as a commercial artist in addition to stints as an art director at Bell Labs amid World War II and art editor for *Home Furnishings* magazine, before Meryl came along. "She started a family when she was 35, which was unheard of," Meryl recalled. "All of her friends were 22, 23 years old." While Mary kept a studio out back, bringing up her three children took priority. "I asked her once, if she could have had her druthers, what would she have done with her life. She said, 'I would have loved to have been a lounge singer.' I think she was telling the truth. She was funny, really funny. Just witty."

The handsome Harry Streep called their daughter Meryl because he liked the name. (Growing up, Meryl would rather have been a Kathy or a Patty.) Mary, whose best friend inspired the middle moniker Louise, could think on her feet. She always had the right thing to say at the right time, where Meryl—an introvert by comparison—had a shy side, more prone to observe than to draw attention to herself. In a 1990 interview with the *Los Angeles Times*, Meryl, usually careful not to reveal too much about her personal life, made a rare confession: "My mother was the pretty one in her family. I wasn't."

Meryl wanted to be like her mother. Mary's comfort taking center stage encouraged the budding artist, who learned that a good actor must not only step into a character's shoes. She must *perform*.

Reach out into the audience and leave them spellbound. Deliver a performance they'll rave about forever, and preserve Playbills and ticket stubs as evidence they were there.

"My mentor was my mother," said Meryl, bragging with obvious pride about Mary, who died in 2001. "She was a mentor because she said to me, 'Meryl, you're capable. You're so great.' She was saying, 'You can do whatever you put your mind to. If you're lazy, you're not going to get it done. But if you put your mind to it, you can do anything.' And I believed her." The steady, reassuring loop of positivity—*you can do anything,* on repeat—instilled in Meryl a preternatural confidence that would help her navigate treacherous waters that swallowed up many an ingénue. Mary "said it from the time I was little. And that made me arrogant."

Like Julia Child, through whom Meryl would channel Mary in *Julie & Julia,* the Streep matriarch radiated joie de vivre, refusing to ruminate on life's setbacks. "I'm much more inclined to want to not say anything in public," Meryl once said. "When I have to be in the spotlight, I think to myself, *Mary could do it.* It's a good thing, to imagine yourself doing something you think you can't. I do that every day, because basically, if I had my way, I'd just stay home and think about what I'm having for supper."

Her father, Harry, had a performative nature as well. According to Meryl, "He wrote songs. He was a great dancer. We used to dance in the living room, he and I and my brother. And he was a really good pianist when he was a young boy, and he got a scholarship to Brown. But they didn't have any money, and when the Depression hit, he had to leave school. He went for a year. But after that he never graduated from college. It was hard. Everyone had to go out and work. And he had so much potential as a person, but at every turn things kind of ran into a wall. He had a tough time with his parents. His mother was very ill, very depressed. And he had a strong streak of melancholy."

23ANDSTREEP

History time! Records show that Englishman Lawrence Wilkinson, Meryl's eighth great-grandfather, was born circa 1620 in England, jumping ship—literally—for the shores of Rhode Island years later as a young man. Old Lawrence signed his name on the colony's 1645 civil constitution and acquired more than a thousand acres in the Providence area, a colonial power grab driving out Native Americans. While Metacom, leader of the Wampanoag people, waged war, descending upon settlers' towns, Wilkinson survived an attack in the spring of 1675, according to an investigation by the PBS series *Faces of America*. "Oh, I'm so sorry to hear this," Meryl told host Henry Louis Gates Jr., adding, "It makes it feel sort of like it's my fault on some level. But it also connects me to those events. Those first encounters between the two cultures must have been raw, terrifying."

Lawrence's descendant, John Wilkinson, was a farmer, Quaker, and father of five in Bucks County, Pennsylvania. Shockingly, John was expelled from the pacifist religion during the Revolutionary War. Why? Along with Ben Franklin, the patriot demonstrated his support for the war by signing a document cutting Pennsylvania's ties as an English colony. Centuries later, Mary Wolf Wilkinson married Harry Streep—and the couple had a daughter, Mary Louise (nicknamed Meryl), and two sons, Harry III and Dana.

"They were all Quakers [on] my mother's side," Meryl explained. "They said 'thee' and 'thou' in my grandfather's home."

Another maternal English ancestor, Silas Crispin, was one of the first to purchase William Penn's stake in Pennsylvania. In 1682, he signed a deed paying the Lenape Indians for their land, unlike Lawrence Wilkinson, who had seized it. That historical footnote pleased Meryl.

The Streep side, meanwhile, harks back to Germany and Switzerland—not Holland, as Meryl had long believed. Though she'd been told the Streeps had Dutch and Sephardic Jewish roots, it turned out they didn't. Her paternal great-great-grandfather, Gottfried Streeb, arrived in the United States sometime during the mid-nineteenth century. (In German, the "b" in Streeb is pronounced "p." Hence the switch to Streep.) A century before, her sixth great-grandfather, Johann Georg Streeb, had been mayor of the village of Loffenau, where more than a dozen Streebs still lived in 2010, the time PBS delved into her lineage. Johann was a "most senior judge," too. "That's why I'm so bossy," Meryl said.

A Swiss great-grandfather, Balthazar William Huber, landed stateside in 1869 on a ship dubbed the *City of Paris,* doubtless hoping for a life of greater prosperity.

"We are nothing but [our ancestors], and as an actor I'm always trying to call up lives. I think we are the sum of all the people that have lived before us," quoth Meryl, the most famous Streep of them all. She mused, "Think about how many lives we all carry around with us. Everything that they learned, everything that wounded them, everything that made them stronger, everything that made them happy, we contain in our little corporeal selves. So that gives me a rush and a kick. I am my people—good and bad."

When Meryl was twelve years old, she wowed the audience at a school concert with her solo performance of "O Holy Night"—sung in French. Soon the gifted tween, a coloratura soprano, was traveling to New York for regular lessons from prominent voice coach Estelle Liebling. She was in stellar company: Liebling had scheduled her young charge following vocal warm-ups with seasoned soprano Beverly Sills. Not that Meryl noticed. She didn't connect the dots until recognizing Sills onstage in *The Wings of the Dove* as the "nice lady who had the lesson before me."

Meryl, it turned out, lacked the passion to sing opera professionally. After four years, she dropped Liebling to concentrate on more important things: boys and cheerleading, Bob Dylan and the

Beatles. Now a student at Bernards High School, she set out to undo
her awkward adolescence—including Mary's "love affair with Bobby
Home Permanents," which explained Meryl's unfashionable frizz—
by staging a makeover she has credited as the first major role of her
life: the American teen beauty queen. "I wanted to learn how to be
appealing," she told Barnard graduates in her 2010 commencement
address, explaining, "This was all about appealing to boys and at the
same time being accepted by the girls—a very tricky negotiation."

As usual, Meryl did her research and then some: She flipped
through *Vogue, Seventeen,* and *Mademoiselle* magazines. She light-
ened up her giggle and her hair, too, applying peroxide and straight-
ening it with a flat iron. She starved herself, consuming "an apple a
day, period." She "demanded name-brand clothes," against Mary's
wishes, and attempted to mimic the perfect '60s dreamgirl-next-
door lipstick and eyelashes. And how could she bat those lashes if
she still wore glasses? Solution: pop in contacts.

It was a complete change, from the outside in and the inside out.
At the time, Meryl wasn't fully aware that she had reinvented herself.
She just did it. "I adjusted my natural temperament, which tends to
be slightly bossy, a little opinionated, loud...full of pronouncements
and high spirits," she recalled. "I willfully cultivated softness, agree-
ableness, a breezy, natural sort of sweetness, even shyness if you
will, which was very, very, very effective on the boys." She continued:

> But the girls didn't buy it. They didn't like me; they sniffed
> it out, the acting. And they were probably right, but I was
> committed. This was absolutely not a cynical exercise.
> This was a vestigial survival courtship skill I was develop-
> ing. And I reached a point senior year when my adjustment
> felt like me. I had actually convinced myself that I was this
> person and she, me: pretty, talented, but not stuck-up. You
> know, a girl who laughed a lot at every stupid thing every
> boy said and who lowered her eyes at the right moment and

deferred—who learned to defer when the boys took over the conversation. I really remember this so clearly and I could tell it was working. I was much less annoying to the guys than I had been....This was real, real acting.

One thing a teenage impersonator masquerading as a popular girl must learn is not to be seen trying *too* hard in class, especially in front of the opposite sex. But although Meryl loathed certain subjects and authority figures (biology, a geometry teacher dubbed "Fang"), she excelled at foreign languages, placing in the advanced French course because she could imitate the accent without mastering the grammar. Indeed, she had a knack for dialects and at one point entertained the dream of becoming a United Nations translator (who lived in a castle with her husband, the Prince of Wales). Rather than make straight As, "mostly I was known for making jokes, making animal noises, and terrorizing the teachers," she said.

When Meryl came home from school, she sang along to her father's Barbra Streisand albums; she knew every song by heart, and Streisand's theatrical track lists doubtless allowed her to feel all the things she kept hidden, like opinions that made boys uncomfortable in the halls of Bernards High. "Ooooo-eee! Ooooo-eee!" she would croon to Mary in mock falsetto, signaling her presence, to which Mary, covering her ears, shouted, "I'm going to strangle you, Meryl dear, if I hear that falsetto one more time!"

Meryl being Meryl, her mother's daughter, she naturally found her way to the stage, winning the lead in high school productions such as *The Music Man,* where at age fifteen she played Marian the Librarian—the Barbara Cook role she had swooned over when she saw the musical on Broadway. "If I can locate the moment when I was first bitten, that was it," said Meryl, remembering *The Music Man.* "The whole audience stood up when I came out."

For an actor, applause can be a drug, and a standing ovation the ultimate high. It's why countless drama kids pursue professional acting careers and the reason famous actors flood your Instagram feeds with a continuous stream of selfies, videos, and inspirational quotes. They're going after "likes." (Meryl, if you're reading this: Please join social media. Signed, everyone.)

Bernards High English teacher Jean Galbraith was stunned to witness "the kid in the first row who sits next to the windows" rehearsing "Till There Was You" like a professional, her singing voice high and light. Next came roles as Daisy Mae in *Li'l Abner* and Laurey in *Oklahoma!*, which also starred her best friend, Sue Castrilli, and her brother Harry III, whom Meryl called "Third." Meryl became the target of jealousy for hogging the limelight—and, really, just being so damn talented. Envy would dog Meryl her entire career, resentment flowing from drama school professors who tried to break her, from film critics who wanted to see her go down, and from conventional beauties losing Oscar-worthy parts to an unlikely movie star.

One way to diffuse the jealousy is to chase likes.

"I thought that if I looked pretty and did all the 'right things,' everyone would like me," she recalled to *Ladies' Home Journal* in 1980. "I had only two friends in high school, and one of them was my cousin, so that didn't count. Then there's that whole awful kind of competition based on pubescent rivalry for boys. It made me terribly unhappy. My biggest decision every day used to be what clothes I should wear to school. It was ridiculous."

She had a steady boyfriend, Mike Booth, a self-described "mediocre football player and even worse student," her date to the prom twice in a row and also to see the Beatles at Shea Stadium (the couple's song: "If I Fell"). With his large, expressive eyes and square jaw, Mike gave off a young Harrison Ford vibe in photos. He would later reveal to *Us* magazine that she thought her singing voice was "shrill" and drew funny sketches of herself "with hairy legs and a protuberant nose." For lunch, she served Mike cakes that she jokingly described as "aged like fine cheese." But, despite her Supportive Girlfriend persona, the cheerleader was not content to clap from the sidelines. She shone the brightest in that relationship, with Mike later admitting, "I was nowhere near as accomplished in anything as Meryl was, but I did write poems for her and somehow managed to keep her interest."

It didn't last long. Itching to escape Bernardsville, Mike let Meryl go and joined the army. Within two weeks, she snagged a new main squeeze: Bruce Thomson, a hunky, confident football jock who helped the dismal Bernards High Mountaineers secure a rare victory against Bound Brook in the fall 1965 season opener. According to Streep biographer Michael Schulman, "His girlfriend was the captain of the color guard. She was a senior, like Mike, and had grown suspicious of Meryl. So had some of the other girls. Meryl was someone who got what she wanted. She wanted Bruce."

Senior year, as expected, Meryl was crowned homecoming queen and Bruce her king. After four years spent undercover, playing a character she would soon shrug off but resurrect when necessary, that was finally a wrap.

Bye-bye Bernardsville, hello Vassar.

Vermont's Bennington College had been Meryl's first choice, but a negative experience during a campus visit scared her away. As Meryl recalled to *Ms.* magazine, "This woman interviewed me. She said, 'Ahhhhh, what books have you read over the summer?' I looked at her. I said, 'What do you mean, books over the summer?!' I had read none. I was on the swim team."

Then she remembered visiting the library one rainy day and discovering *Dreams* by Carl Jung, the godfather of analytical psychology. She devoured the fascinating volume. When the Bennington College interviewer asked who wrote it, Meryl replied, "Carl Jung," to which the Bennington gatekeeper corrected, sounding the *J* as a *Y*: "Please, Jung." Lamented Meryl, "I mean, that was the biggest book that anyone ever read over any summer, and she's yelling at me because I don't say the name right!"

She left the admissions office, telling Harry Streep, "Daddy, take me home."

In 1967, Meryl's small world expanded, along with her mind, when she enrolled at Vassar, the Poughkeepsie-based, all-girls private liberal arts college. Freed from the pressure to conform and please men, Meryl exhaled. She had never been happier. It was liberating to be herself. To not have to be "pretty" all the time. To not care what guys thought. To actually have a thought! She could even say the word "asshole" without consequence. Surrounded by women who became good friends and their earnest discussions about feminism, "I felt a thing emerge, which was my actual personality and my actual voice.... I realized that I was funny and I was allowed to be— and I was allowed to be loud and obnoxious and I took full advantage of it," Meryl said. As a result, she would have no qualms about looking plain or ugly for a role. Vassar sucked the vanity right out of her.

One day her sophomore year, in an intro to drama class, Meryl was asked to read an excerpt from *A Streetcar Named Desire*. Although she could not be further from Blanche DuBois, a southern belle losing her grip on reality, Meryl slipped into character with astonishing ease. Her nuanced interpretation, fueled by instinct and imagination, inspired Professor Clint Atkinson to cast her in the title role in Vassar's production of August Strindberg's *Miss Julie*. It was the first serious play she'd ever seen, and now she was starring in it. The performance turned the theater major into something of a campus star. Her friends asked, *How did you do that?* She couldn't really say. She just knew that she loved it. Atkinson marveled at Meryl's ability to access "the volcano within her"—and plumb the depths of tragic characters in classic plays. She played Miss Julie, a Swedish aristocrat persuaded by her lover to commit suicide, "with a voluptuousness that was almost shocking in someone of that age," he said. On spring vacation her senior year, Atkinson directed Meryl's off-Broadway debut in *The Playboy of Seville* at the experimental

Cubiculo Theatre on April 16, 1971; she played the fishermaid Tisbea opposite Michael Moriarty's Don Juan. Vassar's student newspaper praised her "perfect gestures."

As a change of scenery, she also participated in an exchange program at the all-male Dartmouth College, where she spent a semester studying costume design, playwriting, and dance. She could be seen on campus wearing a cape. Immersed in a bubble of white male privilege, where professors were seemingly generous with As, Meryl observed a marked difference between the classrooms of Vassar and Dartmouth. "I learned a great lesson there. At Vassar, when the professor would ask a question, there would be a silence at first while people were formulating their answers. Then tentatively hands would go up. At Dartmouth, the question wasn't even out of the teacher's mouth and all hands went up," she explained. "The men would answer off the tops of their heads. Sometimes they were wrong. It taught me something: You have to jump in."

Although Dartmouth did not admit women as full-time students until 1972, Vassar had opened its doors to men in 1969. But Meryl—the same Meryl described in her high school yearbook as "Where the boys are"—seemed to regard coeducation more like an invasion, an unwelcome influx of dudes busting up two blissful years of sisterhood. The year they arrived, numbering around forty, campus wasn't quite the same. Meryl watched as the interlopers usurped the counterculture movement from the 1,600 female students who dominated in size but not ego. "I'm so sensitive to theater, and these boys would get up and perform," she said. "Everybody was a mini–Abbie Hoffman in front of this adoring swarm of girls. I just thought it was bullshit." The effect, perhaps similar to the show of machismo at a 2016 Bernie Bro rally, led Meryl to reject the antiwar protests at her alma mater.

After graduation in 1971, she did summer stock for a season in Vermont, through the Green Mountain Guild. The experience

tested Meryl—especially when noisy ski boots disrespectfully interrupted a Chekhov play she was directing at a mountain lodge. But
it also showed how much she cared. Her genuine passion for theater seemed to outweigh lingering doubts about the "absurdity"
of making a living at it. *Should she apply to law school?* No matter
what the very responsible voices in her head advised, Meryl kept
following the uncertain path of the artist. She auditioned to join
the National Shakespeare Company but was rejected for reasons
unknown. Meryl, baffled by the snub, decided to obtain a fancier
pedigree. She applied to two elite thespian incubators, Juilliard and
the Yale School of Drama, but scoffed at the price of admission at
option number 1. "Juilliard had this very uppity, expensive applica-
tion that finally added up to $50," she sniffed. "Yale's application was
$15 and I was making $48 a week. So I wrote Juilliard a snotty letter
saying this just shows what kind of cross-section of the population
you get at *your* school. I applied to Yale and I got in and they gave me
a scholarship."

Once behind those ivy borders, Meryl received an education that
would literally send her to the doctor with an ulcer. Over three rigor-
ous years, she played forty different roles while waiting tables and
typing plays and weathering an assembly line of instructors with
varying methods. One teacher, Tom Haas, put Meryl on academic
warning in her first year. "He said that I was holding back my talent
out of fear of competing with my fellow students," she would recall.
"There was some truth in that, but there was no reason to put me on
warning. I was just trying to be a nice guy, get my M.A. and get out
of drama school."

That period, from 1972 to 1975, is now the stuff of legend. Just
look at the esteemed graduates: Tony-winning playwright Christopher Durang; Wendy Wasserstein, who dubbed the place the Yale
School of Trauma and remembered Meryl wearing overalls a lot;
Sigourney Weaver, who struggled with the judgy, political atmosphere there before finding success in the box-office hits *Alien* and

Ghostbusters; and, of course, Meryl, an unofficial Yale mascot and recruiting tool to rival Juilliard's distinguished roster of alumni (Robin Williams, Viola Davis, and Adam Driver).

Robert Brustein, the program dean and founder of the Yale Repertory Theatre, known for innovative and daring productions that challenged the status quo, was on leave as Meryl began her studies alongside eight other acting students. She dazzled in Drama 118, a class taught by Haas that focused on improvisation, scene study, and masks. On day one, Haas—thirty-four years old and the subject of gossip that his wife left him—ordered the class to improvise their deaths. How did Meryl choose to die? She gave herself an abortion. It was a bold reference to *Roe vs. Wade,* which was months away from a Supreme Court decision. While one of her peers mimed suicide by gunshot, Meryl used the stage to call attention to the dangers women face when they lack access to safe, legal abortions. Oh yes, Meryl *went there,* immediately raising the bar for everyone in the room.

Meryl's abilities amazed her peers, who learned from example "to Streep it up," a mantra meaning "Take the stage. Own your character. Make us look at you," explained classmate William Ivey Long. Another fellow Yale boot camp survivor, Ralph Redpath, recalled, "She was more flexible, more limber, had greater command of her body than the rest of us."

Come spring, Haas marginalized Meryl in a humiliating fashion, stunning her friends. "Our class names ourselves the Meryl Streep Class, and this asshole puts the namesake of the class on probation!" Long told Michael Schulman. "Of course, we all assumed he was jealous of her. Everyone was just in revolt of him because of this behavior."

Was jealousy the issue, or had Haas sensed Meryl's skepticism of his method?

"I love actors who don't let the audience objectify their characters," Meryl declared. "It's the opposite of what Tom Haas said. He said, 'The minute you come into a room in a play, the audience should know who you are.' I feel that the minute you leave a room, half the audience should know who you are, and the other half should be in complete disagreement with them."

When Haas abandoned the first-years to direct a play, the revolving door ushered in Professor Allan Miller, whose midcentury Method approach to acting required pupils to tap into real-life trauma—something that turned Meryl off, as did the time Miller invited her to see a show with him at the Yale Rep. She declined. Miller, making the rounds in the pre-#MeToo era, next propositioned a willing Laura Zucker, and the two paired up—adding an extra dose of weirdness to the dynamic in a class where Miller was the teacher and Zucker his student. Although Miller assigned Meryl the lead in a tense production of George Bernard Shaw's *Major Barbara,* he seemed hell-bent on picking her apart, rather than exploiting her strengths. He christened her the "Ice Princess."

He said: "*Come on, Meryl, let it out.* She whipped around at me with this terrific look of both desire and pain, and then stopped. She stopped the emotional flow. She didn't want to be vulnerable, and that's why her nickname was the Ice Princess."

She said: "He delved into personal lives in a way that I found obnoxious."

Even so, Meryl was at the top of her game, creating complex characterizations without needing to excavate old wounds. Her most brilliant Yale Rep performance: Constance Garnett—a pioneering English translator of classic Russian novels—in *The Idiots Karamazov,* an original play by Durang and Albert Innaurato. Meryl, using a wheelchair, relished the chance to disguise her youthful beauty and portray an elderly eccentric. "I adored playing Constance! Anyone in a wheelchair!" she enthused. "It's guaranteed to be great. It limits you and at the same time it frees you."

Robert Brustein said Meryl's performance "immediately suggested she was a major actress." Robert Lewis, who founded the

Actors Studio and also taught at Yale, said he'd never seen such an imaginative tour de force.

Haas, who directed *The Idiots Karamazov,* advised Meryl to "do less," Durang recalled. "So she did. But when the curtain calls came, Meryl improvised by rolling herself around the stage in her wheelchair, screaming, 'Go home! Go home!' Then she faked a heart attack. It was hilarious. And she got even."

Meryl was frequently cast in Yale Rep shows, and the demands on what little time she had—in addition to school and off-campus jobs—took a toll. She wound up developing an ulcer and made an appointment with a psychiatrist. He told Meryl, "Wait until you leave Yale and it will be alright."

As it happened, the shrink's prediction panned out. The ulcer went away.

۰ ۵ ۰ ۰ ۰ ۰ ۵ ۰ ۰ ♔ ۰ ۰ ۰ ۰ ۰ ۰ ۵ ۰ ۰

MERYL'S FELLOW DISTINGUISHED YALE SCHOOL OF DRAMA ALUMNI

Lupita Nyong'o (Class of 2012): Two years after graduating from the prestigious acting program, Nyong'o won the Best Supporting Actress Oscar for her searing role as Patsey in *Twelve Years a Slave.*

Liev Schreiber (Class of 1992): The Tony Award winner played Meryl's son in the 2004 remake of *The Manchurian Candidate,* where Meryl exuded maximum creepiness as Senator—and supervillain—Eleanor Prentiss Shaw.

Sigourney Weaver (Class of 1974): "She was the immediate star of her class—beautiful, sculpted face, slender body—and she seemed to be about seven feet tall," Weaver's classmate, playwright Christopher Durang, recalled.

Chris Noth (Class of 1985): It's a little-known fact that the TV star better known as Mr. Big comes from a serious theater background. Now if everyone would stop calling him Mr. Big.

Sanaa Lathan (Class of 1995): Lathan has conquered Broadway (*A Raisin in the Sun*) and the big screen (*Love & Basketball*). But did she really bite Beyoncé? That rumor shall never die.

● ● ● ● ●

I could write a book about the exquisite torture of being a struggling artist in New York City. Taking odd, terrible temp jobs to pay the rent. Heading to audition after audition, only to score a small role in a low-budget horror film set on Staten Island. (Here's looking at you, Tom Hanks.) Getting typecast as Pretty Blonde forever. But, given Meryl's meteoric success, that would be alternative history. The truth is, opportunities just sort of fell in her lap.

The twenty-six-year-old moved to Manhattan after Yale, renting an apartment on West Sixty-Ninth Street near Central Park. Everyone she met seemed to be single. "I read three newspapers and the *New York Review of Books*. I read books. I took afternoon naps before performances and stayed out till two and three, talking about acting with actors in actors' bars," she would reminisce.

That was hardly the life of an aspiring movie star moonlighting as a bartender, bike messenger, or part-time hand model. Right off the jump, Meryl became a working actor, and not just any working actor: A Broadway starlet. Meryl had a powerful ally in Joe Papp, the dynamic producer who founded the Public Theater. He hired her for a small part next to Mandy Patinkin and John Lithgow in his 1975 revival of *Trelawny of the "Wells"* at Lincoln Center, which in turn led to a knockout audition to play Flora—a zaftig Mississippi woman-child—in the Tennessee Williams play *27 Wagons Full of Cotton.*

She sported prosthetic breasts to help make the believable transition from slim, sophisticated ingénue to lusty, busty hot mess. The feat earned her a Tony nomination in 1976.

Catching Meryl off guard in a Christmas Eve phone call, Papp asked her to play two coveted roles the following summer in Shakespeare in the Park—Isabella (*Measure for Measure*) and Katharine (*Henry V*). "His conviction about me was total, but somewhere in the back of my brain I was screaming: 'Wow! Wow! Look at this! Wow!'" Meryl later said.

Besides Papp, the theater introduced her to two other important men in her life: J. Roy Helland, the opinionated hair and makeup guru who gravitated to Meryl backstage at *Trelawny* and would stick by her side through thick and thin; and John Cazale, her leading man in *Measure for Measure,* the cutthroat Angelo to her virtuous Isabella. The plot: Angelo, deputy to the Duke of Vienna, is tasked with cleaning up a city that has spiraled downward to become a hotbed of prostitution and disease. As a scare tactic, he sentences Claudio to die for the crime of fornication. Claudio's sister, Isabella, a young nun, begs Angelo to spare his life. But Angelo, who's got a thing for Isabella, says he'll do so if she gives him her virginity. In their scenes together, Meryl and Cazale generated palpable sexual fireworks—her intensity matching his—and they soon became a couple off stage, with Meryl's curiously chapped lips inciting backstage gossip. At forty-one, Cazale had become famous as Fredo in *The Godfather* movies and also starred alongside close friend Al Pacino in *Dog Day Afternoon.* He was strange looking, with a large, round forehead, receding hairline, and dark, sad eyes, yet Meryl—previously drawn to more conventionally attractive boyfriends—fell deeply in love. "He wasn't like anybody I'd ever met," she has said. "It was the specificity of him, and his sort of humanity and his curiosity about people, his compassion."

Cazale, introspective and methodical, a real actor's actor, gave good advice about acting, which Meryl took to heart: "I think probably I was more glib, and ready to pick the first idea that came to me.

And he would say, 'There's a lot of other possibilities.'" His directors would call him "20 Questions" because he would interrogate them incessantly. He was as committed to Meryl as he was to his craft, telling Pacino, "Oh, man, I have met the greatest actress in the history of the world."

She moved into his Tribeca apartment, where they would live together until tragedy ended a love affair for the ages. In the meantime, Hollywood came calling—and Queen Meryl was waiting in the wings.

When Meryl Met Roy

J. Roy Helland has masterminded Meryl's hair and makeup for forty-three years, beginning with her 1975 performance in the stage comedy *Trelawny of the "Wells."* The two became tight backstage at the Broadway production.

"Roy was very offended that the stagehands had all these naked posters of women everywhere, with their tits and ass," Streep would remember. "So in his room he mounted posters of, like, gay porn."

"*Playgirl* centerfolds," corrected Roy, chiming in. "I wallpapered it."

"I had never seen anything like this in my life," Meryl said. "We all gathered often in his room."

This exchange occurred after both Meryl and Roy won Academy Awards for their 2011 collaboration, *The Iron Lady,* where she was rendered virtually unrecognizable as former British prime minister Margaret Thatcher. After winning her (second) Best Actress Oscar in 2012, Meryl thanked both husband Don Gummer and Roy, her "other partner."

The duo has collaborated on a stunning range of characters. Soft and fragile Sophie. Karen Silkwood and her mullet. Vampy Madeline Ashton. The icy editrix Miranda Priestly. "It's fascinating to make her look different," remarked Roy, who has moonlighted as a female impersonator. "A long, long time ago I probably got the best lesson in makeup, which was someone said, 'Don't paint what you see; paint what you want.' So for us—Meryl and I—it's all about not having it be her but having it be whoever the character is."

Over the decades, Roy gained a reputation as Meryl's closest confidante on the set. (Don't you tell your hairdresser all your secrets?) And, throughout many interviews for this book, I've heard him described as her gatekeeper and "security blanket," a consummate professional armed with a sardonic sense of humor. Wendy Finerman, producer of *The Devil Wears Prada,* told me, "It was very important to confer with Roy about Meryl." One thing she learned: when you get Meryl a sandwich, you better bring one for Roy, too.

"I have the technique to create what she dreams up," Roy has said, to which Meryl responded: "He does what I say."

CHAPTER 2

Runaway Meryl

Ted Kramer: Where are you going?
Joanna Kramer: I don't know.

(Kramer vs. Kramer, 1979)

The casting director Juliet Taylor often scouted talent at the theater, and, after witnessing Meryl Streep on stage, Taylor put the promising young actor on a flight to England to meet Fred Zinnemann about a role in the director's new film, *Julia*. If everything worked out, soon Meryl could be starring opposite Jane Fonda as a woman who joins the Resistance ahead of World War II.

Allow me to describe the plot of this 1977 gem of a movie that you should drop everything (except this book) and watch immediately: Adapted from a chapter in Lillian Hellman's *Pentimento*, a memoir that flirted with fiction, *Julia* tells the story of the deep, undying friendship between childhood friends Lillian and Julia, who left the United States to study at Oxford and the University of Vienna. When Lillian, a playwright, learns that Julia has been injured in a Nazi attack at her school, she flies to Vienna—but there is no trace of Julia. Later, Lillian receives an invitation to a writers' conference in Russia, and Julia resurfaces with a dangerous assignment to smuggle money out of Berlin en route to Moscow as part of a mission to help Jewish people targeted by fascists. I'm not about to spoil the ending, but know this: Lillian's train ride into Russia is one of the most suspenseful moments in cinema. I will forever be haunted by it and in awe that a period picture showcasing brave women fighting evil, rather than discussing men, was even made at all.

Julia had everything: Drama. Mystery. Intrigue. Heroines on the right side of history. JANE FONDA.

A few weeks passed until Meryl heard from Zinnemann. He delivered the news that the venerable Vanessa Redgrave was going to play Julia to Jane's Lillian. *Would Meryl accept a smaller role?*

"Well, you know, I'll check my book," Meryl recalled herself saying. She liked the part—snobby girl-about-town Anne Marie—and she found a celebrity mentor in Jane, who took the rookie under her wing. "She had an almost feral alertness, like this bright-blue attentiveness to everything around her that was completely intimidating and made me feel like I was lumpy and from New Jersey, which I am," she remembered.

Meryl, then twenty-eight, was to film all of her scenes with Jane. The prospect induced anxiety, which manifested itself in hives. On her first day, she and Jane rehearsed just once before shooting a scene. By the second take, Meryl was loosening up, feeling good, when Jane told her, "Look down." *What?* "Over there. That green tape on the floor—that's you. That's your mark. And if you land in it, you will be in the light. And you will be in the movie."

Jane encouraged Meryl to improvise; the rookie made her laugh so hard she cried. After *Julia* wrapped, Jane spread the word around Los Angeles. "I found out she'd gone back to California and told everyone who would listen about this girl with a weird last name. And opened more doors than I probably even know about today," Meryl said.

Unwittingly, Jane imparted an object lesson in kindness. As a result, she inspired Meryl to pay it forward when setting an example for younger, less experienced costars (most of whom were terrified to breathe the same air as she).

Alas, Zinnemann was forced to cut Meryl's role. She briefly appeared in two scenes and oozed passive-aggression during an encounter where Anne Marie insults Lillian's spirit sister: "By the way, I tried to see Julia again but she wouldn't see me," sneers the socialite, sporting a fur stole, pearls, ginormous red hat, and unflattering black wig. "She's leading a strange life, pretending not to be rich. Doing something called...anti-fascist work."

Despite mixed reviews, *Julia* garnered eleven Oscar nominations and a Best Supporting Actress trophy for Redgrave.

Meryl, meanwhile, was uncertain about this whole movie thing. She made her screen debut in the March 1977 made-for-TV sports drama *The Deadliest Season,* playing the wife of a hockey pro who accidentally kills another player on the ice. *Julia* premiered that October. It unsettled her that in its final cut, the dialogue she spoke in one scene had been transferred to another. She thought, "I've made a terrible mistake, no more movies, I hate this business." Unlike doing a play, where she unleashed her energy in two or three hours, making movies was a tedious, drawn-out process that required a lot of waiting. It seemed like the only people having fun were the gaffers and lighting technicians. Meryl would not have fun until she mastered the tricks of the trade.

But the theater devotee continued to take high-profile work on camera, joining her partner, John Cazale, in the Vietnam War epic *The Deer Hunter.* She played Linda, a small-town girl whose boyfriend, Nick (a foxy Christopher Walken), goes AWOL following a traumatic experience overseas. Linda seeks comfort in the arms of Nick's best buddy, Mike (an emo Robert De Niro), but he is more devoted to his missing friend. (Mike returns to Vietnam to find Nick; it does not end well.) Unlike the guys' roles, Linda barely existed on the page. "She's the kind of girl I went to high school with," observed Meryl, who also drew from her cheerleading past. "The kind who waits to be asked to the prom, who waits to be asked to get married, and who waits for her lover to come back from the war."

After seeing Meryl on Broadway in *The Cherry Orchard*, De Niro encouraged director Michael Cimino to bring her aboard *Deer Hunter*. "They admitted they didn't have any idea what the girl would say in any of these situations," she said. "And I'm like, 'Oh, my God.' Whatever I thought—would be appropriate. On one hand, you could think of it as negligence. On the other hand, it was great artistic freedom for me because I really could make my performance."

There are a lot of tears shed in *Deer Hunter*, but, to me, the biggest heartbreaker happens at the very beginning: The submissive Linda, who lives with her abusive, alcoholic father, is getting ready for a friend's wedding when she discovers the deadbeat in a drunk, incoherent state. She tries to put him in his bed, but he smacks her to the ground. She gets up, forces a smile, and pleads, "Daddy, no, it's me!" He slaps her again, screaming, "All bitches, I hate 'em!" Including his own daughter. In the span of a few minutes, Linda's despair—familiar to women stuck in toxic relationships from which they can't escape—elicits as much audience empathy as does the pain endured by Vietnam veterans Michael and Nick, though hers is less central to the story line.

A cautious Linda, wearing a bruise on her cheek, asks Nick whether she can stay in his trailer. Nick, who is gentle and loving, rejects her offer to pay rent, consoling, "It's me you're talking to." It's no wonder Linda's drawn to him. Nick makes her feel safe. Working with minimal dialogue and maximum emotion, Meryl helps us understand *why* Linda would wait for her lover to come back from the war instead of catching a bus to literally anywhere else—and never looking back. (The thing is, nobody ever told Linda she could *do* that—just leave. As part of her bleak character study, Meryl put Linda's voice and agency on mute to reflect an authentic female experience for women rooted in their hometowns, conditioned to serve men, for better or worse.) "I wanted the audience to feel another dimension to her," Meryl explained. "She's the forgotten person in the screenplay and also in the characters' lives."

Off camera, she endured heartbreak in real time: Cazale was suffering from lung cancer. Despite his illness, he wanted to do what he loved with the person he loved. Cimino, who cast him as Stan, a working-class Pennsylvania townie, arranged the shooting schedule to film Cazale's scenes first. De Niro paid the insurance required to keep Cazale in the film. Meryl paid his medical bills. After wrapping *Deer Hunter,* Meryl traveled to Vienna to film a role in the NBC miniseries *Holocaust* as the Christian wife of a Jewish artist (James Woods) sent to a concentration camp. The shoot took 2 ½ months, and Meryl ached to get home. Returning to New York, she cut back on work to take care of Cazale, whose disease had spread to his bones. "She was always at his side," Joe Papp later said. "It was such a statement of loyalty, of commitment. She never betrayed any notion that he would not survive. She knew that he was dying, but he knew only in the way that a dying man knows it. She gave him tremendous hope."

With Meryl nearby, Cazale closed his eyes in the middle of the night on March 13, 1978. A doctor said he was gone. Meryl was so overcome by grief that she pounded on his chest, crying. But then, reported Michael Schulman in *Her Again,* Cazale opened his eyes briefly and said, "It's all right, Meryl," before closing them forever.

Afterward, in a wounded state of mourning, she stayed at a friend's house in the Canadian countryside where she drew sketches of Cazale and Joe Papp.

The next month, *Holocaust* aired in four installments. The series was hugely popular, snagging Meryl an Emmy Award for Outstanding Lead Actress in a Limited Series. But she refused to accept the honor at the televised ceremony later that September, declaring, "I don't think performances should be taken out of context and put up against each other for awards."

Money motivated her decision to appear in *Holocaust,* and she wasn't about to apologize for needing the cash. As her profile rose, she started to get recognized on the street—*that* made Meryl uncomfortable. One day, she was riding her bike in Chelsea when four men in a Volkswagen began yelling out the window at her. *Hey, Holocaust! Hey, Holocaust!* "It's absurd," she complained, "that that episode in history can be reduced to people screaming out of car windows at an actress."

Nevertheless, Meryl jumped into work: she shot *The Seduction of Joe Tynan* with Alan Alda shortly after Cazale's death, which left her devastated but determined to heal. In *Joe Tynan,* she adopted a butterscotch Louisiana accent to charm Alda's Joe Tynan, a liberal US senator and presidential hopeful, into cheating on his wife. Alda had written a star vehicle for himself, and, in his screenplay, the Other Woman was an ambitious labor lawyer named Karen Traynor. "When I want something, I go get it—just like you," she tells Joe. Karen wore elegant separates and her hair upswept in a chignon. In a 1980 *Newsweek* interview, John Lithgow, a theater colleague, described Meryl's angst over a love scene with Alda: "It's a scene that demands tremendous high spirits and a good deal of sexual energy, and at the same time, right after John Cazale had died, Meryl was in no mood for either. And she was embarrassed by the scene. She said she would perspire until she was dripping wet from embarrassment."

WHEN THE QUEEN MET THE CANADIAN PRIME MINISTER

This story soon became legend at the Public Theater in New York. As the lore goes, Pierre Trudeau (Justin's father) went backstage following one of Meryl's performances and asked her on a date. She politely turned him down, remarking to a colleague, "I don't understand it. Why do famous people only want to meet other famous people?"

Juliet Taylor also tapped Meryl for a small but memorable role in the Woody Allen comedy *Manhattan*. For his leading ladies, Woody ensnared Diane Keaton and Mariel Hemingway in a love triangle with his alter ego, divorced forty-two-year-old comedy writer Isaac Davis, at the center. Mariel was sixteen years old, an age difference that seemed to unsettle Meryl, even in those wild and woolly times. "When people asked me what it was like to work with Mariel Hemingway on *Manhattan*, I said, 'I never even met the child,'" she told *Cue* magazine. The hyperefficient writer-director had an aloofness that irked Meryl. She tried improvising to no avail. Woody wanted actors to stick to his script. (Meryl later "realized Diane Keaton could say whatever she wanted.") She deemed him "a womanizer, very self-involved," at the expense of his art. "It's sad, because Woody has the potential to be America's Chekhov," she said in 1980, raising eyebrows among cinephiles who admired him. "But instead, he's still caught up in the jet-set crowd type of life and trivializing his talent." Where other actors might refrain from knocking Woody in public, lest they get black-listed, Meryl didn't appear to care: "I don't think Woody Allen even remembers me."

The *camera* certainly worshipped her. As Isaac's ex-wife, Jill, she had never looked more glamorous, radiating urban goddess energy with cool, collared blouses and hair as long as Rapunzel's. Jill had left Isaac for a woman, marking Meryl's first gay role, and she panicked the neurotic by writing a tell-all book, *Marriage, Divorce, and Selfhood*—an early inspiration, I like to think, for Nora Ephron's *Heartburn*, a thinly veiled account of her disastrous split from Carl Bernstein. Jill was fierce, angry, strong, and cold, the Ice Princess who rejected Yale professor Allan Miller.

According to Bob Greenhut, *Manhattan*'s executive producer, Meryl never had to read for Jill. Taylor, Woody's longtime casting guru, had said, "There's this wonderful Yale grad who's just, like, knocking everybody's socks off in auditions and everything and you

Meryl in 1979 looking normcore-fabulous outside the Public Theater.

really should take a look at her." Greenhut told me, "Boy, was she attractive. I mean, everyone was, like, in love with her. 'Who is this girl?' And plus, she nailed the part."

Growing buzz—and a pushy agent—got her in the door to see director Robert Benton, producer Stanley Jaffe, and their star, Dustin Hoffman, about *Kramer vs. Kramer,* a drama based on Avery Corman's controversial novel depicting a housewife and mother walking out on her family. The story is told from the male perspective, a one-sidedness angering feminists, who complained that the wife had been shamed for wanting her own career and identity outside of marriage. It was zeitgeisty as hell. A "male nightmare"—to borrow a favorite Ephron-ism—plaguing husbands anxious that the women's movement of the 1970s would lure their wives away from home, leaving behind chores, child-rearing, and other unpaid labor.

Benton and Meryl shared a powerful representative: Sam Cohn, who dominated the New York talent market at ICM, despised Los Angeles, and had a curious habit of eating paper. Benton came very close to casting *Charlie's Angels* star Kate Jackson, but producer Aaron Spelling would not alter his TV production schedule to accommodate Jackson. That was after Jackson and Dustin reportedly partied at Studio 54 after reading together. Sensing an opening, Sam phoned Benton.

"Would you look at this young actress, Meryl Streep?"

"She's a lovely actress," said Benton, who had seen Meryl in *The Cherry Orchard*. Now she and Raul Julia were sparring in an electric revival of *The Taming of the Shrew* in Central Park. Still, he thought it was too late in the process to consider her.

"Please do it for me," Sam implored.

As a favor, Benton and company agreed to meet Meryl at the Sherry-Netherland on Fifth Avenue.

"Meryl showed up and she sat there," he recalls. "I don't think the interview took more than 15 or 20 minutes maximum, and it was...the worst single interview I have ever had with an actor in all my years in Hollywood. The worst. The worst. She walked out the door, and Dustin looked at me, and I looked at Dustin and we said, 'That is Joanna Kramer.'"

Stanley Jaffe pulled strings at the studio, Columbia Pictures, urging executives to take a risk on an unknown actress with an unconventional face. Neither *The Deer Hunter* nor *The Seduction of Joe Tynan* had been released in theaters yet.

Bigger names had been considered for Joanna: Ali McGraw. Faye Dunaway. Jane Fonda, although Jane projected an inherent strength—a feral alertness, if you will—undermining her believability as the fragile Joanna. *Fragility*. That's the essence of what Benton desired in his female lead but couldn't articulate until Meryl sat down. Dustin, trained in the Method at the Actors Studio, would go deep into Ted Kramer, blurring the line between character and self. At the time, his separation from wife of nearly ten years Anne Byrne, the mother of his two daughters, was giving him plenty of material to mine. Anne yearned to focus on her career in show business; in Meryl, he viewed a partner in pain. He was aware that she'd lost Cazale earlier that year and, based on her behavior, observed a lingering numbness. She could use that. And Dustin would have something real to act against.

Although Dustin remembered Meryl not saying a word at the meeting, in her recollection, she aired concerns about the screenplay. Joanna came across as the bad mommy—a selfish princess who requests custody of seven-year-old son Billy after a year of "finding herself" in California. The ensuing courtroom battle echoed a Salem witch trial. Meryl had read Corman's book, which *Ms.* lambasted as "an antifeminist backlash novel" riding a wave of hatred toward women, and thought Joanna should be treated sympathetically in the script. Internally, she wondered, "The woman in *Kramer* is like a Tennessee Williams person, one who bruises. How can I play her? I'm not a mother....I don't live on the Upper East Side. But people outside of an experience sometimes have a greater insight than those living it."

With whirlwind speed, Meryl was running toward motherhood. Don Gummer, a handsome sculptor and friend of her brother Third, helped mend her broken heart. "Three weeks after

John's death, a former girlfriend of John's materialized from California and reclaimed our apartment," she recalled in an interview with *Ladies' Home Journal*. "It turned out that she and John had signed a lease together a few years earlier, but had never lived there together." Third, a modern dancer, had moved into Cazale's Tribeca loft. "Then suddenly when this woman appeared, we had to leave. So within a period of three weeks, I not only lost John but our home."

Don offered to help Meryl and Third move their stuff to storage, and anything left over he would keep safe in his Soho loft/studio. Meryl went off to Washington and Baltimore to shoot *Joe Tynan*, and, when she got back to Manhattan two months later, Don told the Streep siblings they could live at his place while he embarked on a trip around the world.

"I started writing to Don while he was away," she said. "He and my brother had been friends for years and I had met Don two or three times, but I honestly didn't remember him. We really got to know each other through our letters. Then when he returned to New York, he built me a little room of my own in the loft, and told me I could stay. And twenty minutes later we got married! No, actually, it was two months later. It just seemed right. A lot of men had asked me to marry them, but it had never really seemed right before."

Dear reader, I know what you're thinking. *If Meryl was still grieving over Cazale, how on earth could she move on to another man so quickly?*

The thirty-one-year-old Yale School of Art graduate projected an alluring groundedness. He was born in Louisville, Kentucky, and raised among five brothers in Indiana, where he married his college sweetheart. A divorce followed after he moved to the East Coast to expand his horizons at the Boston Museum School and Yale. He found his artistic voice creating large-scale, abstract sculptures crafted from such natural materials as wood, stone, and soil. Don's aesthetic impressed Richard Serra, who selected him to launch a solo show in 1974 at Artists Space on Wooster Street. Don grew up assembling model airplanes and tree forts, and he was destined to build things with his hands. During the day, he worked as a union carpenter in Midtown Manhattan's Olympic Tower. He had a dark mop of curly hair and a quiet, calm demeanor—like Meryl, he would shatter the notion that an artist had to be a wild neurotic to be successful.

"He's like me," she gushed. "I mean, he's very private. And he never says anything he doesn't mean. He's warm, strong, gentle, funny, kind, understanding, very creative. I couldn't live with someone who wasn't creative."

She felt as though she'd "fallen into heaven." When you know, you know. Also, Meryl disliked dating, preferring the stability of marriage and the contentment it brought her. They exchanged vows in an Episcopal ceremony at her parents' Connecticut home on Saturday, September 30, 1978. Don was on crutches from a motorcycle accident in Thailand. The speedy progression to the altar appeared to perplex Meryl's mother, who asked Joe Papp, "What is she thinking about?" Weeks before on the set of *The Taming of the Shrew,* Papp noticed she was still mourning Cazale. But he supported her decision. "She does the right thing for herself at the moment," the producer would say.

Several days after saying "I do," Meryl went back to work.

◊ ◊ ◊ ◊ ◊

Perhaps you're aware that Meryl and Dustin clashed on the set of *Kramer vs. Kramer.* If not, prepare for a cautionary tale in how not to treat your coworker.

Several years before, Meryl encountered Dustin while auditioning for a Broadway play he directed called *All Over Town.* She was in school at Yale; he made a terrible first impression. "I'm Dustin

Hoffman," he said, burping and groping her breast. Little did she know that someday this brute would be her movie husband. (Dustin is said to have apologized later for that incident.)

Like Billie Jean King preparing to outplay Bobby Riggs, Meryl had done her warm-ups. She hung around Upper East Side playgrounds to watch young, nonworking moms dote upon their kids and began to empathize with her character's internal struggle: "Joanna's daddy took care of her. Her college took care of her. Then Ted took care of her. Suddenly she just felt incapable of caring for herself." Meryl, of course, had experienced none of that in her scrappy life. "I wanted to play a woman who had this feeling of incapability, because I've always felt that I can do anything."

On the second day of shooting, Dustin crossed a line. They were filming Joanna's dramatic exit at the very top of the film, when a

Dustin and Meryl.

distressed Joanna, trying to keep it together amid tears, bluntly informs Ted that she doesn't love him and she's leaving—without their son, Billy. According to Meryl, "We were supposed to emerge out into a hall, so we started out in the room, behind the door, and they said 'Action,' and Dustin turned around and...slammed me in the face." The slap left "enormous red finger marks on my cheek," she said. Benton was in shock. Meryl, ever the professional, continued with the scene, which involved Joanna escaping down the elevator in the hallway outside the Kramers' apartment. Later, as the camera captured her emotional goodbye, she heard Dustin, the Method man, attempt to provoke her by mentioning Cazale. Such was his warped approach to get under Meryl's skin and elicit the performance that *he* wanted.

Meryl hardly needed Dustin's help. She was angry. After *Kramer*, Dustin would never push her around again.

"It was overstepping," she reflected in 2018, months after #MeToo exposed Dustin's history of sexual misconduct and boorish behavior toward female colleagues. "But I think those things are being corrected in this moment. And they're not politically corrected; they're fixed. They will be fixed, because people won't accept it anymore."

SOME SHIT MERYL SAID ABOUT DUSTIN HOFFMAN

"He's just got the devil in him, you know? He's always making trouble. And that's the way he works. He gets it all happening. He gets everybody on pins and needles."—*Good Morning America* interview, February 18, 1983.

"What Dustin really wants to do, you know, is give birth. But he's still glad he's got a penis."—Responding in 1982 to the actor's commentary that men and women "relate totally differently" and "have no idea what it's like to be the opposite sex."

"He's mad! He's totally out of his mind.... But he's such a good craftsman and he really loves his work."—Talking *Kramer* in the December 1979 edition of *Ladies' Home Journal*.

"Redford, marry. Maybe. *Yeah,* okay. Jack, shag. Dustin...[mimes slitting her throat]."—Playing "Shag, Marry, Kill" on *Watch What Happens*, August 9, 2012.

Another unscripted moment was the restaurant scene where Joanna announces her intent to assume custody of Billy. The screenplay called for Joanna to break the news right away and then explain, "All my life, I've felt like somebody's wife or somebody's mother or somebody's daughter—even all the time we were together, I never knew who I was." However, Meryl wanted to say this *before* dropping the Billy bomb as part of her mission to humanize Joanna. Benton agreed, but Dustin was fuming.

"I finally yelled at her," Dustin said. " 'Meryl, why don't you stop carrying the flag for feminism and just act the scene!' She got furious. That's the scene where I throw the glass of wine against the wall and it shatters. That wasn't in the script, I just threw it at her. Then she got furious again. 'I've got pieces of glass in my hair!' and so on."

For the courtroom scene, Benton—who wrote the script and willingly tweaked it with Meryl's input—asked Meryl to rewrite Joanna's monologue on the witness stand. "I think I've written it as a man, not as a woman would say it," he told her. "Take the speech, keeping the points that were made, but put it in a woman's voice."

When the time came, Meryl brought a legal pad and a page and a half of handwritten dialogue. Benton thought, *Oh my God, what have I done? I'm going to lose a friend and two days of work. This is going to be awful.* He braced for the worst. Then he read her revise, and—*phew*—it was about a third too long but perfect. Even better: he didn't have to worry about hurting Meryl's feelings or losing her as a friend. They trimmed the speech together, cutting two lines, and handed it to the script supervisor.

Action.

She nailed the first take, prompting a stunned silence from everybody in the room. Benton began to worry that Meryl would use up all of her powers because this was going to be a long day and he had much more footage to film, including reaction shots. Benton approached her and warned, "Meryl, please don't. You're new to this. Please don't blow this early because there's a lot." He urged her to "save it for the close-up."

Meryl didn't listen. Take after take, she delivered her lines as if it were the first time she said them. "It was never mechanical," says Benton. "After maybe the third or fourth time that she did it, I suddenly realized I was scared shitless of her. That control, and the depth, was unbelievable."

Joanna was coming into her own but in a very different way than Meryl had on the set of *Julia*. Where the feminist, outspoken Jane Fonda proved an enthusiastic advocate for Meryl, the erstwhile Mrs. Kramer was a lonely island in uncharted seas, advocating for herself without another woman to help her. An excerpt of Joanna's original speech, as written by Benton: "Don't I have a right to a life of my own? Is that so awful? Is my pain any less just because I'm a woman? Are my feelings any cheaper?"

Meryl doesn't get enough credit for her writing skills. The way she tweaked Benton's attempt, she toned down the theatrics and went straight for the emotional jugular, rendering an utterly sympathetic, discreetly feminist portrait of Joanna that endeared the character to skeptics predisposed to villainize her. "I was incapable of functioning in that home, and I didn't know what the alternative was going to be," she wrote. "So I thought it was not best that I take [Billy] with me.... I was his mommy for 5 ½ years. And Ted took over that role for 18 months. But I don't know how anybody can possibly believe that I have less of a stake in mothering that little boy than Mr. Kramer does. I'm his mother."

She triggered Benton with the word *mommy*. And Dustin, up on his old tricks, triggered Meryl with the words *John Cazale*. He whispered them into Meryl's ears and briefed her to look directly at him when Ted's attorney says, "Were you a failure at the most important relationship in your life?"

She followed his advice, and, upon making eye contact, Dustin's response touched the heart: he shook his head, ever so slightly, creating an interlude of tenderness between the foes—and letting Meryl/ Joanna know that he didn't think she had failed.

Meryl had given him something real to react to. And Benton, eager to keep the magic going, had Dustin repeat his micro-gesture so he could capture it on film.

It seemed as though Meryl, four movies in, was finally getting the hang of it. But the theater held a special place in her heart. There, she didn't run the risk of losing what made her great. She could let loose and play someone grittier than a supporting starlet who exists only to let the Dustin Hoffmans and the Robert De Niros and the Alan Aldas chew the most scenery.

"Working on movies is very economical, clean, pared down," she said in 1979. "You can afford to do so little. You don't even have to be a good actor, or even an actor, to be effective in movies. But when you get a good actor, like Brando or Olivier, there's a difference— when somebody takes a part by the throat and sings with it. My fear is that in doing so little, I will not be able to do what I do on stage, which is to be brave, to take the larger leap."

Somewhere around this time, Meryl saw Liza Minnelli perform at the Winter Garden. The ambassador of show tunes, sequins, and classic New York knew how to give it her all. And if you've ever seen

Liza in concert, you know what that means: A confetti explosion of razzle-dazzle and old-time showmanship. No inhibition. No shame. No dull moments.

It made Meryl think. There was more to acting than focused characterization. You had to give 'em a show. Make it sparkly and exciting. Meryl would take Liza's cue and attempt to transform Hollywood into Broadway—but on her terms. Impossible, right?

CHAPTER 3

Mother Meryl

The truth does not make it easier to understand, you know. I mean, you think that you find out the truth about me, and then you'll understand me. And then you would forgive me for all those...for all my lies.—Sophie Zawistowska

(*Sophie's Choice*, 1982)

Scene: A Manhattan restaurant. August 1979. Meryl, now thirty years old, was expecting her first child and being interviewed by *New York Times* reporter Janet Maslin about *The Seduction of Joe Tynan*. But Meryl teased the better movie, *Kramer vs. Kramer*, slated to hit theaters in December. "I'm set up as a villain," she said, "so I like the idea of reappearing and trying to turn that around."

Meryl would come to find motherhood enriching, and her superhuman ability to toggle between a quiet family life and movie stardom would astonish friends, who wondered how she did it. But onscreen during the 1980s, intriguingly, she continued to portray atypical mothers, like Joanna Kramer, making hard choices in movies where women struggled to survive in a man's world. Exhibit A: *Sophie's Choice*. If Meryl helped expose women's history through her art, giving voice to the voiceless, then it's no surprise that part of her duty as a feminist included shattering ideals and revealing painful truths about a hallowed role—mother—that hardly anyone, even Meryl Streep, can possibly live up to.

On hiatus from moviemaking, Meryl was happy to discuss husband Don's new, thirty-five-foot sculpture at Castle Clinton in Battery Park. ("It's a real big deal for him.") The piece, called *Surrounded* by *Divisions,* marked a milestone that introduced his artwork to the masses. As an artist, she innately understood the drive to create, say, an understated wall relief in painted wood. And Don doubtless appreciated her passionate turn as Kate in *The Taming of the Shrew*—breathing fire and ice at the Delacorte Theater. She didn't have to explain herself to Don, and vice versa. "She's learned how to look at objects and I've learned how to look at people," he said. An insecure husband might worry that his gorgeous and talented wife, a soon-to-be superstar, might leave him in the dust or, worse, trade up to Harrison Ford. Don exuded nothing but confidence. "There are many different levels of love," he explained. "Ours is founded on a very deep-rooted feeling of trust. We're best friends."

The year before, Meryl graced the cover of *Horizon* alongside three other actresses—Swoosie Kurtz, Jill Eikenberry, and Tovah Feldshuh—whom the arts magazine identified as the next generation "of young screen stars, augmenting the recently heralded ranks of Jill Clayburgh, Diane Keaton, and Lily Tomlin." In the accompanying article, Meryl revealed that she'd paid off her Yale debt partially thanks to *Joe Tynan* and *The Deer Hunter.* Though the middle-class girl from Bernardsville earned substantially less than her male costars, those paychecks bought security, relieving the stress of working overtime to survive in the big city. She could afford to take a break. But greater financial freedom came with a side effect: losing her prized anonymity, which allowed her to observe human behavior—an actor's sustenance. She and Don unlisted their phone number after fans, tracking down "Gummer" in the phonebook, began calling for Meryl.

The Beverly Hills Hotel was another story. The staff of the swanky institution failed to recognize her when she stayed there for the 1979 Academy Awards. Meryl was unschooled in the protocol of performative glamour and fake-it-'til-you-make-it, committing a severe social faux pas: she actually *swam* in the pool—a place to see and be seen and not get wet! If she had played the "Do you know who I am?" diva card, then hotel employees would have been made aware of the Oscar nominee in their midst: a critical, if controversial, darling, *The Deer Hunter* had been nominated for nine awards, including Best Supporting Actress for Meryl. It was her very first nomination; on this special occasion, she wanted to wear something that would make Mary Streep proud, so she picked up an elegant, if unremarkable black silk dress at the department store Bonwit Teller.

On the big day, antiwar protesters gathered outside the Dorothy Chandler Pavilion to demonstrate against *The Deer Hunter*, which stoked outrage and accusations of racism for its one-sided take on Vietnam. The Viet Cong, for instance, are shown torturing De Niro and Christopher Walken with a sadistic game of Russian roulette; De Niro seizes a machine gun and kills them all. Then there's the last scene, where Meryl leads a singalong of "God Bless America," the first time she sang in a movie. She chose to remain neutral amid the fuss, saying *The Deer Hunter*, named Best Film by the New York Film Critics in 1978, "shows the value of people in towns like that." (She had seen it six times, once with John Cazale's brother, Stephen. The torture parts were too much, but she liked watching Cazale.)

Ironically, the Best Picture category pitted *The Deer Hunter* against *Coming Home*, a politically liberal picture starring Jane Fonda (a.k.a. "Hanoi Jane") as a VA hospital volunteer who falls for a paraplegic Vietnam veteran played by Jon Voight. The Academy's voters crowned *Deer Hunter* the winner, also bestowing the Best Director and Best Supporting Actor statuettes to Michael Cimino and Walken, respectively. De Niro, up for Best Actor, was apparently so anxious he stayed home. Jane, who called *Deer Hunter* "racist" and refused to acknowledge Cimino backstage, won Best Actress. The actor-activist held no grudge toward Meryl, her up-and-coming *Julia* costar, whom she once suggested for a part in *Coming Home*.

A starstruck Meryl sat near Gregory Peck, Sir Laurence Olivier, and Bette Davis. "It was intense," she said later. "I was completely in awe. It wasn't like now, where everybody's always everywhere publicly. Those people lived in rarified Hollywood and you only saw them on screen or in the most controlled ways—in magazines or something." The inaugural nominee smiled while losing to *California Suite*'s Maggie Smith. Clearly, she was changing her mind about awards recognition. The truth: Meryl did love to win on some deep level, and this competitiveness prevailed over the part of her that felt it was unfair to rate one excellent performance above another. As she admitted in 2014, "I don't like it, but I crave it." (That Emmy she didn't accept for *Holocaust*? A journalist spotted the trophy sitting atop a cabinet in her apartment.)

Film reviewers heaped praise upon Meryl in *Deer Hunter*. Vincent Canby of the *New York Times* called it "smashing," and Pauline Kael, the *New Yorker* legend who later became Meryl's greatest critic, wrote that she "has the clear-eyed blonde handsomeness of a Valkyrie—the slight extra length of her nose gives her face a distinction that takes her out of the pretty class into real beauty. She doesn't do anything standard; everything seems fresh. But her role is to be the supportive woman, who suffers and endures, and it's a testament to Meryl Streep's heroic resources as a mime that she makes herself felt—she has practically no lines."

Months afterward, Meryl mesmerized critics in *Manhattan*, *Joe Tynan*, and *Kramer vs. Kramer*. They championed her screen presence, eager to introduce a rising star to fellow film buffs. The positive feedback helped establish Meryl as the Best Actress of Her Generation—buzzier than Swoosie, Jill, and Tovah—while she embarked on a challenging role that would require long stretches at home, changing diapers, not dialogue.

On November 13, 1979, Henry Wolfe Gummer arrived three weeks late, a breech baby delivered by C-section. "There was nothing to it," Meryl said. "Don was with me and held the baby right after it was born. It seemed the most natural thing in the world." She'd wanted children since girlhood; now she was among the first of her career-focused friends to have a kid. "I think they're important to have around," she remarked, "so I'm going to manage, however it's possible."

The new mother vowed to raise Henry in her parents' tradition. "They were consistent with me. It's important not to say one thing one day and then say 'Oh, it's all right' the next. You need some kind of structure. I had that consistency as a child and it gave me a battering ram, a good thing to rebel against. I've been reading Dr. Spock and I think he's been misinterpreted. He doesn't advocate allowing children to do anything they want. He says *listen* to what your children are *saying* to you."

In interviews, Meryl took parenting as seriously as her profession, betraying what appeared to be an anxious, albeit entirely rational, outlook for Henry's future. "This child," she told *Ladies' Home Journal*, "will have to get us into the next century. His generation will have to deal with problems of survival that our generation never even thought of: pollution, depletion of natural resources, population control...."

She was careful to own her special privilege as a successful working mom free to take Henry on a movie set and breastfeed him in a trailer. However, she noted, "it's very difficult for women with other jobs. It's odd that there are all sorts of incentives for women to enter the workforce, but little provision made for their children."

During reshoots for *Kramer vs. Kramer*, Robert Benton heard pregnant Meryl say that had she been "offered this role now, I couldn't have taken it."

The divorce drama premiered December 19, 1979, just in time for the holidays. Even though Joanna appeared only in the beginning and end, Roger Ebert commended the balanced perspective that Meryl brought to the table. Sure, he hogs most of the screen time with his button-cute son (Justin Henry), but Ted Kramer—an advertising executive and absentee husband and father—is certainly no saint. "Right away we're close to choosing sides and laying blame: How can she walk out on her home and child? we ask," wrote Ebert.

> But we can't quite ask that question in all sincerity, because what we've already seen of Hoffman makes it fairly clear why she might have decided to walk out. She may be leaving the family but he's hardly been a part of it. Harassed, running late, taking his son to school on the first day after his wife has left, he asks him: "What grade are you in?" It's the first. Hoffman didn't know.

Dustin, for his part, "saw Kramer as a lousy father who became a good father and who learned to be a mother." Taking over Joanna's role as primary parent, Ted experiences the penalties women confront in a hostile workplace when they become mothers. He gets fired for assuming a traditionally female role and making time to care for his son. He also masters how to cook french toast without burning it. Welcome to being a woman in 1979! When the court judge grants custody to Joanna, we do feel for Ted. He's grown as a human being. He knows our pain.

Like many feminists, *New West* columnist Jeanie Kasindorf was unamused. "Many critics who have reviewed *Kramer vs. Kramer* have praised the film for its evenhanded treatment of the two parents in the custody fight. That is patent nonsense," she wrote. "For almost two hours we watch Ted Kramer struggle with the demands of a single parent....The only hint of evenhandedness is a stunning courtroom speech" by Meryl. Where were the movies about a working mother's struggles? As Kasindorf argued, "Filmmakers, like many other men and women, think that cooking french toast in the morning is nothing special when a woman does it because it is what is 'expected' of women. So there is nothing special to watch on a movie screen."

On April 14, 1980, Meryl won an Academy Award for her break-through role. She triumphed over supporting actress contenders Candice Bergen and Barbara Barrie as well as her costars Jane Alexander (*Kramer vs. Kramer*) and Mariel Hemingway (*Manhattan*). Right before Jack Lemmon announced the result, Meryl grinned with giddy, nervous energy—as though Lemmon had already called her name. And when he did: *Ahhhhhh!* She kissed Dustin on the cheek and floated up the steps like Cinderella, accepting the award in a cream gown and jacket. Meryl's long, Disney princess hair bounced off her shoulders. She was an Oscar-worthy shampoo commercial.

"Holy mackerel!" she proclaimed, deferring to *Kramer*'s men. "I'd like to thank Dustin Hoffman and Robert Benton, to whom I owe this. Stanley Jaffe, for giving me the chance to play Joanna. And Jane Alexander and Justin"—blowing her screen son a kiss—"for the love and support during this very, very delightful experience. Thank you very much."

She seemingly recited the speech from memory, struggling a bit to remember her lines amid the excitement. She radiated *happy* and *humble* and *I hope you like me*. The character, if you'll remember: Teen Beauty Queen. Meryl could resurface the Bernards High babe when surrounded by powerful men and skeptical women whom she needed to win over to survive the social spiderweb of the entertainment industry. Dustin, homecoming king, took home Best Actor, while the Academy awarded Benton the trophies for Best Director and Best Adapted Screenplay. Last but not least, *Kramer* was named Best Picture—the rare character drama picture to achieve both critical acclaim and massive commercial success. Proving that Hollywood still produced movies for grownups, it made a whopping $106 million in an era when blockbusters such as *Star Wars* and *Jaws* topped the box office. "It was a movie that spoke to a lot of people's lives," says Benton, citing the timely rise in divorce.

BIG IN CHINA

"I am, weirdly. I mean, I was really surprised! The first time I went was about six years ago. We went to Beijing and Shanghai, but also went to Xi'an—I'd never heard of this city. Only, you know, half a billion people. But I got off the plane and many, many people recognized me and I was really, really surprised. I found out later that the very first film to be released in China after the cultural revolution was *Kramer vs. Kramer*. And every single person in China saw that movie."— Meryl, casually mentioning her Tom Cruise–level international fame on *Jimmy Kimmel* circa 2012.

Backstage in the Oscars press lounge, gossip columnist Rona Barrett said feminists felt the movie "was a slap to them." Dustin countered, "I can't stop people from feeling what they are feeling, but I don't think everyone feels that way." Then Meryl showed up, metaphorically removing her teen-queen gloves to reveal the Vassar hippie underneath. "Here comes a feminist," she declared. "I don't feel that's true at all. I feel that the basis of feminism is something that has to do with liberating men *and* women from prescribed roles."

Meryl defended her characters. Joanna was suffering from depression, an invisible, misunderstood illness at the time. She'd managed to take action, entrusting Billy with Ted, a stable provider, so she could get help. Shouldn't art provoke conversations? Reflect modern life in illuminating ways? Why did everything—every female character—have to be so black-and-white?

Kramer vs. Kramer boosted Meryl's visibility at warp speed for a newcomer. *Newsweek* splashed her on the cover of its January 1, 1980, issue. The headline: "A Star for the '80s." In his glowing profile, senior editor Jack Kroll enthused that Meryl "may become the strongest performer of her generation, the first American woman since Jane Fonda to rival the power, versatility, and impact of such male stars as Dustin Hoffman, Robert De Niro, and Al Pacino." Kroll waxed poetic, pondering, "Can one face express all these warring emotions, with a grave dignity that adds a deeper beauty to the physical structure?"

Sometimes important magazines can jump the gun, as when ingénue Gretchen Mol graced the September 1998 edition of *Vanity Fair* alongside the coverline "Is She Hollywood's Next 'It' Girl?" She wasn't. But, with Meryl, the hype happened to deliver. The exposure unsettled her, though. She wondered whether she deserved the attention. "It is the weirdest feeling," she remembered. "A strange dissociation. You ride the subway and see something on the ground and look at it closely and see my face. There I was, all over the place. It made me feel mortal and made me feel how ephemeral the whole thing was. And sort of a little bit silly."

WHEN THE QUEEN MET THE QUEEN

On March 17, 1980, Meryl shook Queen Elizabeth II's hand at a screening of *Kramer vs. Kramer* in London. Her Streep-ness wore the off-white gown she would repeat to accept her Oscar for Best Supporting Actress the next month. (Hey, this was well before the Internet and *Us Weekly* began monitoring celebrities for fashion faux pas such as recycling outfits on the red carpet.) I hereby deem Meryl and Elizabeth's groundbreaking first encounter a national holiday in America and around the world. Both women are forces of joy. Since Meryl has played Margaret Thatcher, among other British roles, I'm of a mind that the Queen should knight her American counterpart.

After *Kramer*, she told Sam Cohn, "I've got to do something outside of Manhattan, outside of 1981, outside of my experience. Put me on the moon; I want to be someplace else. I want to be held in the boundaries of a different time and place."

She longed to dive with childlike abandon into a new life. "I had just done three movies, and I needed to jump and leap and feel the way I see my little boy play," she said later. "And I wanted to forget the way I look, to become un-self-conscious, to have that freedom children have when they're doing something in the middle of a room full of adults looking at them—and they just totally don't care. Sure, maybe I can go to an analyst to try to not be self-conscious, but it never occurred to me to do that."

Enter Sarah Woodruff, the Victorian-era outcast of John Fowles's novel *The French Lieutenant's Woman*, which Harold Pinter adapted into a screenplay. The film had a dual structure. In the main narrative, Sarah, the village pariah who wears a witchy, brown cape, seduces paleontologist Charles Smithson (Jeremy Irons), whose life turns to shambles when he leaves his well-to-do fiancée to pursue her. After Sarah bolts to parts unknown, he's nearly driven mad. *Has she become a London street urchin? A prostitute?! The disgrace!*

Three years go by. Finally, Sarah reaches out with an update: She's living a happy, healthy life as a governess in northwest England. The news infuriates Charles, who pays her a visit. But rather than exchange a polite hello, he pushes Sarah to the ground. How dare she desert him! "It has taken me this time to find my own life!" she asserts, explaining that she wanted her freedom. Now, she seeks Charles's forgiveness. ("I must forgive you," he relents.) Despite the physical violence and emotional manipulation, Sarah and Charles get a happy ending: a pleasant boat ride on Lake Windermere.

While all that's happening, a parallel subplot partners Meryl and Jeremy as modern-day actors who strike up an affair on the set of—how meta—*The French Lieutenant's Woman*. Meryl's character, Anna, returns to her husband as if the showmance never happened, leaving Mike (Jeremy) heartbroken.

From May to September 1980, Meryl relocated to the UK for the shoot, which took place in the seaside town of Lyme Regis, among other locations. She and her family rented a home in London's tony Kensington neighborhood. According to a *People* dispatch, Meryl "needed an extra inducement before United Artists could lure her to London." The icing on the cake: "a studio and raw materials for her sculptor husband, Don Gummer, so he can create while she films." United Artists, the movie's distributor, had offered to pick up the tab.

She experienced preshow jitters, confiding to a friend, "I'm so frightened, I'm so frightened about something as important as this." *French Lieutenant* tested her star power: if she successfully carried the romantic drama, then more leading lady roles would follow. She knew there were people out there who wanted to see her fail following so much success—no doubt actors in actors' bars talking smack. She had battled anxiety before opening nights and big premieres, telling brother Third, "This is the worst thing I've ever done." To which he would reply, "Don't you remember? This isn't the worst thing. The *last* thing you did was the worst thing."

For Meryl, who wanted to do well, the fear of failure seemed to be a propeller: get gritty, do the work, and—fingers crossed—thwart public humiliation. She faced pressure not only to perform but *transform*, assuming a character's troubles, tics, and accent. "Meryl was very concerned at first," recalled Karel Reisz, her director. "We even had it up our sleeve that we could lip-sync some of those parts if it was necessary."

To capture Sarah's nineteenth-century speech, Meryl hired a voice coach and read aloud from Jane Austen and George Eliot. She studied photos of geisha women "because they demonstrated a highly formalized kind of femininity," she said. "I give a lot away with my face and I wanted to work on revealing less; so much of Sarah is hidden, covered up—that's what entices Charles and makes him give up his whole way of life." Wearing a dramatic, if harsh, red wig and full corset for ten-hour stretches helped Meryl get into character.

She made unexpected choices, like giggling instead of crying when Charles assaults Sarah. "That was one of the most miraculous acting moments I've ever seen, but the punchline is that they did six takes and she only did that once," the director Mike Nichols later marveled. "To be able to tap into your inner responses and know that's the deepest part of the character is to be a great film actress."

Jeremy Irons was classically trained at Britain's Old Vic Theatre School, founded by Laurence Olivier, and had played Petruchio in a West End revival of *The Taming of the Shrew*, bonding him closer to Meryl, who'd played Kate in New York. At first, Jeremy had been intimidated by Meryl's work ethic and strong will. "Whenever she suggested something, I at least tried it," he recalled. "If ever there was a possibility of confrontation, I tried it her way." She pushed Jeremy to match her stamina. "When we shot the barn scene, where Meryl wakes up to me watching over her, it wasn't going well after many takes. So she came over to me and physically shook me and said, 'It's hard, it's hard. You have to do it though, it's never easy.'"

In an interview after filming ended, Jeremy suggested their intimate scenes were authentic. "In order to reach the right emotional pitch, Meryl and I had to experience emotionally almost what the characters were experiencing," he said. "So for the day we shot our love scene, Meryl and I had an affair. And when the cameras stopped, our affair stopped." Meryl responded to clarify that she and Jeremy were "two good pals" who had been "playacting under the direction of Karel Reisz."

She would be swarmed with awards, including a BAFTA and Golden Globe for Best Actress, as well as another Oscar nomination (she lost to Katharine Hepburn for *On Golden Pond*). But, in hindsight, she still believed she hadn't done enough. "I didn't feel I was living it," she confessed on the *Graham Norton Show* in 2016. "You always want to do something better after the fact." And watching *French Lieutenant,* "I couldn't help wishing that I was more beautiful." She has said, "There comes a point when you have to look the part, especially in movies. In Victorian literature, passion, an illicit feeling, was always represented by darkness. I'm so fair that dark hair makes me look like some old fish, so I opted for auburn hair instead. I really wish I was the kind of actress who could have just stood there and said it all."

On the flip side, what Meryl lacked in the feline sex appeal of, say, Jessica Lange, whom she alternately admired and envied, lent a layer of intrigue to Sarah Woodruff. Moviegoers wondered, What *was* it about her, exactly? *She's so plain. But she's not* not *pretty.* Meryl would use her polarizing visage to great advantage—it allowed her to sidestep the typecasting that discarded leading ladies who only played beautiful characters as soon as they hit forty, only to replace them with younger models. Because Meryl's looks did not define her, she was liberated to become anyone she wanted. As a human being in a beauty-obsessed industry, she wasn't immune to self-doubt. "I wasted so many years thinking I wasn't pretty enough and why didn't I have Jessica Lange's body or someone else's legs? What a waste of time," she would reveal decades later.

Meryl had no interest in making "soft-core" fare that exploited a woman's sexuality. She'd seen those scripts before, where a woman "emerges in half-light, half-dressed," the sort of "character who doesn't even have a name before they write the third draft." She was "drawn to complicated, attractive, prickly women. I like them because I like difficult people in life."

Her next challenge: Sophie Zawistowska. In April 1980, rumors swirled that Meryl was going to portray the Holocaust survivor in the big-screen adaptation of *Sophie's Choice*, potentially with Al Pacino. Goldie Hawn campaigned for the role, and Barbra Streisand offered to take a pay cut. But Meryl interested writer-director Alan J. Pakula from the beginning. The problem: she asked to read his shooting script, and Pakula didn't yet have one. He moved on to an obscure Slovak actress, Magda Vásáryová, who conveyed European authenticity but had little grasp of English (an eventual deal breaker). Finally, there was a script. Sam Cohn got his hands on a copy and sent it to

Meryl. "I really *wanted* that part," she said. "I went to Pakula and threw myself on the ground. 'Please, God, let me do it,' I begged."

Pakula had pictures of Magda—*whatever her name was*—all over his office. "You can't let her play it!" she recalled saying. "I have to play this part! You don't understand. I can do it." Without question, Meryl had the talent. But he worried her "technique" would become a problem. Could this strong, self-assured professional lose herself in an unguarded, sensual performance? Equally important: *Could an American actress convincingly pull off the role?*

Several weeks later, he offered Meryl the part. (You have to wonder whether he was making her sweat as penance for the screenplay request. According to Meryl, Pakula had been "mad" at her.)

Meryl recommended that Kevin Kline, thirty-three years old and already a two-time Tony winner, play Sophie's vibrant, volatile lover Nathan. (Pakula's short list of potential Nathans had included De Niro, Pacino, and Dustin Hoffman, all of whom he judged unfit.) The baby-faced Peter MacNicol, who starred in the Pulitzer Prize–winning play *Crimes of the Heart,* joined the cast as Stingo, a genteel southern writer who befriends Sophie and Nathan in 1947 Brooklyn.

Sophie was Meryl's most complex character to date—soft yet strong, sexy and enigmatic, with warm humor masking terrible pain. After World War II, the Polish Catholic refugee flees to New York, vulnerable and broken, unable to speak English. Nathan, oozing charisma and manic energy, takes pity on Sophie and teaches her to read. They move in together, starting a codependent, roller-coaster relationship tethered to Nathan's violent mood swings. Meeting the dysfunctional couple for the first time, Stingo witnesses a belligerent Nathan shake Sophie amid a temper tantrum. "I need you like a case of anthrax!" he screams. Also, "Go back to Krakow, baby!" Sophie, indebted to his sporadic kindnesses and grappling with undiagnosed PTSD, takes him back hours later.

Unbeknownst to Sophie and Stingo, Nathan is hiding the fact that he suffers from a debilitating mental illness: paranoid schizophrenia.

As Stingo grows closer to Sophie, he begins to unravel the mystery of her past. Like Nathan, she's perpetuated a lie—reframing her father as a hero and intellectual in defiance of Nazi Germany.

When Sophie owns up to the truth, the film switches to devastating flashbacks that reveal her life as a tragedy of unfathomable torment: She hated her dad, a law professor with anti-Semitic views from which she recoiled. His ideology offered no protection when the Nazis, coming for the intellectuals, sent the academic as well as Sophie's husband to a German work camp, where they were both killed. Sophie, part of the underground Resistance, was arrested and deported to Auschwitz with her two young children, a boy and a girl. A sadistic Nazi officer ordered her to choose between them—sparing one child's life and sentencing the other to die in a gas chamber. Sophie, hysterical, picked her daughter, Eva, a subconscious sign that she valued her son Jan's life more; he was taken to a children's camp, never to be seen again. Sophie, whose German was flawless, became a typist in the home of an Auschwitz commander. Miraculously, she survived starvation and the threat of death, but eventually succumbed to the guilt that would compel her to join Nathan in suicide by cyanide.

Though Meryl was prepared to do Sophie right, at first she struggled to find common ground. "The problem was that Sophie was such a victim," she said. "She really let the tanks run over her." The tanks, of course, were manned by the patriarchy: Nathan, her abuser in New York, isolates the immigrant within their small, prisonlike apartment, knowing she has nowhere else to turn. Soon enough, however, "I saw little bits of me in her," said Meryl. "I found she had some spirit, a little backbone." She admired Sophie's resilience, how she weathered setbacks "with a lot of life and vitality."

Given Meryl's publicly voiced outrage over the human casualties of war—particularly, mothers grieving their children—the film historian Karina Longworth surmised that "this compassion for the price inflicted on women as collateral damage from the political conflicts of men helped her to connect to Sophie."

It wasn't until studying Polish that Meryl really got to know her. While shooting the Brooklyn scenes, she brought a trace of her Polish accent home, upsetting Henry. Meryl underwent five months of tutoring to learn the language. "I thought it would be a piece of cake, like picking up Italian or French or something—but it's not," she said. "It's a lot like Latin because there are seven cases, I think—my teacher will kill me if I don't get this right—grammar wasn't my strong point, I can get the accent. Anyway, because of that it was real hard to learn, you have to parse every sentence as you speak it, every word changes its ending according to whether it's the object of a sentence or the subject or the indirect object. It's really wild."

Before moving to Zagreb, Yugoslavia, for three weeks to film the concentration camp sequences alongside a European cast, Meryl was now required to learn a new tongue during her break. Pakula wrote the wartime scenes in English but believed, at the last minute, that they should be filmed in Polish and German, which meant a crash course in the latter for Meryl. "Get me a German teacher," she told Pakula.

Overseas, Meryl faced a dilemma: Don was mounting a solo show at a Manhattan gallery. "I know how you're going to feel about this, but please consider it anyway," she wrote in a note to Pakula. "Don's always there for me. Now I'm eating myself up that I can't be there for him." Pakula, at a loss, fielded advice from someone who said, "Tell her, 'no,' Alan, and put her out of her misery. Meryl just has guilt feelings. It's up to you to relieve her of them." Instead, Pakula trusted Meryl to pull through—and she did not disappoint. After less than twenty-four hours in New York, she made it to the set, conjuring Sophie with no apparent sign of jet lag.

Pakula had invited Kitty Hart-Moxon, who grew up in Poland and survived Auschwitz-Birkenau as a teenager, to help her understand what it felt like to be imprisoned in a camp. Meryl shed a dramatic amount of weight through a rigid diet that involved eating foods mixed in a blender and drinking few fluids. On camera, she was all skin, bone, and angles—a sliver of Brooklyn Sophie—with a short wig, discolored teeth, and sad, watchful eyes that managed to reflect conflicting emotions: despair and hope. Later, in America, Sophie was voluptuous and vivacious, yet her face (altered by Meryl's prosthetic teeth) simultaneously conveyed sadness that memory could not erase.

Meryl read the scene where Sophie makes her choice only once. "I didn't want to think about it," she said. "I had memorized it because it was, like, engraved on my heart. When we shot it, I didn't want to do it again. I didn't want to be there. And we got it done. I didn't need to think about, 'What if I had to leave my son?' I didn't want to think about that *at all!*"

It is painful to watch, but, like testimony from Hart-Moxon, the ordeal serves to remind us that the atrocities of the Holocaust occurred not long ago, in broad daylight. We must keep the memory alive so that we never forget.

○ ○ ○ ○ ○

Like a shot of espresso, *Sophie's Choice* invigorated Meryl. She received a buzz from the spontaneity of acting opposite her costars; no amount of research could prepare her for what developed when the camera started rolling. "Kevin and Peter MacNicol and I really fell mutually in love, just as the characters did in the film," she said. According to an unnamed source in the December 1987 edition of *Life* magazine, Kevin was "smitten." (At one point, Peter felt left out because Meryl, echoing Sophie, was paying more attention to Kevin on the set.) Meryl, you'll continue to read, had that effect on her leading men. Here's how Mike Nichols, who directed her in three movies and one TV miniseries, described it: "As she becomes the person she is portraying, the other performers begin to react to her as if she *were* that person. Whoever is playing the lover falls in love with her, whoever is playing the villain is frightened of her, whoever is playing her friend becomes her friend, and so on. She changes the chemistry of all the relationships. I've never seen anybody else do that."

Kevin and Meryl.

The impact: a stronger performance by Meryl, who must *feel* that Sophie loves Nathan. In turn, her excellence trickles down to strengthen the cast as a whole—even actors with far less talent than Kevin Kline.

Oh, *him.*

"Kevin is a dream! He's heaven. He really is," she said. "It's a terrible job, you know. I mean, loving all those handsome and fascinating men.... Come *on!* It's fun! It's fun to recreate those feelings—and not have any of the repercussions."

Come on! Wouldn't you?

Kevin met few people who enjoyed their work as much as Meryl. He found her to be "one of the most blithely assertive people I've ever met. She has no neurotic self-absorption. She can make points as they evolve, spontaneously, moment to moment, without having to apologize for having an idea."

Do go on.

"She's healthy and sane," he continued. "She's also unencumbered by prejudgments about what one should or shouldn't do."

Pakula didn't always approve of Meryl's experimentation. When she insisted upon drinking real alcohol in a scene with Peter, Pakula agreed to her request but soon dismissed the footage as excessive. Otherwise, the star left the director in awe.

One night, he returned home in high spirits. He told his wife that he thought Meryl was a "genius," a word he didn't use unless he truly meant it. After *Sophie's Choice* finally wrapped in New York in April 1982, Meryl and the crew "had a drunken evening," and she "cried and cried." She had felt alive—joyously, rapturously alive. Would she ever find a character like Sophie again, or had she peaked at thirty-two?

CHAPTER 4

Meryl Goes Nuclear

*Drew: Sweetheart, it's like you're two people. I'm in love with
one of them. But the other one's . . .
Karen: Just a real pain in the ass.*

(*Silkwood*, 1983)

There was little time to mourn Sophie. Meryl soon relocated to Dallas
to assume the identity of another tragic heroine: Karen Silkwood, the
real-life Oklahoma plutonium plant whistleblower whose mysterious
death in a 1974 car crash stoked speculation that the twenty-eight-
year-old had been run off the road.

Meryl's growing political activism mirrored that of her character.
Before filming *Silkwood*, Mike Nichols's biopic of the activist, Meryl
was among the thousands who flocked to Central Park on June 12,
1982, to protest nuclear weapons. Bruce Springsteen, James Taylor,
and Joan Baez performed for the peaceful crowd. The cause moved
Meryl. "We've got to do everything we can to make ourselves felt and
not just *talk* about the nuclear threat," she said at the time. "We've
got to write letters to our congressmen and read books like Jonathan
Schell's *The Fate of the Earth*. We can't withdraw into a deadening,
frightening, end-of-the-world fear, so deeply rooted that we don't
even recognize it in ourselves. I keep thinking all the time that, in
the year 2000, Henry will be only 21."

Silkwood (original title: *Chain Reaction*) was trapped in limbo for
seven years. The long-gestating project gathered steam once Meryl
expressed interest, turning the movie into a sudden hot property. Nora

Ephron and Alice Arlen cowrote the screenplay, which Nichols signed on to direct. In 1968, he won an Oscar for his groundbreaking dramedy *The Graduate* but took an eight-year break from movies after directing a succession of mid-1970s stinkers (*The Day of the Dolphin, The Fortune*). For Nichols, Meryl was the bait to lure him back behind the camera. If she wanted to do *Silkwood,* then so did he. Now, the filmmaker *could* have made a flashy thriller pitting Karen against corporate goons in dark suits and Ray-Bans, but instead he collaborated closely with the screenwriters to focus on her personal story—specifically, how an apolitical working-class woman becomes radicalized.

Karen Silkwood had a target on her back. A Texan, born and raised, Karen was a straight-A student who excelled in science and had been the lone girl in her high school chemistry class. She married young, at age nineteen, and seven years later, in 1972, she left her three kids and cheating husband behind for the supposedly greener pastures of Oklahoma City. She soon found a steady gig at the Kerr-McGee Corporation, a powerful energy company. Her work as a chemical technician involved making plutonium pellets for nuclear reactor fuel rods. The process risked exposing her to a toxic substance that, even in small doses, leads to radiation poisoning, cancer, and death. By 1974, Karen had joined the Oil, Chemical and Atomic Workers International Union, becoming the first female Kerr-McGee employee on the union bargaining committee. She participated in a strike against the company and raised alarm about workers' health and safety after uncovering evidence of spills and leaks. She testified before the Atomic Energy Commission, saying she'd been exposed to unexplained radiation there.

Against a backdrop of rising environmental activism, Kerr-McGee was a thousand lawsuits waiting to happen, and Karen a pest who wouldn't go away. On November 13, 1974, she was to meet *New York Times* reporter David Burnham and show him the contents of a manila folder containing documents that purported to reveal unsafe conditions inside the plant where she worked. En route to the meeting, Karen's car careened off a country road and crashed into a culvert, killing her. The Oklahoma Highway Patrol called it an accident. Perhaps she'd fallen asleep at the wheel—after all, quaaludes were discovered in her bloodstream. But, in a conflicting report, the Atomic Workers Union cried foul, alleging that another vehicle intentionally forced Karen's fatal swerve. Adding to the creepiness: that manila folder was MIA.

"Just before her death Silkwood had charged that the plant had strayed so far from the federal nuclear code that it posed a danger to its workers and the public, and she allegedly had been collecting proof of that," *Rolling Stone* writer Howard Kohn reported in 1977. "Some investigators later theorized that Silkwood had also unwittingly uncovered a smuggling ring at the plant and that her documents held information about missing plutonium."

Two weeks before Karen died, she underwent decontamination after repeatedly testing positive for plutonium. A federal investigation confirmed many of Karen's allegations, and, in 1979, her estate was awarded $10.5 million in damages in a civil suit. Seven years later, an impending retrial sparked Kerr-McGee—which had since shuttered its nuclear plants—to settle with Team Silkwood for $1.3 million. Even in death, Karen, a hero to feminists and antinuclear activists, seemed to eclipse the defendant in power. She had become a martyr.

ABOUT THAT ENDING

Mystery surrounded the sequence of events that precipitated Karen Silkwood's fatal car crash. Did she fall asleep at the wheel, or was it murder? She had been driving to meet *New York Times* reporter David Burnham to reveal health and safety violations at Kerr-McGee, her employer. Curiously, documents containing proof of wrongdoing had gone missing from the scene of the accident.

Silkwood director Mike Nichols had intended to show that Karen had been murdered. In the director's original finale, Karen left a union meeting at a coffee shop with papers she was going to present to the journalist. She "said goodbye to her friend, got into her car then started it," the film's editor, Sam O'Steen, wrote in his book *Cut to the Chase*. "The moment she pulled into traffic, the headlights blinked on in the car parked behind her. This was an 'oh, oh' moment. But I had to take that out, the shot of the lights blinking on. Now all you see is a time jump, where she's driving at night and sees headlights from the car behind her in her rearview mirror. The next shot is of her wrecked car. So in the final cut it wasn't as clear that someone was following her."

The legal ramifications of keeping the scene as it stood—of taking a side—proved too risky, as Kerr-McGee Nuclear Corporation had threatened the film. "Mike was upset about it, but there was nothing he could do," O'Steen said. "He did consult with a heavy-weight lawyer at one point to see what he could get away with."

Nichols wound up adding the disclaimers that the death was judged a single-car accident, that Karen had alcohol and a tranquilizer in her system, and that no one could confirm the papers were meant for Burnham.

Meryl had thoughts on how Karen died but did not share them publicly.

"I really don't think we can know much about people after they're not there to tell us," she explained. "All their real, real secrets die with them. At the end of this whole experience of making this movie, I thought about those minutes before Karen's car went off the road, and I missed her."

❂ ❂ ❂ ❂ ❂

Sure, Nora Ephron was a seasoned journalist, but that didn't mean the mother of two small boys could research the convoluted Silkwood saga all on her own. Accuracy was essential; one egregious error could spell legal trouble. She needed help digesting the facts and synthesizing them into a script that would manage to tell a compelling story about a red-state rebel. Nora, who grew up in Beverly Hills before becoming a New Yorker for life, had no clue what it was like to be Karen Silkwood. So she hired Alice Arlen, who knew the lawyer on the Silkwood case. (Alice told me that Nora visited her family ranch and "thought I knew more about rednecks than she did.")

The screenwriting duo enlisted the expertise of *Silkwood* executive producer Buzz Hirsch, who had already done extensive interviews with players such as Karen's boyfriend, Drew Stephens, who said Karen once flashed him at work. "I knew exactly who she was at that moment," Nora said. "She was a provocateur."

When Meryl arrived to the set, "she still looked like Sophie," Hirsch remembers. "She was still sort of in character. And it was only when Roy Helland cut her hair and dyed it and gave her the Karen Silkwood 'do that—bam—she changed. It was really amazing. She became Karen Silkwood." Out went Sophie's golden locks; in came a brown mullet. Meryl resembled a low-key Williamsburg hipster. (Some might call that #goals.)

Most of the production took place in Irving, Texas, at the Dallas Communications Complex, which houses studio soundstages. The VIPs among cast and crew took temporary apartments near each

Meryl's mullet.

other. On weekends, Don and Henry would visit Meryl and swim in the pool. Even with her husband and toddler son, Meryl "was Karen Silkwood all the time," Hirsch observes. One day, Meryl surprised him during a break between takes. "She came over and just sat in my lap, which kind of shocked me and was just really flirty," he recalls. "And when filming started again, she got up, and as she was walking away, I said, 'I'll save your seat for you.' And she turned around and gave me a look, like, 'Well, that was fresh.' But it was the character that was doing this."

Off camera, Meryl spoke in a Texas twang. She told Hirsch that she would go and sit in shopping malls and just listen to the way people talked. Although Karen's father, Bill, complained that *Silkwood* made his intelligent daughter "look not very bright and a hick Tobacco Road type," Drew Stephens was amazed. "He couldn't believe how she had captured Karen," Hirsch says. Nichols chose the fun-loving Kurt Russell to play Drew. As for Karen's best friend, Dolly Pelliker, he chose a woman who needs no introduction: *Cher.* The role required the entertainer to tone down her aspirational flamboyance. She was prepared to do just that if it would advance her acting career.

Cher sparkled like the view from the Hollywood Hills on a smogless night, but Meryl—Meryl was sophisticated, chic without trying. An Ivy League smartypants. Cher had been nervous to meet her costar, whom she compared to the pope. What if Meryl thought she was a bad actress?

The first day on location, Meryl gave Cher a warm welcome, like Karen greeting Dolly. "My friend is coming," she thought, "I have someone on my side." But she could not ignore the celebrity in her midst. "Cher! You know, from 'I Got You, Babe' and all those other records I bought....[O]n the other hand, apparently [she] had an image of me as sitting at the right hand of Dame Edith Sitwell. I think she was intimidated by my rep."

All told, Cher was hardly an acting novice. She soared to fame alongside then-partner Sonny Bono as a chart-topping '60s pop duo while simultaneously launching a successful solo career. Then, in 1971, Sonny and Cher debuted their popular CBS variety hour, where Cher sharpened her comic timing in a range of character sketches. Three years later, she won the Golden Globe for Best Actress, Television Series Musical or Comedy. Meanwhile, the couple was on the brink of divorce, prompting their series' 1974 cancellation. Cher next headlined a short-lived eponymous show, performing opposite big names from David Bowie to Bette Midler. On television, her glamorous, show-stopping ensembles cemented her legacy as a style icon. After completing a two-year Vegas residency in 1982, the entertainer starred on Broadway as a James Dean fangirl in the play *Come Back to the Five and Dime, Jimmy Dean, Jimmy Dean* as well as in Robert Altman's film adaptation.

Following *Silkwood,* Cher would garner glowing reviews in the 1985 drama *Mask* and the 1988 romantic comedy *Moonstruck,* for which she snagged the ultimate Streepian prize: the Oscar for Best Actress.

According to Hirsch, Meryl immediately sought to ingratiate herself with Cher. "And Cher," he says, "would just love the idea of being great friends with Meryl. I would hear Cher. 'Will you come and visit me, and stay with me in LA? I really would love it if you came and stayed with me.'"

Cher had been in show business for two decades, but not until *Silkwood* did she think people took her seriously. Meryl shared acting advice and never made her feel less than. In a case of art imitating life, Cher—the devoted Dolly to Meryl's Karen—would talk about moving across the country to be closer to Meryl. The improbable friends (call them "Cheryl") were more alike than one might expect. "She is a lot like me, my real personal self," Meryl said back then. "She has a lot of humor, is a little sassy, gets a lot of people mad at her, and she does what she believes she has to do."

Cher relished this new, exciting friendship. "If she were my own sister, I couldn't love her more," she gushed. "People don't realize it, but Meryl's a funny, funny lady."

At the start of the *Silkwood* shoot, Meryl mocked Cher's fashiony, fish-out-of-water approach to dressing. "Give it up Cher—not here, not in Texas. Send all that crap home," she'd say, to which Cher retorted, "Mary Louise, you've got to learn how to *dress*."

It drove Cher crazy when Meryl insisted on ironing her own clothes, and Meryl's jaw basically dropped upon seeing what Cher wore to visit Six Flags. "Cher had this pink miniskirt on that was maybe six inches long in the back," Meryl said. "And she just blithely walks through the place. I mean, I'd wear a wig, sunglasses, and a trench coat. But Cher doesn't mind being the center of attention. It isn't agony for her."

What did agonize Cher: Nichols's vision for her character's aesthetic. Dolly had originally been written as a "glamorous barrel rider," said Cher, who screen-tested that look for Nichols. He ultimately disliked it, advising her to scrub her face. Then, Nichols and costume designer Ann Roth outfitted the glamazon in "some horrible men's bowling shirt and awful chino pants, with two pairs of jockey shorts underneath to make me look heavier."

Nichols was happy, but when Kurt Russell spotted her, he said, "What the fuck are *you* supposed to be?"

Cher ran to a bathroom and "cried her eyes out." She was *supposed* to shine. Instead she looked dreadful. However, Cher came to embrace the frumpier Dolly, a "female version of a good ol' boy," and her slouchy, utilitarian wardrobe of T-shirts and jeans. It seemed that Meryl's lack of vanity had rubbed off on her. Without makeup, Cher felt free.

"Meryl made her look good," says Hirsch. "She wasn't in the same league with Meryl, and that film was sort of [edited] for Cher. We had to get those good takes of Cher because Meryl was always good.... It wasn't often that we did a lot of takes. Mike just didn't work that way.

But if there was more than one take, Meryl never did it exactly the same twice. It was always perfectly tuned to what she was receiving from Kurt or Cher, from whatever actor was on the set."

Meryl could spot the difference between a natural actor and a bad actor from a mile away. A natural actor cannot ring a false note; she always responds to the truth of the character and scene. On the contrary, a bad actor will force emotions she doesn't feel to appease a director. Cher managed to exceed her high standards.

"She's a completely natural actress," Meryl raved. "No artifice, no effort, just intuitive. You'd think that somebody that was so involved in artifice, and style, and the sheen of it, would have difficulty in knocking that off, getting underneath. And she didn't at all." Most impressive, "Cher just *felt* things—with the camera going. And that's a very strange thing, to feel things with the camera going. And Cher was raised in Texas, y'know. And they didn't have much money. So she came from that part of the world, and she was able to fall right into it again."

MERYL AND CHER: A TIME LINE OF THE GREATEST FRIENDSHIP IN MOVIE HISTORY

1982: The legends quickly bonded on the set of *Silkwood*, where Meryl starred as Karen Silkwood and Cher played her best friend, Dolly. "I thought it was going to be like having an audience with the Pope," Cher recalled of meeting Meryl. Instead, the Oscar winner "just came up, threw her arms around me and said, 'I'm so glad you're here.' She's all communication and warmth and friendship with a great sense of humor."

1984: Meryl's fifth Academy Award nomination was fated, but OMG: Cher earned a nod for Best Supporting Actress! Dressing down to play Dolly had paid off, as had Meryl's acting guidance. On

Oscar night, Cher ruled the red carpet in a sparkly nude gown by her favorite designer, Bob Mackie. She wore massive diamond earrings and Val Kilmer on her arm. When Cher got an early look at Meryl's ensemble, she said, "You can't wear that." So she lent her friend a white, knee-length Sonia Rykiel dress with intricate embroidery. Meryl's accessory: Don Gummer.

1988: Are you sitting down? Because Cher and Meryl were—gasp—up for the same Oscar in a major category: *Best Actress*. While Meryl tugged at the heartstrings as a homeless woman in the bleak Depression-era drama *Ironweed*, Cher dazzled opposite Nicolas Cage in *Moonstruck*. The optimistic romantic comedy outperformed *Ironweed* at the box office. Not that anyone's keeping score! When Cher's name was called as the winner (!!!), Meryl (who already had two Oscars) stood up and applauded. In her speech, Cher thanked "Mary Louise," saying it felt "so unbelievable that I did my first movie with her, and now I was nominated with her, and I feel really thankful."

1990: Cher joined Meryl onstage to sing "What a Wonderful World" at a charity concert for the environmental group Mothers & Others, which Meryl formed in 1989 to raise awareness of toxic pesticides used in food production, among other health hazards. The event, dubbed "An Evening with Friends of the Environment," summoned other divas, including Bette Midler, Olivia Newton-John, and Goldie Hawn. Everyone dressed like a '90s mom except Cher. Wearing ripped rock-chick jeans, she looked like she'd crashed a PTA meeting in Connecticut. Surprise, surprise: Meryl, having a ball on stage, did a note-perfect Louis Armstrong impression.

2002: Oh no! In the December 2002 edition of *More* magazine, Meryl—experiencing a career renaissance with roles in *The Hours* and *Adaptation*—revealed that she and Cher were no longer besties. Basically, Cher had ghosted Meryl. "I was very, very close to her; then she sort of dropped out of my life," Meryl said. "It was a weird thing. She's a really interesting person—really smart and really funny. I called her a few times. She just kind of disappeared." However, Meryl wasn't letting herself off the hook. She wished "I had been a better friend and more in the lives of my friends during the years when I felt I just couldn't get a breath."

2003: Cher must have read that interview because, one year later, the two made joint, unexpected cameos in the Farrelly brothers comedy *Stuck on You*. Did Cher phone Meryl to make amends and invite her long-lost pal on the set? I am pretending that was the case. The crass yet surprisingly sweet movie officially costars Matt Damon and Greg Kinnear as Bob and Walt Tenor, conjoined twins who move to Hollywood so Walt can pursue his movie-star dreams. Lucky him, he strikes up unlikely friendships with both Cher *and* Meryl, playing themselves. The best moment occurs at the end, when Meryl steals the show in a community theater production of a musical based on Bonnie and Clyde.

2004: Cher honored Meryl at an American Film Institute tribute to the decorated Oscar veteran. "Meryl Streep is also an incredible singer," she said. "She uses her voice like she does everything else, with amazing grace." The "amazing grace" was a reference to Meryl's haunting performance of the hymn in *Silkwood*.

2012: In a rare appearance on Bravo's *Watch What Happens*, Meryl told host Andy Cohen a bit of trivia I shall carry with me forever: Cher smells like "patchouli." *Who knew?* Cher: Please bottle your scent for mass consumption and label it Confidence. (Hat tip to Cher expert Hilary Weaver for bringing Meryl's scent revelation to my attention.)

2018: Worlds collided at the London premiere of *Mamma Mia! Here We Go Again*, and once again, the Internet capsized on itself. While posing for photos, Meryl and Cher locked lips in an instantly iconic kiss. I can only describe it as equivalent to a Care Bear Stare expelling rainbows across the universe—the antidote to the negative news cycle and the toxic cesspool that is Twitter. Despite a three-year age difference, Cher played Meryl's mother in the ABBA-riffic sequel. "It was great, and [Meryl] was hiding watching me sing, and I was so excited," she said. "I didn't find out until afterwards—I would have been more nervous."

Like Nora, Meryl had a tough time nailing down Karen's personality. "I very quickly found I didn't know whom to believe," she said. "Everybody who had known Karen had a different image of her. There were a few things people agreed upon, but there were so many differences. It was as if I was hearing about several different women.... I realized that the more I knew about Karen, the less I knew her. She was very hard to find. Everything else about the film and everybody else in it exists. But there's no way I could catch her out of the air, as if I was a psychic picking up clues from the other world."

During the rehearsal phase, Meryl pored over court documents and other material that Hirsch and his producing partner Larry Cano assembled in their efforts to get *Silkwood* off the ground. She heard a recording of Karen's low, slow alto voice. It depressed her. "I listened to it again and again, but it turned out to be one of the least helpful things for me," she recalled. "Maybe the phone call was in the middle of the night and she was tired; maybe it was the recorder." Soon enough, "I stopped listening to it. It became disconcerting, and it upset me. The more I got into her life and death, the sadder it made me."

An old ID photo of Karen haunted Meryl. To flesh out this enigma and bring this *ghost* back to life, she seemingly drew from her own experience as a concerned citizen growing into her activism. Was Meryl a flirtatious nine-to-fiver? No way. Would she be the thorn in Kerr-McGee's backside? No doubt.

She patched together a character so specific that it required constant fine-tuning. To make a sports comparison: imagine a young Michael Jordan, already the best in the game, practicing for hours to help take the Chicago Bulls to the NBA Finals. Meryl was always perfecting Karen Silkwood. That might explain why Buzz Hirsch saw Karen, not Meryl, swimming in the pool away from the set.

"I really loved playing her," Meryl would later tell *Marquee Magazine*. She felt closer to Karen than other characters she'd played and called her "a pain in the ass. She was no saint, but a real, contradictory human being." Meryl once said that her contradictions were the part of her that always showed on film; acting, she thought, wasn't about becoming a different person. Rather, "It's finding the similarity in what is apparently different, then finding myself in there."

While making Silkwood, Nichols caught a screening of Sophie's Choice. He assumed that "Silkwood Meryl was the real Meryl." Sophie, however, made him rethink the woman he thought he knew. "Who the fuck is that?" he wondered. "She's absolutely real! Which one is she?!"

Despite belonging to different social classes, Meryl and Karen shared a rebellious spirit: both were walking contradictions, taking on noble causes—and personas—with a change of scenery. The nonconformists found purpose in pushing back against expectations. If Nichols failed to figure out the real Meryl, then maybe ambiguity was the point. Meryl, in her various forms, confounded Nichols and kept him guessing. She wasn't boring or predictable. You never knew what she was going to do next, and that made her thrilling to watch. In fact, her next major role would be the exact opposite of Karen Silkwood: elegant, aristocratic, and the center of one of the sexiest film scenes ever.

Meryl's Antinuke Crusade

On June 12, 1982, one million peaceful demonstrators descended upon Central Park to resist nuclear power and call for an end to the Cold War arms race. Never before had so many people assembled to protest for the cause, and Meryl Streep was among them. The antinuclear movement spilled over from the '70s into the '80s, gaining urgency with the election of President Ronald Reagan, who announced a nuclear buildup after taking office in 1981. The proliferation of weapons of mass destruction gave Meryl and many other Americans intense anxiety. What if an unstable individual hell-bent on annihilating the human race controlled the button that released the Bomb?

Heavy, terrifying stuff.

Initially, Meryl shied away from publicizing her concerns because she thought reporters would "invariably make some crack about Jane Fonda." Jane, remember, drew backlash for her vocal anti–Vietnam War activism. Coincidentally, the *Coming Home* star had been interested in playing Karen Silkwood but backed out to headline 1979's *The China Syndrome,* a fictional nuclear cautionary tale with a courageous female protagonist.

Meryl's self-conscious silence did not last long. She began to voice her opinions loudly, saying she wanted peace on earth for her son, Henry. "I've found that as my responsibilities multiply, so does my own stake in the future of the world," she said.

At the massive Manhattan rally and march, activists brandished signs that read "Bread Not Bombs," "Reagan Is a Bomb—Both Should Be Banned" and "A Feminist World Is a Nuclear-Free Zone." Addressing the crowd, Coretta Scott King, the widow of Dr. Martin Luther King, said, "We have come here in numbers so large that the message must get through to the White House and Capitol Hill."

Surrounding the event, Meryl helped organize the New York premiere of the Oscar-nominated documentary *Eight Minutes to Midnight,* which profiled

Dr. Helen Caldicott, a pediatrician and founder of Women's Action for Nuclear Disarmament (WAND). That summer, Meryl began filming her *Silkwood* role as lab technician and labor union activist Karen Silkwood, who was contaminated at the plutonium plant where she worked. "I look for good art, and when I find it, it always in the end seems to be politically right, too," she said.

In 1984, Meryl received the Helen Caldicott Leadership Award at a gala fundraiser for WAND's education efforts. The same year, Los Angeles TV stations declined to air a public service announcement that featured Meryl delivering some bad news to fellow moms: *there's no cure for nuclear destruction.* One broadcaster tried to explain that there were "two sides" to the issue. "Yeah, those who *bomb,* and those who are *bombed,*" wrote the *Los Angeles Herald-Examiner* in response.

Meanwhile, Meryl took the threat seriously enough that she literally built her life around it. "I'm hyper-alert to all signals," she told the *New York Times* in 2004. "When we picked our house in Connecticut—this was after I played Karen Silkwood—it was because it was 90 minutes from any nuclear facility. We actually drew the circles on a map." She added, "When I moved out of New York it was because of Ramzi Yousef saying 'I'm going to come back to the World Trade Center.' And I think I'm the only human being who believed him."

She liked to recommend *The Fate of the Earth* by Jonathan Schell, first published in 1982.

"What profoundly disturbed me about Schell's book on nuclear proliferation was the idea of global interconnectedness, that what we were doing was going to affect the climate," she said. "It turned out to be mostly true, although the predictions were more dire about the Earth freezing instead of the polar caps melting. I don't know why I read that book. But it's in the power of the great universities and colleges to plant ideas and curiosity and not just mills for turning out hedge fund managers."

CHAPTER 5

Meryl the Lion

I had a farm in Africa.—*Karen Blixen*
(*Out of Africa*, 1985)

Meryl was frustrated. She tried to connect with her character, with the script, and with her costar, but doing so seemed impossible. This time, she had a problem—and didn't know how to fix it.

"I just couldn't get a scene right," Meryl said of *Still of the Night*, an Alfred Hitchcock homage written and directed by Robert Benton. "The dialogue seemed false. I got madder and madder because I knew the answer lay within me, but I couldn't wrestle it up. I sulked all day—something I never did before. There's a lot of tension toward the end of a film, because the answers *have* to be there."

While *Silkwood* wound down in Texas, a new Meryl—a femme fatale with a shady past—was slinking into movie theaters nationwide on November 19, 1982. In Benton's whodunit, originally titled *Stab*, she played Brooke Reynolds, a glamorous auction house employee and suspected psycho killer. Things go awry when Manhattan psychiatrist Sam Rice (Roy Scheider) becomes obsessed with the murder of a married patient. The mistress, Brooke, is chilly, self-possessed, and opaque, a real Hitchcock blonde. But did she do the dirty deed? (I won't spoil it for you.)

Meryl shot the thriller between *The French Lieutenant's Woman* and *Sophie's Choice* and now considers it a blip in her filmography.

Her frustration produced friction with costar Scheider, which affected their chemistry on screen. "Scheider and Streep are no [Cary] Grant and [Grace] Kelly," wrote *Newsweek* film critic David Ansen. "You can't strike a flame with two metallic matches."

Au contraire, Meryl and Kevin Kline set off palpable sparks in *Sophie's Choice*, which opened the next month to largely positive reviews—for Meryl, not the movie itself, which *Variety* dubbed "handsome" yet "astoundingly tedious." *Still of the Night* was already a forgotten fluke. Everyone was talking about Sophie. To Janet Maslin of the *New York Times*, Meryl had accomplished "the near-impossible, presenting [the character] in believably human terms without losing the scale of Mr. Styron's invention." Her performance perplexed *Vogue*'s Molly Haskell, who argued, "Alan Pakula's scrupulously faithful and richly atmospheric adaptation gives full rein to Streep's chameleon-like inventiveness in her most physical performance to date. She trips over 'the English' in her charmingly comical Polish accent, falls on the floor with anemia, blossoms under the solicitude of her mad lover Nathan…in the end, her guilt defines her, and we know no more about her interior life than we did in the beginning. What was missing from the character to begin with is still missing: some core identity that is just what Meryl Streep, a mistress of self-disguise who will never be accused of just 'playing herself,' can't supply."

As a result, Haskell became "more intrigued by the actress than moved by the character." Pauline Kael, the most prominent reviewer this side of Roger Ebert, unleashed a contrarian opinion in the *New Yorker* that accused Meryl of…acting. "She has, as usual, put thought and effort into her work," sniffed Kael. "But something about her puzzles me: after I've seen her in a movie, I can't visualize her from the neck down. Is it possible that as an actress she makes herself into a blank and then focuses all her attention on only one thing—the toss of her head, for example, in 'Manhattan,' her accent here?" That approach, she pondered, "could explain why her movie heroines don't seem to be full characters, and why there are no incidental joys to be had from watching her."

Ouch. Meryl seemed to make Kael uncomfortable. Her inscrutable alter egos, from Sarah Woodruff to Sophie Zawistowska, suffered more than they laughed. The women lacked roundness because their identities weren't fixed. They were running from the past, starting new lives, and dodging quicksand underneath. Rather than present Sophie's foundation as consistently solid, Meryl served the character by vividly internalizing her struggle to overcome survivor's remorse. A strong, complex personality born before Technicolor and raised in an era when movie stars were movie stars, Kael was prone to champion actors whose raw sexuality colored their screen presences. She refused to drink the Meryl Kool-Aid. This oddball It Girl, with her patrician chill and self-possession and limitless tones, failed to thrill Kael as she had captivated other major (predominantly male) critics. But there was joy, as Haskell suggested, in watching the artist create.

"It killed me," Meryl has said of Kael's criticism. In 2008, she conceded to the *Guardian* that she was "incapable" of ignoring it. "And you know what I think?" she said, breaking her interview persona (classy, warm, likable) to deliver a low blow. "That Pauline was a poor Jewish girl who was at Berkeley with all these rich Pasadena WASPs with long blonde hair, and the heartlessness of them got her. And then, years later, she sees me."

On April 11, 1983, Meryl and Don arrived at the Dorothy Chandler Pavilion for a super-fancy, high-pressure date night: the Fifty-Fifth Academy Awards. *Sophie's Choice* had scored five Oscar nominations, notably Best Actress for Meryl. It was the Holy Grail of awards. The year before, Katharine Hepburn took home the prize, but this time Meryl wasn't the dark horse. In January, she won the Golden Globe for Best Actress, establishing her front-runner status.

The Academy snubbed newcomers Kevin Kline and Peter MacNicol and, most glaringly, *Sophie's Choice* as Best Picture. It faced stiff competition: *Gandhi* (the winner), *E.T.* (the cultural phenomenon) and *Tootsie* (Dustin Hoffman in drag), each making the cut—plus more money at the box office. (*Sophie's Choice* pulled in a decent $30 million on a $9 million budget.) Also up for the top prize: *Missing,* a historical drama starring Sissy Spacek and Jack Lemmon, and *The Verdict,* a legal drama with Paul Newman.

Meryl was up against three fellow cool kids—Spacek, Jessica Lange (*Frances Farmer*), and Debra Winger (*An Officer and a Gentleman*)—as well as a beloved icon: *Victor/Victoria*'s Julie Andrews. Meryl looked nervous but resplendent in a loose-fitting gold gown that concealed some personal news: she was pregnant with baby number two, due later that summer. When Sylvester Stallone introduced the nominees, Meryl drew an enthusiastic round of applause. She smiled, looked down, touched her chin and glanced to her right, where Don, the embodiment of Zen calm, sat stoically.

Finally, after ninety seconds that seemed like two years, Stallone announced her name. She kissed Don and made her way to the stage, dropping a piece of paper on which she wrote her speech. She retrieved it and then hovered at the podium for a few seconds, bubbling with happiness. Finally, she spoke: "Oh boy! No matter how much you try to imagine what this is like, it's so incredibly thrilling right down to your toes." She thanked Pakula, Roy Helland, her Polish coach, her German coaches, and, last but not least, Kline and MacNicol, to whom she dedicated her second Oscar in four years.

Five months later, she welcomed her second child in four years.

Daughter Mary Willa, whom Meryl called Mamie after her grandmother, was born in New York on August 3, 1983, weighing 7 pounds and 1 ½ ounces. While in utero, Mamie had an arrhythmic heart. A doctor assured Meryl that in 60 percent of instances, the condition was temporary. Meryl worried Henry's sibling would fall

Meryl's second Oscar win!

"into the 40 percent" category, winding up with "severe cardiac disease." Compounding her fears, the hospital placed fragile Mamie—greeting the world for the first time—in infant intensive care. The good news: she was OK.

Afterward, according to the April 1984 edition of *Ladies' Home Journal*, Meryl suffered a bout of postpartum depression. She would turn on the TV news and cry. When Mamie was six weeks old, Meryl brought her along to an interview with *Ladies' Home Journal* to promote *Silkwood,* slated for release in December. Mamie's nanny had the flu, and a mother's got to do what a mother's got to do. The housewives who read the magazine would approve. With Mamie in tow, Meryl presented a sweeter, more wholesome image that countered the tragic malcontents she portrayed on film. She was just a nice, normal mom taking a year off from acting to focus on family.

"Successful women are people whose life has more of an ebb and flow to it," she told Claudia Dreifus, her interviewer. "It's certainly true of me. I have this period of great activity, and then I pull away. It isn't because my interest wanes. It's because it's necessary. You can't have two young children and be away on location. I *had* to take time out to have a baby. I just couldn't have balanced it all physically. Motherhood has a very humanizing effect. Everything gets reduced to essentials."

She said of her husband, "Don and I are a lot alike. He's a hermit and so am I. We like to be alone—with each other and with our kids. We don't like the razzmatazz, the photographers, and the glitz. We hardly ever go to Broadway openings because of all that. Some of our happiest times are when we're alone together in the country."

The Gummers bought a ninety-six-acre Christmas tree farm upstate in 1980, though they continued to make Manhattan their home base. The couple divided childcare duties, with Don taking Henry to school in the mornings and Meryl picking him up in the afternoons. Meryl cooked; Don tidied up. Besides a nanny, they employed a housekeeper.

Meryl and Don left the kids at home to attend *Silkwood*'s Los Angeles premiere on December 12, 1983. Ebert gave the movie four out of four stars, writing, "The movie isn't about plutonium, it's about the American working class. Its villains aren't monsters; they're organization men, labor union hotshots, and people afraid of losing their jobs." He lauded Meryl's attention to detail. "Silkwood walks into the factory, punches her time card, automatically looks at her own wristwatch, and then shakes her wrist: It's a self-winding watch, I guess. That little shake of the wrist is an actor's choice. There are a lot of them in this movie, all almost as invisible as the first one; little by little, Streep and her co-actors build characters so convincing that we become witnesses instead of moviegoers."

Vincent Canby called *Silkwood* "unlike anything [Meryl has] done to date, except in its intelligence. It's a brassy, profane, gum-chewing tour de force, as funny as it is moving." Even Pauline Kael admitted that Meryl had delivered a "very fine performance," even if "she's the wrong actress for the role."

Like clockwork, the Academy bestowed a Best Actress nomination upon Meryl as well as nods for Cher (Supporting Actress), Mike Nichols (Best Director), and Nora Ephron and Alice Arlen (Best Original Screenplay). Nobody won, but, according to Arlen, it truly *was* just an honor to be nominated. Meryl lost to Shirley MacLaine, who broke hearts in *Terms of Endearment*, a heartwarming, apolitical blockbuster that better matched the climate of Reagan-era Hollywood. Oh well. You can't win 'em all. Buzz Hirsch saw Meryl at dinner following the ceremony. She seemed quite different from the Texas spitfire he remembered.

"How can I describe it?" he recalls. "She just had taken on this persona of a very fragile, easily broken, overly sensitive, almost frightened person. Just me theorizing: It was the Meryl who she felt she had to present publicly, because she was this woman who was getting all this acclaim and all these nominations. Meryl's very smart. She was smart enough to know that, 'Hey, if you're gonna climb to the heights, don't go the glamour route.' I watch the Oscars every year, and she's always there. It amazes me how frumpy she makes herself look. She deliberately does this. And it's because she knows how jealous people can be of her success, and when you get up to a place as she has, there are a lot of people who are going to want to take you down."

AN EXCERPT FROM MERYL'S SPEECH TO VASSAR'S CLASS OF 1983

Fame came with certain rules: *thou shalt not talk politics in the political sphere.* Meryl resented having to be extra cautious about giving her opinion freely. So she let it rip (sort of) while addressing graduates at her alma mater:

> When I was going to California for the Academy Awards, my dad called and said, "If you win, when you get up there, keep it short, sparkling and nonpolitical." I told him my dress would sparkle enough for both of us, and if I could get up at all at that moment, I promised I wouldn't say one word about the [Meryl makes the sound effect for a bomb exploding]. That's a nice-sized audience, 300 million people, and the desire to say whatever you want to say to everybody on earth in two minutes is strong. However, on that occasion I could see his point about what was appropriate to the moment. But when he gave me the same advice today, I had to disagree. Because we are all political actors, aren't we, to be judged by our sins of omission as well as commission, by our silence as much as by our expressed opinions, by what we let slide as much as by the things we stand up for.... I think we feel in this country that it's "inappropriate" for even the most vaguely expressed political views to intrude on what should be short, sparkling, and entertaining. Anyhow, I'm not going to try to make you share my political views today, but I do exhort you to investigate your own and follow through on them. Even at inappropriate gatherings like this.

Following maternity leave, Meryl cleared her schedule for three disparate films: the infidelity drama *Falling in Love,* opposite Robert De Niro; the stage-to-screen adaptation of David Hare's *Plenty,* produced by Broadway guru Joe Papp; and the epic romance *Out of Africa,* costarring Robert Redford.

First, she filmed *Falling in Love,* an obscure but affecting little movie about a topic that touches lots of marriages. It reveals how good people can surprise themselves by having affairs—and wrecking families in the process. Frank (De Niro) is a sensitive architect with two young kids; Molly (Meryl) is a shy, winsome artist who lost a child two years earlier. Both commute to New York from Westchester County on the Metro-North train. They meet-cute in a Manhattan bookstore, and casual friendship turns into romantic love. The star-crossed cheaters part ways before consummating the relationship, thereby rendering them more likable to moviegoers for whom sex crosses the line. Ultimately, Frank and Molly leave their spouses and reconnect after bumping into each other via the Metro-North.

Could it be...a happyish ending? "My mother says if I die one more time, she won't speak to me again," Meryl explained. She had been eager to do a love story and reteam with *Deer Hunter* costar De Niro, whom she idolized since *Taxi Driver.* "That's the kind of actor I want to be when I grow up," she told herself in 1976. Flash-forward seven years later: They were colleagues. Collaborators. Members of the same food group. Meryl and De Niro had initially planned a project based on the Ferenc Molnar play *The Guardsman.* But that fell through. They found the script of *Falling in Love,* written by Michael Cristofer, and decided to give it a go. As a scene partner, De Niro was meticulous in his pursuit of the perfect take.

Meryl much preferred De Niro to Charles Dance, the Englishman who played her beleaguered husband in *Plenty.* After completing *Falling in Love,* Meryl headed to London to shoot the period picture with Charles and Australian director Fred Schepisi. She was playing Susan Traherne, an irascible housewife. The cast included Tracey Ullman as her bohemian best friend and Sting (yes, *Sting*) as her fling at whom she fires a gun (yes, a *gun*) amid a violent tantrum. Kate Nelligan originated the juicy role in London's West End, and the film version proved catnip to Meryl, who lived to flex her theatrical muscles. Don, Henry, and Mamie joined her on location.

David Hare adapted the script from his award-winning play. He was inspired to write *Plenty* after reading a startling figure: 75 percent of married women who worked as British spies during World War II got postwar divorces. His antiheroine, Susan, had been a spy in occupied France; she longs to relive her exciting wartime mission, which filled her with purpose. Back home, Susan marries courtly diplomat Raymond Brock (played by Charles in the movie) but feels trapped in her secondary station as Raymond's wife, relegated to keeping the conversation flowing at stuffy social events. Susan begins to make life hell: she embarrasses Raymond in a dinner-party scene, going off on a rant that Ullman's character, Alice, amusingly labels "psychiatric cabaret." When Raymond tells Susan to stop talking, she screams, "I WOULD STOP, I WOULD STOP, I WOULD STOP FUCK-ING TALKING IF I EVER HEARD ANYBODY ELSE SAY ANYTHING WORTH FUCKING STOPPING TALKING FOR!"

(Otherwise, she spoke in a breathy Princess Diana voice.) Meryl crushed both the part and that memorable one-liner, one of Meryl's all-time favorite bits of dialogue. She and Charles, a tall ginger in his late thirties, did not see eye to eye. They had different working methods. Charles, known for playing bureaucrats and villains, was part of the Royal Shakespeare Company before moving on to the television series *Father Brown* and *The Jewel in the Crown*. Generally, the pace of a TV production is faster than it is in the movies. A TV actor might require a take or two, nothing more. Now, Meryl wasn't overly precious about her work, but she did aim for precision in terms of emotional truth and the details of a scene. Schepisi did a lot of takes, milking actors' performances, and Meryl, within reason, would do as many takes as necessary to deliver a better performance. Charles once praised Shirley MacLaine, his costar in ABC's 1987 miniseries *Out on a Limb,* at Meryl's expense: "Where Meryl Streep is intellectual, Shirley follows her gut. I like that better."

Of Meryl, "Let's just say I found her a little distant," he confessed. "I hardly got to know her. We had dinner a couple of times, but she only spoke about work. I didn't find her easy to work with, but it's not her job to make it easy for me."

Ian Baker, the cinematographer, wondered whether she "deliberately" alienated Charles. In a pattern Mike Nichols observed, could it be that Meryl had re-created their characters' animosity for the movie's sake? Did Charles dislike Meryl…or Susan? On the flip side, Meryl and Ullman became close friends, echoing Susan and Alice. Toward the end of filming *Plenty,* the partners in crime survived a near-death experience on a crowded flight home from Tunisia, where they shot several scenes. They were drinking champagne and talking smack about Charles. "Guess what happens? An engine blew on the plane, and the other one cut out," Ullman recalled. "And we began to descend. And the lights went out. And a young air stewardess started crying, which is never a good sign. And after the initial screams, we both went very pale, and we held hands and we became reflective."

From 30,000 feet, Meryl worried, "Oh damn, that woman who's writing that horrible unauthorized biography on me will have a terrific ending!"

Diana Maychick, author of the 1984 book *The Reluctant Superstar,* would not get to write a tragic final chapter to an extraordinary life: the plane made an emergency landing in Nice, France, where the French ground staff treated passengers—even Meryl—like dirt.

Midair panic attacks aside, Meryl was "cool as a cucumber" on *Plenty,* says Baker. When Schepisi and company captured footage she wasn't in, she stayed on the set and curled up like a cat, reading a book.

Perhaps she had been studying Karen Blixen's memoir, *Out of Africa,* in preparation to portray the Danish writer on the big screen. Next, Meryl would fly to Kenya, joining Redford (and some rented lions), for Universal Pictures' adaptation of the book. Blixen (pen name: Isak Dinesen) was a baroness and owner of a coffee plantation near Nairobi. In 1913, she moved to the East Africa Protectorate, a British colony, and married her second cousin, Swedish Baron Bror von Blixen-Finecke. They purchased a farm, hiring Kikuyu tribespeople to cultivate land that belonged to the tribe before colonial occupation. Blixen started a school on the premises for the tribe's children. Within eight years, she divorced her husband and ran things solo. The farm fell into debt for various reasons, including soil conditions and the plunging price of coffee. Blixen sold it in 1931 and returned to Denmark, publishing *Out of Africa* six years later.

The book was bound to reach the movie theater sooner or later, especially given Blixen's love affair with Denys Finch Hatton, a charismatic big game hunter born into British aristocracy. The same year Blixen gave up her farm, Hatton died when his biplane crashed after takeoff. She documented the tragedy in *Out of Africa*'s final chapters.

Director Sydney Pollack, who previously helmed the Oscar-nominated *Tootsie,* met with Judy Davis and Julie Christie about playing Blixen. Jane Seymour screen-tested with Redford. Kate Capshaw appeared to lobby for the role in a note to Pollack with letterhead from Copenhagen's Hotel d'Angleterre: "Somewhere in my heart, it feels that I have also come full circle with 'Out of Africa.' And now finally I can lay it to rest and be at peace with my creative exploration with this fascinating lady," she wrote, praising Pollack. "You have helped me define yet further the quality of peers I strive to work with."

Sam Cohn pitched Meryl, but Pollack wasn't interested. Meryl persisted until the director reluctantly agreed to meet with her. She heard through the grapevine that he didn't think she was sexy enough to play Blixen. "I went out and got a padded bra, one of those dreadful frilly low-cut blouses for our first meeting—and I got the part," she recalled. "Now, I'm sure it was because of my Danish accent and my intelligence and my ability to portray a writer. But it also probably had something to do with the cleavage."

Pollack disputed Meryl's account. "She tells the story that she wore this push-up bra, and that's why I hired her. You have to trust; it wasn't the push-up bra," he insisted.

Once Pollack glimpsed Meryl face-to-face, Pollack forgot Sophie, Silkwood, and Joanna. He believed he could see the real Meryl and that she was absolutely right for Blixen. During 101 days of filming in Africa, Meryl's endurance impressed him. ("Everybody got sick but her," he said.) She played it cool when things got rough, like a stage actor adapting to a prop mishap in real time. While filming a long, seamless take of Blixen arriving at her farm, Meryl was totally composed. "But the instant Sydney said 'Cut!' her face contorted and she smashed her fist against her chest and she yelled, 'Get this *thing* out of here!'" witnessed *Out of Africa* screenwriter Kurt Luedtke. "The costume person tore open her dress, and out fell an enormous insect! It had been crawling around in there all through the scene, but she had forced herself to ignore it."

In another feat of courage, Meryl took over for her stunt double in the scene where Blixen fends off a lion who raids her campsite. The beast terrified the stunt double. "That girl was really scared, you know, and she had the sense to be scared," Meryl remembered. "I didn't. I was out there with all I had." Meryl grabbed the whip. "Well, that lion wouldn't do anything to get excited, so Sydney untied the lion while I was whipping it—and didn't tell me because he wanted the shot. It was the last shot of the film, before we got to go home. I could have killed him."

Pollack denied advising the lion trainer to let the animal off leash, instead blaming Meryl's "creative memory." The director

recruited at least six trained lions and lionesses to join the production, and hired crew to stand by with fire extinguishers in case shit
went haywire. Pollack's goal: to *contain* a rogue lion, not hurt it. But
Meryl's inventive mind—a potent force when acting in the moment
and responding to threats, real or imagined, in the world around her
character—could not so easily be contained.

⍥ ⍥ ⍥ ⍥ ⍥

Pollack preferred that Meryl stay blonde, even though Blixen
was brunette. Meryl and Roy Helland overruled him, deciding to
go dark. "She'll never be prettier," Roy told Pollack. Meryl's right-
hand man consulted on *Out of Africa*'s most erotic—er, *iconic*—
interlude: when Denys shampoos Blixen's hair by the riverside. The
sudsy round of foreplay provoked watercooler conversation akin to
Demi Moore and Patrick Swayze's lusty pottery sequence in *Ghost*,
but with extra sexual tension because Blixen had not yet slept with
Denys. Redford solicited Roy's advice on how to wash Meryl's mane.
"Pretend like you're in there with dirty socks," Roy said.

"A lot of people thought Bob was wooden in *Out of Africa*," Meryl
said. "I didn't. I thought he was subtle—and just right. But then I'm
the worst one to ask. I had a big crush on him. He's the best kisser I
ever met in the movies. Anyway, Sydney had the idea that Redford's
essence lined up with Denys Finch Hatton's, and I agree. Redford
is that kind of guy. He's an adventurer and loves to put himself in
danger. He cares about the disappearing wilderness. He likes to be
alone. He likes a good story. And good wine. And he's a heartthrob,
you know."

Redford "fulfills what's usually the woman's part," Meryl continued. "Where there's a central male character, there's the elusive
woman he's always trying to get. Meanwhile, he can't sleep and his
job is going to hell because there's this spectre of love and happiness out there and he just—can't—get—her! Anyway, in *Out of
Africa* the roles are flip-flopped. The woman is central, the man is

unattainable. Bob felt that was the balance, and he very generously played it that way."

He and Meryl "probably got along too well," Redford recalled, according to his biographer Michael Feeney Callan. "It caused ripples. We liked to talk. We'd be off camera, between takes, taking it easy. We had a sense of humor in common. But Sydney didn't like that. He would break it up. It bothered him that I was connecting with her in some way that didn't fit his picture of me, or of us as a team. That wasn't easy to deal with, because I felt I was in a vise and I became resentful."

In Redford's view, Sydney encouraged Meryl "to fly" but treated Denys as "a symbol, not a character." Redford was essentially asked to play an even more swashbuckling version of "Robert Redford" the movie star. Meanwhile, Meryl loved Nairobi, "but Redford didn't," she said. "He couldn't go out—even there. He was self-conscious all the time. I went everywhere, saw whatever I wanted to see." She felt sorry for him. He was too famous. The deeply private matinee idol and father of three offered a parenting pointer that Meryl took to heart. He said of her children, "They are not your props."

To Meryl, Kenya was "paradise." The country had a positive effect on Don, too. Later, he painted watercolors featuring animal skulls and African artifacts and sold the paintings for about $5,000 apiece. The couple's serene, isolating experience helped inspire their move to a $1.8 million estate in rural Salisbury, Connecticut, a two-hour drive from New York. The property boasted a forty-seven-acre lake and spacious studio for Don. "What we really bought was privacy," Meryl explained. "A house that can't be seen from the road. In Kenya when we woke we looked out the window at Mount Kilimanjaro in the mist. And I thought, 'After this, can we really go back to Eighty-Seventh Street, where the only place the kids can play is in a dog park full of poop and diesel exhaust?'"

When Pollack showed her the first print of Out of Africa, Meryl's doubts crept in. Would a mainstream audience pay to sit through nearly three hours of Meryl attempting yet another accent to play an imperious, lovesick aristocrat?

She went home and cried. Despite her perfect image, Meryl wasn't immune to insecurity—especially during dark nights of the soul when the mind tends to ruminate on uncertainty, regret, and rejection. This would make her an inspired choice to play Nora Ephron in *Heartburn*.

The Meryl Effect

If it hadn't been for Meryl Streep, Diane Kamp—manager to Hollywood's most in-demand dialect coaches—might be doing something else professionally. *Sophie's Choice* was a "watershed moment," Kamp says. "It was effortless, it seemed. You forgot it was her."

When Meryl won her Best Actress Oscar in 1983, the acting community paid more attention to the value of dialect training. It became a prestigious pathway to an Academy Award. Meryl, a self-professed "mimic," mostly learned new accents without a coach's help. Her self-guided research involved watching and listening to how people speak. However, to play Holocaust refugee Sophie Zawistowska, she was required to learn Polish and German as well as develop an authentic Polish accent while speaking Sophie's broken English. She worked with tutors for both languages, going above and beyond the call of duty in an industry where accents were afterthoughts.

To moviegoers, her effort conveyed: acting is a serious, legitimate profession.

To peers, it signaled: holy shit, I better catch up.

But what do you do when you lack the gene for mimicry? You call a dialect coach.

Before Meryl, "you used to be able to screw up all the time," Kamp says. But, after *Sophie's Choice*, actors began to turn to experts such as accent whisperer Tim Monich, a former Juilliard professor who helped Gary Oldman, a Brit, transition into American roles. Monich also taught Cambridge, Massachusetts–born Matt Damon to impersonate a South African in *Invictus*.

Actors who abstained from accents would suffer the consequences—especially if Meryl upstaged them. Robert Redford tried out an English accent opposite Jane Seymour in early screen tests for *Out of Africa* but decided to Americanize his character, Denys Finch Hatton, just several days before filming began. "We were concerned that audiences might be thrown by Bob as an Englishman," explained director Sydney Pollack, "so we forgot about it."

It seems that Pollack unwittingly sabotaged Meryl's efforts to emulate Karen Blixen's specific, upper-crust Danish accent, which Meryl could master using old recordings of the *Out of Africa* scribe. "When I did it for Sydney, he said, 'Oh, no!' It was too much....Sydney thought that audiences would cringe if I talked like that. So I pulled back a bit," she recalled.

Meryl called Jeremy Irons, who had a Danish nanny, "and he made her read poetry into a tape, which I listened to on the way to Africa," she told the *Guardian* in 2006, revealing, "The depths of my preparation were not that great."

The result backfired in Denmark, which raised an eyebrow. "Obviously, Meryl gives another perfect performance," says my friend Rocio Rodjter, who's Danish. "But her accent is more Swedish than Danish. She sounds like someone from ABBA (a foreshadowing of *Mamma Mia?*). Getting Karen Blixen's accent right is a challenge, because her Danish accent sounds incredibly affected to modern ears because she was an aristocrat and was also born in the 19th century. It's a double challenge to translate that into English." Rodtjer's final verdict: "It's perfectly serviceable but falls apart if you start picking it apart. Like basic Ikea furniture."

Certainly Meryl gets an A for even daring to accept the mission to learn Scandinavian Blueblood in record time. Criticism hardly kept her from next attempting, with better success, such accents as Australian, Italian, and Irish, not to mention different timbres of American.

Demand for dialect coaches grew during the 1980s, thanks in part to the proliferation of cable channels and the implosion of the British film industry, which sent Oldman to seek fame and fortune in the United States. "The world was getting smaller," Kamp says. "We could hear that there were all kinds of accents and dialects, all over the place."

Meryl was up for the challenge. Quoth Kamp, "She must have a perfect ear."

Why hire Henry Higgins when you *are* Henry Higgins?

CHAPTER 6

Meryl the Heartbreaker

I'm never getting married again. I don't believe in marriage.
—Rachel Samstat

(*Heartburn*, 1986)

While shooting *Out of Africa* in 1984, Meryl thought about her next big role. She was looking for a character who had—unlike Karen Blixen—a sense of humor, but not much amused her. As she read the screenplay for *Heartburn*, which Nora Ephron adapted from her roman à clef of the same name, she found herself drawn to its lighter moments. After *Sophie's Choice* and *Silkwood*, *Heartburn* seemed uproarious, even though it's about a bitter divorce.

Ephron's novel was a thinly disguised version of Nora's disastrous marriage to journalist Carl Bernstein, whose reporting on the Watergate scandal helped bring down President Nixon—and transform Carl into a hero alongside Bob Woodward, his partner at the *Washington Post*. Nora was also a media celebrity, a sharp-witted, must-read essayist and magazine writer who loved gossip and suffered few fools on the page or in person. You did not want to get on her bad side; Carl made that mistake.

In 1979, Nora discovered Carl was cheating on her when she was seven months pregnant with their second child. The other woman: Margaret Jay, the wife of Britain's ambassador to the United States. Nora was humiliated. She left Carl in Washington, DC, and moved back to New York to write a revenge roman à clef, as one does. Four years later, Nora published *Heartburn*, sending "how *could* she" shockwaves throughout clubby literati circles in Manhattan and the Hamptons. Nora turned her alter ego, "Rachel Samstat," into a food writer. Carl was "Mark Feldman," a political journalist "capable of having sex with a Venetian blind." Margaret was "Thelma," who had "a neck as long as an arm and a nose as long as a thumb and you should see her legs, never mind her feet, which are sort of splayed."

Like Meryl, Nora had a strong mother who shaped the adult woman she would become. Phoebe Ephron raised Nora and three younger sisters in Beverly Hills while working as a successful screenwriter in the '40s and '50s. Phoebe's greatest hits included *Daddy Long Legs, Desk Set,* and the movie adaptation of Broadway's *Carousel.* She was an emotionally distant parent, conditioning Nora not to come to her with a sob story unless she could make it funny. Only then would Phoebe listen. According to her philosophy, rooted in Jewish comedy, "When you slip on a banana peel, people laugh at you. But when you tell people you slipped on a banana peel, it's your laugh." Unfortunately for Carl, Nora applied the banana-peel lesson—*brand yourself the hero rather than the victim of the joke*—to their breakup story.

"Ninety percent of the things I get I don't think are funny," Meryl said. "The ones that are made, I sit there in the theater and think 'What are they laughing at?' Am I alone here? I'm from Mars, probably. But *Heartburn* was funny and it also had some impact, and that's great. The combination is so nice. The movies that I love the most have humor in them, and yet are poignant."

The highest-grossing film of 1984, *Beverly Hills Cop,* starred a comedic genius, Eddie Murphy, while dude-centric offerings like *Ghostbusters, Police Academy,* and *Revenge of the Nerds* clustered the market, targeting teenage boys who liked to watch Goofy Guys Get the Girl. The '80s leading lady wasn't supposed to outshine the male star and be funnier than him. (That would be a turnoff.) The star's ideal girlfriend was a trophy: elegant yet sexy, the Sloane to his Ferris. *Chicks didn't need jokes—they just had to laugh at them.*

Meryl avoided doing films that sexualized her or made her a prop to a male lead. She had two Oscars to her name and unbridled ambition. *No, she wasn't going to let some guy steal all the best lines.*

Still, Meryl's detractors wanted to see her loosen up. Pauline Kael, leading the backlash, sniped, "If only she would giggle more and suffer less." Her performances were dissected and dismissed as overly technical, receiving a level of scrutiny unknown to the equally committed Marlon Brando. Much criticism reeked of unconscious, internalized misogyny. Meryl was an easy target for displaced resentment toward uppity women who work hard and succeed at what they do. And Meryl's success arrived early and easily, a fact that created a bigger bull's-eye on her back. In the *Hollywood Reporter*, Scott Brown wrote that "Streep can come off like a piece of fine china, white, hard, perfect. Indeed, one can almost appreciate colleague Jane Alexander's complaint that the media have treated Streep as though she were royalty, something, Alexander sniffed, that *she* was never part of."

See also: Virginia Campbell's sour essay in the October 1985 edition of *Movieline* magazine. "She has been harshly criticized for her 'Streepisms,' the blatant tics she gives to the more nervous of her generally nervous heroines," said Campbell.

But audiences like Meryl Streep, and by extension like the movies she appears in, even when these movies are not in themselves very good, which is too often the case. Meryl Streep's popularity is a fascinating phenomenon when you consider the roles she has played—with few exceptions, characters who are neurotic, clinically hysterical, or otherwise highly disagreeable women. She is loved either in spite of, or who knows, because of the contrariness and self-involvement she projects. It may be that her ideal audience would be a convention of psychiatrists.

Campbell went on to suggest that Meryl should've known better than to do *Falling in Love,* given the "positively inert script," asking, "Now that Meryl Streep has reached a point where she can take on only Big Roles in Big Movies, will there ever be a Big Role in a Big Movie that is also a Great Movie?"

The writer had yet to see *Out of Africa,* a not-great movie due for a holiday opening. *Falling in Love,* which premiered in November 1984, collected just $11 million and sat out the awards circuit. *Plenty* debuted in limited release the following September, earning $6 million at the box office. It disappeared from theaters after four weeks.

At the time, Meryl was filming *Heartburn* under the direction of Mike Nichols. The project had a rocky beginning. For starters, Carl Bernstein scored the right to review Nora's screenplay during their protracted divorce proceedings. Per the terms of the legal deal, Nora was required to portray Mark Feldman as a good father at all times. (She also changed "Feldman" to "Forman" in what now seems a concession to shroud the identity of the notorious Watergate source known as Deep Throat. Nora had correctly identified Mark Felt years before the former FBI agent unmasked himself in 2005.)

Adding to the drama, Nichols fired Meryl's leading man, Mandy Patinkin, after the first day of shooting in New York and replaced him with the inimitable Jack Nicholson. (Dustin Hoffman declined the part; he'd already portrayed Carl in *All the President's Men.*) Mandy was neither right for Mark nor entirely jazzed about starring in *Heartburn.* Nonetheless, the Tony-winning Broadway star felt pressure to launch a movie career. Sam Cohn, who represented Mandy, had pushed Nichols to cast him. "We're at the table read, and Mike leans in and says, 'How do you feel about blue contact lenses?' And I was like, 'What?'" Mandy later told the *New York Times.* "We got to the first shot, which was on 81st Street at Pizzeria Uno, the cameras were across the street, Meryl and I were in the window playing the scene, and I remember Mike said, 'Just try to imagine a golf ball running down your leg,' to try to get me to lighten up and laugh.

That was right after we did a scene in bed, naked. This was the first day, a scene in bed, naked—and now a golf ball running down my leg, and the next day I was fired. I thought my life was over."

The studio, Paramount Pictures, had been happy that Mandy "was cheap," says *Heartburn* producer Bob Greenhut. But Nichols noticed an absence of chemistry. In the meantime, "Meryl sort of kinda wanted to be left out of it," Greenhut recalls. "She was fine. She had no problems with Mandy and she didn't want to have herself put in the position of having to subjectively look at the film and say, 'Oh, yeah, something's not working.'"

Enter Jack.

Nichols had directed the actor before, in 1971's *Carnal Knowledge,* and begged him to help rescue *Heartburn.* Jack did *not* come cheap. However, he'd wanted to work with Meryl since his 1981 remake of *The Postman Always Rings Twice.* She turned down the part that went to Jessica Lange. "Jack kept reminding me that there would be a lot of nude scenes, so I said, 'Right, but I expect you to be equally sexually explicit,'" Meryl said. "He wasn't so keen on that."

Jack was close to Nichols. He decided to do his pal a solid, pocketing $4 million up front. (Meryl, according to the *Los Angeles Times,* had recently earned $3 million for *Out of Africa,* half Redford's salary.) In Manhattan, Jack met Carl, an acquaintance, for a power lunch at the Russian Tea Room, reassuring him that he had nothing to worry about. "I was specifically hired *not* to play [Carl]," Jack said in an interview with *Rolling Stone.* "Mike and Nora and Meryl were very anxious to move the film into fiction. And since I had no desire on a couple of days' notice to do a biographical portrait, that suited me just fine."

According to Bob Greenhut, Jack developed strong feelings for Meryl: "He shows up and it's a little clumsy at the start. He's not the best student in terms of memorizing lines and things like that. He knows it's last minute anyway, he's trying to get up to speed. He starts falling in love with Meryl.... You know, 'Let's go over our lines together later.' 'Maybe we can have dinner.' I mean, he really had the hots for Meryl. And, of course, she's married and Mike, meanwhile, is very protective of her."

Nor did Nichols hide his "severe crush on Meryl," though Jack was "much more demonstrative," remembers Greenhut. "Meryl was good at defusing all this but she had a good way of throwing cold water on Jack whenever he got a little too friendly. She used to just blow him off in a very creative kind of way that wasn't mean or uppity. She handled him very well."

In his 2013 biography on Jack, Marc Eliot cited reports that Meryl "threw him out of her hotel room and vowed never to make another movie with him. The story was widely reported in the British press, and Streep denied it happened, but sources said the reason was Jack's relentless sexual overtures."

Later, she spoke admiringly of Jack's social nature, how his thirst for new experiences drove him to participate in life rather than observe it. She and Jack would reunite in the 1987 drama *Ironweed*, playing two Depression-era vagrants who lean on each other during hard times.

Heartburn marked the screen debuts of Meryl's mother, Mary, and brother, Dana, who made cameos as dinner party guests. Mamie, who turned two years old during the shoot, played Rachel's mini-me daughter, Annie. And Meryl, who was in the first trimester of her pregnancy with her third child, wore a prosthetic baby bump. Rachel was much further along. Meryl intuitively understood Rachel, an urbane, harried mother, and created the character as a composite of savvy women she knew. "They're friends of mine," she said. "I don't think anybody would ever be a friend of mine if they knew how many times I'd used them. Jewish girls I knew, city-bred girls.... And I stole things from Nora that were just patently obvious, like her glasses. Her terrible posture. I tried to get as *thin* as she was but I never could. That always... pleased her."

If Meryl didn't do an out-and-out impersonation of Nora, then how to explain the thick, dark, shoulder-length hair? The high-pitched, slightly nasal voice? The 1980s-chic wardrobe?

There's a scene in *Heartburn* that showcases Meryl at her best: women's intuition leads Rachel to rummage through Mark's drawers, scouring them for evidence of his affair. She finds receipts from gifts to *Thelma*. She hears Mark arrive home, so she pulls out a drawer and brings it with her into a bathroom, pretending to shower. Heavily pregnant and in the throes of despair, Rachel emerges from the steamy bathroom to confront a guilty, shell-shocked Mark, pleading, "Don't do this! We have a baby, Mark! We have another baby coming! Don't you even care about them?"

In a decision of which Phoebe Ephron would approve, Meryl infuses humor into Rachel's meltdown. Witness the sight gag of wild-haired Rachel in the doorway, wearing a muumuu and surrounded by steam. It's really funny! But she is so vulnerable, sad, and desperate that instead of mocking Rachel's pain, you want to reach through the screen and give her a hug.

MERYL'S MARRIAGE ADVICE: DON'T BE COMPLACENT!

"I guess all I can say about marriage is that I think you have to look at it as sort of a muscular organism that you have to keep working out," Meryl told the *Chicago Tribune*'s Gene Siskel in 1986. "To continue the workout analogy, you have to, as they say, 'go for the burn.' You have to work hard at it, exercising every part of it."

"That's the real Meryl, that's Meryl exposing her heart," thought Nichols, apparently still trying to unlock her true identity post-*Silkwood*.

Then he watched *Out of Africa,* marveling at Karen Blixen's steely response to the news that Denys, the love of her life, had died. Meryl-as-Karen's reaction was the opposite of expected behavior: instead of sobbing hysterically, she took a stiff upper lip. When Blixen processed the tragedy with "the barely perceptible tremor in her cigarette hand, and went back to reading, I thought, 'No, *that's* the real Meryl,'" Nichols said. "The truth is that it's all the real Meryl, and she can actually change herself within."

Hitting theaters December 20, 1985, *Out of Africa* stunned Meryl by drawing her biggest audience to date. It was a global event, raking in $228 million worldwide. Unlike the drawer where Mark hid his deceit, those were *good* receipts. Triumphant, actually. As Beyoncé says, the best revenge is your paper.

Out of Africa's commercial success accompanied controversy over the problematic way it depicted Africa and Africans—through the colonial lens of a European white woman who behaved as though she owned the Kikuyu tribespeople on her payroll.

In his *New York Times* review, Vincent Canby wrote that Meryl played a believable writer, recouping "any losses sustained by her performance" in *Plenty* (which he panned seemingly out of frustration with the "chilly and distant" troublemaker Susan Traherne, probably Meryl's most unlikable character ever).

Blixen, he said, "sweeps grandly into Africa as if entering a world created for her own intellectual stimulation. She's nothing if not possessive. She speaks of native servants as 'my Kikuyus.' The plantation is 'my farm.' The continent is 'my Africa.' She eventually comes to understand, as [Denys] tells her, that 'we're not owners here, Karen. We're just passing through.' Yet there remains the suspicion throughout the film, as well as in her writings, that Africa exists only as she perceives it—an exotic landscape designed to test her soul."

The government-owned *Kenya Times* slammed Karen Blixen as "downright racist" amid reports that Blixen's book made Kenyans feel "embarrassed." According to Karina Longworth in her Streep-centric tome, *Anatomy of an Actor,* "Black extras discovered they were being paid less than white extras, due to what a publicist described as 'a simple matter of supply and demand.'"

Malick Bowens and Mike Bugura, who played Farah and Juma, respectively, were among the African members of the cast and crew who defended *Out of Africa* in a 1985 letter to the *Kenya Times,* writing that "none of us involved in this film has made any public complaints.... The claim that Karen Blixen was a racialist woman is also false. This is borne out by her several works on Africa. Further testimony can be obtained from the Kenyans who are still alive and who had dealings with her. In the script her sympathies throughout lie with the Africans in a very positive form."

Still, it's hard to argue with Longworth's view that director Sydney Pollack embodied a "colonialist perspective," as when he described "the pictures unfolding in my mind of a landscape nobody knew."

Pollack's cinematographer, David Watkin, framed the majestic expanse of Kenya's countryside—its rivers, plains, wildlife—as unexplored territory, a new land for Karen and Denys to discover together. Many Americans had never seen anything like it, and they lapped it up. Several months before *Out of Africa* opened, a Universal Studios analyst tracking audience feedback to the trailer informed Pollack that viewers twenty-five and up found the scenery breathtaking. "Robert Redford was an overwhelming positive among both males and females," noted the analyst, David Saunders. "Streep, however, was favored more by females who admire her strong female roles and who do not feel threatened by her 'looks.'" In a ridiculous move, Universal decided to give Redford top billing over Meryl—the main event.

The epic swept the 1986 Oscars in seven categories, including Best Picture, Best Director and Best Cinematography. Meryl was nominated for Best Actress alongside Geraldine Page (*The Trip to Bountiful*), Anne Bancroft (*Agnes of God*), Whoopi Goldberg (*The

Color Purple), and Jessica Lange, whose acclaimed turn as Patsy Cline in *Sweet Dreams* triggered Meryl's jealousy. The biopic, directed by Karel Reisz, "was Jessica's from the beginning, even though [Reisz] was a good friend of mine," said Meryl, who nevertheless "couldn't imagine doing it as well or even coming close to what Jessica did because she was so amazing in it."

Page won the Oscar, and after the ceremony Meryl hung out with Jessica and Sally Field at Spago, the Beverly Hills see-and-be-seen haunt. A few weeks later, Meryl gave birth to daughter Grace in New York, making the Streep-Gummers a family of five. She went on hiatus from filmmaking but made herself available to promote *Heartburn* in media interviews. She held the infant while meeting a male journalist for the *Washington Post*—a choice that could be read as both necessity and act of subversion, her way of signaling that mothers ought to bring their babies to work and men had better accommodate them. "She's much more sensitive than my other kids, more sensitive to touch and noise," Meryl said. "Yeah, I sort of felt, 'Well, this is my third, I can just glide along with this one, I'm a pro.' Meanwhile, this one is so skittish. She's like a pixie."

When *Heartburn* premiered in July 1986, critics lobbed tomatoes. One of them, Roger Ebert, accused Nora of harboring "too much anger" and writing a "bitter, sour movie about two people who are only marginally interesting." As for Meryl and Jack, "Here is the story of two people with no chemistry, played by two actors with great chemistry," he complained. "The only way they can get into character is to play against the very things we like them for. Streep seems dowdy and querulous. Nicholson seems to be a shallow creep. Their romance never really seems real, never seems important and permanent. So when he starts fooling around, we don't feel the enormity of the offense. There's not much in their marriage for him to betray."

With all due respect to the late, great Ebert, you've got to wonder whether he disliked *Heartburn*, and by extension Nora, because it exposed an ingrained male fear: *A nasty woman seeks revenge by writing a tell-all. What if my ex got the same idea?* While reviewers took aim at Nora/Rachel, Meryl was off the hook—apparently viewed as an unwitting victim in Nora's devilish ploy to get back at Carl.

Meryl, taking the road less traveled, hopped from one extreme to another, bringing a piece of herself to every part. Her unpredictable path continued to produce fewer hits than misses, eventually leading our heroine to a dark, disturbing place as true-crime villain Lindy Chamberlain.

CHAPTER 7

Meryl the Martyr

The dingo took my baby!—Lindy Chamberlain
(A Cry in the Dark, 1988)

Meryl was in her element: virtually unrecognizable and onstage, belting a song. She loved to sing, especially for an audience, this time pouring her heart out, Liza Minnelli–style, to perform "He's Me Pal" on the set of *Ironweed*, her second movie with Jack Nicholson. Her teeth were discolored, her clothing tattered and her eyes red-rimmed. The performance induced tears. According to actor Fred Gwynne, "There wasn't a dry eye in the house. Her voice was like an angel's. Oh, God, it was beautiful!"

Despite the tepid response to the first Meryl-Jack pairing, the two joined forces once more to film *Ironweed* in February 1987. If you haven't seen it, brace yourself: this extremely depressing film, based on William Kennedy's Pulitzer Prize–winning novel of the same name and directed by Héctor Babenco, features Meryl in a supporting role as a homeless woman without hope for the future. Her character, Helen Archer, is the companion to Jack's Frances Phelan, an alcoholic who blames himself for accidentally dropping—and killing—his baby son. Turning to the streets, Frances finds a supportive partner in Helen, who once sang professionally before she fell through the cracks. In the heartbreaking "He's Me Pal" scene at a saloon, Helen imagines rapturous applause from the crowd. The reality is much grimmer: when she finishes the song literally one person claps. Helen's humiliation underscores a cruelty toward poor people that pervades across history: if the derelict can't pull herself up by her own bootstraps, it's her own fault and the result of her own moral shortcomings. Through her empathetic portrait of Helen, Meryl appeals to our common humanity.

Meryl and Jack "were practically inseparable—no one could get between them," Gwynne, who played bartender Oscar Reo, told *Ladies' Home Journal.* Their friendship even fueled speculation of a showmance, which both denied. Sure, Meryl had dinner at Jack's rented house in Albany, where *Ironweed* was filmed, though her bodyguards reportedly tagged along. She needed extra security to protect her from autograph-hungry fans on location. Yet Meryl was no diva: most days, she would make the ninety-minute drive each way to Connecticut to spend time with her family—not Jack.

That October, Meryl ventured Down Under for her next movie, *A Cry in the Dark.* The docudrama was inspired by the real-life witch hunt that wrongfully landed Lindy Chamberlain behind bars for killing her two-month-old daughter, Azaria. Lindy's trial captivated Australia with breathless news coverage not unlike the O. J. Simpson obsession in the United States a decade later. It all started on the night of August 16, 1980, when Azaria disappeared during a family camping trip to Uluru, then called Ayers Rock. Lindy and her pastor husband, Michael Chamberlain, believed that a dingo, or wild dog, had run off with the baby, but the Australian media—sniffing a hot true-crime story—cast Lindy as the villain who had done the unthinkable. The anti-Lindy contingent defended the dingo as an animal too innocent to commit such an act. The bogus conspiracy theory emerged that the Chamberlains murdered Azaria as part of a creepy religious sacrifice.

Lindy, already guilty in the court of public opinion, didn't stand a chance to walk free, nor had she done much to downplay those nasty-woman qualities that riled her haters: she was firm and resolute in maintaining her innocence and didn't seem to care what they thought. Her steeliness raised suspicions: *Why no tears or prolonged, public grief? What kind of mother was she?* Lindy refused to conform to what society deemed acceptable female behavior and, as a result, would be sentenced to life in prison with hard labor. Michael was found guilty on charges of being an accessory to the crime, but he was permitted to stay home with their other children while Lindy served time. After nearly four years, a tiny matinee coat—which Lindy claimed Azaria wore when she went missing—was discovered near Uluru, confirming her story and placing blame on the real killer: a dingo.

"I loved the problem set up in that, which was the woman was vilified by how she appeared," Meryl explained. "That interested me because it was like if she'd only been a better actress, then people would have thought she was innocent. And I wanted to defend her from the inside and not change a thing about the outside of her."

The English producer Verity Lambert sent Meryl a copy of John Bryson's *Evil Angels,* a book about the Chamberlain case. Meryl read the first forty or so pages when Grace was around three weeks old. "This is really, deeply, deeply upsetting," thought Meryl, deciding not to finish it. One year later, the screenplay adaptation arrived at her doorstep. It stood out from other scripts she was reading. "My God," said Meryl, "anything that has residual power like this, that plays to our deepest fears as parents…there's something compelling in the story."

A Cry in the Dark, produced by Lambert, partnered Meryl with *Plenty* director Fred Schepisi and costar Sam Neill, playing a tanned and toned Michael Chamberlain. Unlike her portrayals of the two Karens (Silkwood and Blixen), Meryl's Lindy was a work of faithful precision. She wore an unflattering short black wig shaped like a bowl and floral dresses that made her look as though she were always going to church. She gained weight, which her image-conscious contemporaries almost never did. She mimicked the unique dialect—Australian tinged with the accent of New Zealand, where Lindy was born—as well as a precise way of talking that irked misogynists. Said Meryl, "I'm fascinated by that stuff, by how females have to be liked, by the fact that you have to break down and cry to be vulnerable, by the fact that what she was telling was the truth but how she told it was annoying or unattractive or unsympathetic."

Lindy gave *A Cry in the Dark* her blessing. As usual, Meryl had read every bit of research on Australia's most notorious woman— but nothing prepared her for meeting in person. "She came with her Bible and she said 'I want you to have this for the duration of the shoot' and inside of [the Bible] was something she'd carried to jail with her and in the margins of certain psalms and certain passages where she took strength," said Meryl.

The Aussie press monitored Meryl's every move, confusing actor and subject. Reporters scrutinized Meryl as they did Lindy. A truck parked outside her house and shined a light into the windows at night. Nobody pulled that crap back home. At the time, journalist Mike Hammer reported that photographers disturbing the set at Uluru caused Meryl to "burst into tears. She was even teased by the media when she inhabited a picturesque country mansion near Melbourne early in the shooting." The headlines snarked: "A Fortress Fit for a Hollywood Queen."

All told, the negative attention might have actually helped Meryl feel the weight of the judgment hounding Lindy. Forget Pauline Kael. This was life or death. No public apology from the government— which wrote Lindy a check for $1.3 million in 1992—could ever fully rectify the character assassination. "There's still people today who do believe she killed the child," says Ian Baker, Schepisi's cinematographer. "Somewhere in Australia, two guys in a bar will [say], 'The bitch killed her.'"

Recently, while traveling to Palm Springs, California, I asked my Lyft driver, an Australian, whether he thought Lindy murdered Azaria. His response, paraphrased: *She did, didn't she?*

"It's her personality," Schepisi, who's very pro-Lindy, tells me. "She just seems an unbearable nuisance to people because she's hard-nosed and confronting with men.... Inadvertently, she was her own worst enemy."

Meryl had been at the fame game for nearly a decade. Unlike Lindy, she knew how to manage her public persona with finesse. In order to keep doing high-profile, meaningful work, she had to stay politic. But soon enough, Meryl, with those high principles and that deep-rooted pursuit of fairness, found it harder than ever to resist opening her big mouth.

NOT-SO-METHOD MERYL

In a press conference to promote *A Cry in the Dark* in 1988, Meryl was asked whether she brought Lindy Chamberlain—the character, not the real woman—home with her each night, thereby confusing her husband and three young kids. "Well, they're used to seeing me pregnant so the weight doesn't bother them and I take my wig off before I come home and they see me scrubbed and who they think they're gonna see when I walk in the door," she answered. "I don't bring the part home. I mean, it's too long a day with [Fred] Schepisi hours, you know. It's too long. I want to come home. I want to forget it and it's a relief to do that and if you have children, you know they demand your attention and something's shaking."

Less than two months after an Australian court overturned Lindy and Michael Chamberlain's convictions, *A Cry in the Dark* hit theaters in the United States and Australia, where it was called *Evil Angels*. The November 1988 release ensured Warner Bros., the film's American distributor, a position in the thick of awards-season hoopla. The strategic timing panned out: although Meryl was the only member of the movie nominated for an Oscar (she lost to Jodie Foster in *The Accused*), the international film community recognized *A Cry in the Dark* as an outstanding achievement. The AACTA Awards, Australia's version of the Oscars, bestowed trophies in nearly all categories, including Best Actress. The Golden Globes, judged by the Hollywood Foreign Press, lavished nominations upon the movie. Nobody took home a Globe, but, in May 1989, the Cannes Film Festival crowned Her Streep-ness with its prestigious Best Actress prize.

The box office results told a different story. Stateside, *A Cry in the Dark* lasted just a few weeks before it was pulled from 319 screens with meager earnings of $7 million. Most surprising, given the spectacle of the Chamberlain trial, it grossed only $3 million in the Chamberlains' home country. Maybe people were suffering from Lindy fatigue syndrome, brought on by media overexposure. Or perhaps they stayed away because they hated the woman. Either way, there were negative opinions about the authenticity of Meryl's accent, which contained traces of Kiwi. "It was perfect," says director Fred Schepisi, her sounding board while learning to speak Lindy. "Critics didn't realize that Lindy had spent time in New Zealand."

Their American counterparts didn't seem to notice. "Streep—yes, with another perfect accent—brings her customary skillfulness to the part," wrote the *Washington Post*'s Rita Kempley. "It's not a showy performance, but the heroine's internal struggle seems to come from the actress' pores." Ebert raved, "In the lead role, Streep is given a thankless assignment: to show us a woman who deliberately refused to allow insights into herself. She succeeds, and so, of course, there are times when we feel frustrated because we do not know what Lindy is thinking or feeling. We begin to dislike the character, and then we know how the Australian public felt. Streep's performance is risky, and masterful."

Meryl only wished the rest of America had the chance to see it. "*A Cry in the Dark* was a wonderful movie, but you can't see a movie if it's not everywhere," she said. "I suppose distributors would rather have what they consider a blockbuster."

Three years later, *Seinfeld* reintroduced millions of Americans to the movie when Elaine, affecting an Australian accent, exclaimed: "Maybe the dingo ate your baby!" Suddenly, *A Cry in the Dark* became part of the cultural lexicon, even if fans didn't immediately get the reference.

In December 1988, Molly Haskell wrote a shrewd essay for *Ms.* magazine, observing "something defiantly perverse in choosing a character who, though a byword in Australia, is remote from movie-goers' experience to begin with, and then giving her disconcertingly unsentimental characteristics. This is no small act of defiance when you consider that *Ironweed* and *Plenty*, two of Streep's recent films, were box-office duds, and she could have used a more conventionally romantic vehicle, something on the order of *Out of Africa,* to shore up her waning audience appeal and keep her career afloat.

"But if there's one strand running through Streep's chameleon-like range of roles and impersonations," Haskell continued, "it's precisely this 'alienation effect,' her determination to be an actress rather than a star in the old-fashioned sense, and to do idiosyncratic, theatrical roles in a medium in which success depends on being loved by huge numbers of people. In her willingness to forgo easy identification, Streep brings to dramatic point something that has been nosing its way to the forefront of consciousness for some time: the whole issue of a woman's lovability."

Haskell chalked up Meryl's contrarian choices to a combination of actorly seriousness and "the inhibitions of a well-bred Protestant"— the sort who might dismiss "playing oneself" in every role, à la Bette Davis, as a gauche demonstration of ego. "One feels a certain con-descension in Streep, as if she were slumming, coming to cinema to save it from its own vulgarity," Haskell ascertained, pondering,

"Does she obscure her 'beauty' in order to be taken seriously, or are her disguises distractions from what she perceives as a lack of beauty? Or is it just 'play-acting'—a refusal to play the movie-star game? The enigma remains."

All of the above, possibly. In nearly all my interviews for this book, Meryl's colleagues remarked, unsolicited, that she is more beautiful in person than on the screen. The fact that she resembles a movie star IRL, not always in her work, still seems to startle and confound them. But Meryl has downplayed her luminous features, attributing career longevity to a nontraditional appearance—unlike sexier actresses, tossed aside as they age, she is valued purely for her skill. Here's Haskell again:

> Hard-core movie lovers and aestheticians have always resisted Streep. Andrew Sarris sounded the note of opposition when he wrote that he preferred more intuitive and less controlled actresses, women with a sense of abandon. But intuitive actresses require someone to use them correctly. Debra Winger, Jessica Lange, Kathleen Turner are dependent on others and have their ups and downs, while Streep endures, her performances independent of her directors. Control is, of course, a key word with Streep. It's what prevents us from warming to her, yet it's part of her mystique....More than Olivier, Streep sometimes appears to be running for cover while displaying her wares, hiding behind her talent rather than enjoying it. Acting is the art of revelation as much as concealment, and Streep reveals little of herself. If she were to reveal more, she might involve us in the destinies of her characters, make us feel what it is we share with them rather than what divides us.

Yet Haskell also theorized that throngs of young women admired Meryl *because* she projected control, strength, and independence.

Meryl apparently read the Haskell piece. She repeated the writer's language in a 1990 interview, saying, "I always think that if I've made a connection with my character, and I've gotten into her heart, then they [the moviegoing public] can get into yours. I always think about that invisible connection among us all, what we have in common as opposed to what divides us."

That was Meryl's roundabout way of saying that Haskell misread her intentions without acknowledging the writer by name—and letting on that she cared about the article. Such a confession would suggest that Meryl wasn't impervious to the judgment of those who struggled to understand her. In these moments, she seemed torn between let it slide and let it rip. "I always wanted to get together a group of actors and talk about the process and then write it all down and send it to all the major critics so they'd know what actors do," Meryl told Yale classmate Wendy Wasserstein in 1988. "Most of them—even the most sophisticated—are swept away by whether it's a character they like or dislike. They confuse the dancer with the dance. With my work, they get stuck in the auto mechanics of it— the most obvious stuff, like what's under the hood. They mention the accent or the hair—as if it's something I've laid on that doesn't have anything to do with the character. It's very ingenuous, really. They're like children who want to believe in Santa Claus. Some critics categorically refuse to believe Santa Claus is their dad with a beard."

Meryl thought "it might have something to do with the loss of icons from the '30s and '40s." Stars whose personas defined them. Katharine Hepburn. Cary Grant. Lauren Bacall. Or a new old-fashioned star like Jack Nicholson, who was born in 1937 but perpetuated a larger-than-life brand of Humphrey Bogart cool even sitting courtside at a Lakers game. Meryl could *bring it,* if she wanted too. Was she trying to dim her own light? Should she reveal more of herself?

CHAPTER 8

Middle-Aged Meryl

Mom! You don't give children sleeping pills when they can't sleep!—Suzanne Vale

(Postcards from the Edge, 1990)

Tick, tock. Was the end near?

As Meryl approached her fortieth birthday, she felt comfortable in her own skin. But she also feared that time was running out. While in her early thirties, she predicted her leading roles would expire within fifteen years. By the time she turned thirty-eight, she said to Don, "Well, it's over." *A Cry in the Dark* was her third box-office clunker in a row. "She began to tell friends she was tired of the whole seriously suffering Meryl Streep persona," wrote Rachel Abramowitz in her book *Is That a Gun in Your Pocket: Women's Experience of Power in Hollywood*. "She didn't want to be out of touch with the way films were being made."

The top-grossing films of 1988 and 1989 centered on men: *Rain Man* starred Tom Cruise and Dustin Hoffman as brothers; *Batman* pitted superhero Michael Keaton against Nicholson's Joker. Other big draws were *Die Hard* (Bruce Willis's righteous macho rage saves the day), *Indiana Jones and the Last Crusade* (Harrison Ford and Sean Connery fight Nazis), and *Who Framed Roger Rabbit,* in which slinky Jessica Rabbit—a cartoon with Kim Kardashian measurements—commanded the juiciest female role. *Real* women actors saw their options shrink. While Meryl's mojo fizzled, big, comic personalities such as Bette Midler and Kathleen Turner were selling tickets in *Beaches* and *The War of the Roses,* respectively.

In this bro-centric climate, Meryl surrendered to the market, signing up for a pair of comedies that would mark a significant shift to lighter, funnier fare. *She-Devil,* a deliciously dark feminist farce directed by Susan Seidelman (*Desperately Seeking Susan*), matched her opposite the brash comedian Roseanne Barr, while she was to reteam with Mike Nichols on *Postcards from the Edge,* Carrie Fisher's adaptation of her witty autobiographical novel.

Meryl didn't need to travel far—New York and New Jersey—for *She-Devil,* which began shooting in April 1989. The script was based on Fay Weldon's book, *The Lives and Loves of a She-Devil,* about a plain housewife seeking revenge on her cheating husband and his mistress, a rich and famous romance novelist. You'd expect Meryl to want to portray jealous suburban scourge Ruth Patchett, but no: she gravitated toward Mary Fisher, a self-absorbed, super-feminine, slightly deranged version of Danielle Steel. "It was so different than characters she had played in the past," says Seidelman, who pitched Meryl through Sam Cohn. Initially, Meryl considered Ruth, a part that happened to fit Roseanne, the breakout sitcom star, perfectly. Cher's name did come up, though she couldn't pull off *ordinary* as well as Roseanne could. For the role of Mary's foil, Meryl thought it was important to cast "somebody who wouldn't stand out in a crowd," Seidelman recalls. "Somebody who wasn't in any way seemingly privileged or exceptionally glamorous or any of those things, just to be in contrast to the Mary Fisher character."

A plot refresher: Mary meets Ruth's husband, Bob, an accountant, at a fancy charity benefit in the Guggenheim Museum, and even though Bob (a game Ed Begley Jr.) embodies Boring Middle-Aged Dad, she falls *hard.* "Writing can be...so lonely," she coos. Bob walks out on Ruth and their children to live with Mary. "I don't even think you're a woman," he shouts at Ruth. "You're a she-devil!" She schemes to destroy him. She sets the house on fire and drops the kids at Mary's tranquil estate, throwing Mary, who's less than maternal, for a loop. Ruth starts a job at the nursing home where Mary keeps her elderly mother (whom she never visits). Thanks to Ruth's machinations, Mrs. Fisher moves in with her deadbeat daughter, bursting the carefully cultivated fantasy bubble Mary created to erase her former identity and reinvent herself as a character from one of her novels. The spark dies between Bob and Mary, who must adjust to the realities of domestic life and managing a dysfunctional family. Mary's latest book, the laundry-themed *Love in the Rinse Cycle*, doesn't sell.

While Mary's in hell, Ruth blossoms as a successful entrepreneur. She founds an employment agency for disenfranchised women who can't catch a break and discovers that Bob has been stealing money from clients (including Mary!). Ruth reports the creep to the authorities, thereby fulfilling her grand plan to take him down. A woman judge sentences Bob to eighteen months in prison. Mary, a "former romance novelist," remakes herself anew—trading poofy pink for bookish glasses as the best-selling author of *Trust and Betrayal: A Docu-novel of Love, Money and Skepticism*. The last scene: Roseanne, sporting suffragette white, is shown walking the New York City streets, flanked by her feminist army of women she's helped.

So, yes, *She-Devil* is amazing. It's a shame that Roseanne is not as progressive and enlightened as Ruth Patchett. As for Meryl, "I knew she was a great actress, so I hoped she'd be funny," says Seidelman, her first-ever female director. "With comedy you really need to know when you can push it and go for that moment—just go all out for that moment and make it work. And she had the skill and smarts to know when to do that and when to pull back as well."

Meryl's timing impressed the director, who points to a scene that begins with a close-up: "She's in bed and you think she's having sex with maybe Ed Begley, and as the camera pulls back you realize her dog is licking her feet. And you just watch her face go from the beginnings of pleasure to ecstasy to surprise to horror in one continuous motion. That's hard to do and pull off, and she does."

Off camera, Meryl was nothing like Mary. She was professional. Generous. Normal. She was lampooning traditional notions of beauty and the way women alter their voices when addressing men, but the joke flew over crew members' heads. They treated her "real nice" when she put on Mary's Barbie outfits, lacquered makeup, and fake nails. Funny how that happens.

On June 22, 1989, Meryl turned the big 4-0. *No, it wasn't over.* Several months later, she relocated to Los Angeles for the higher-profile *Postcards from the Edge,* channeling none other than Carrie Fisher: author, brainiac, addict, Princess Leia, daughter of Debbie Reynolds. Carrie's debut screenplay mirrored the honesty that made her book, published in 1987, such a pioneering piece of addiction literature. Comparing *Postcards* to Bret Easton Ellis's *Less Than Zero,* the *Los Angeles Times* critic Carolyn See wrote, "This is not an inspirational novel, but something on the order of a tough look at reality; a 'serious' piece of work....The outtakes from the life of an actress are sobering, sad, and—again, the word keeps coming back—*interesting.* Will Suzanne ever fall in love, get married, live a normal life? It's an iffy concept, because she's been programmed to like swine: 'I know boring men are the ones to go for but all I can see is the light glinting off the edges of the interesting ones.'"

MERYL ON TURNING FORTY

"I've always thought of myself as 40," she told *Vogue* in 1992. "I mean, even when I was 17, I never felt ingénue. I missed that. So the day I arrived at 40, I felt comfortable for the first time. My daughter

Mamie is like that; she's just who she is, she stands on the balls of her feet. I don't imagine she'll ever be different. I respond to the spirit of people, divorced from their chronological whatever. Some of my closest friends are women who are ageless—Carrie Fisher, Tracey Ullman—and I had the horrifying revelation that they're seven and 10 years younger than me; another friend, [costume designer] Ann Roth, is 59, but to me, she's like me: she's a kid."

Carrie had intended to turn *Postcards* into a one-woman show, but Nichols—snapping up the rights—guided her to make it a movie that focused more heavily on the mother-daughter dynamic. The women were front and center, the men merely supporting players. Meryl laughed while reading the script on a snowy night, brimming with excitement. "I never really get offered parts like that," she said. "I was happy. I was really happy." She leaped at the chance to take on a character as warm, candid, and fascinating as Carrie—er, Suzanne. "When I read the book, I thought: Here is somebody who has endless resources to survive. She is relentless about her demons but is equally relentless about her humor. She serves her jokes like dessert for her own amusement, and it makes everybody else feel good, too."

The Carrie character, Suzanne Vale, attempts to get her acting career back on track following an overdose and a stint in rehab. Her poison: cocaine and Percodan. Her mother, Doris Mann (Shirley MacLaine), is a showbiz veteran with a larger-than-life personality not unlike Reynolds. Suzanne, in recovery, reluctantly moves into Doris's home so that she'll be insured by a movie studio—and thus approved to keep working. She films a humiliating role as a cop in a B movie. A caddish producer (Dennis Quaid) seduces her, then reveals his true colors. Suzanne and Doris engage in a shouting match, with the former accusing the latter of giving her sleeping pills as a child. "They were not sleeping pills!" Doris responds. "It was store-bought and it was perfectly SAFE! Now don't blame ME for your drug-taking! I do not blame my mother for my misfortunes or for my drinking!"

Gradually, Suzanne gets her life together. Then poor Doris— tipsy from wine and Stoli smoothies—crashes her car into a tree; she lands in the hospital, where mother and daughter make amends. Hilariously, Suzanne turns down a date with the doctor (Richard Dreyfuss) who pumped her stomach after she OD'd. The final scene is a triumph: she performs a spirited rendition of a country song, "I'm Checkin' Out," for a new film she's in that won't require her to wear a police badge. Success!

Meryl and Carrie became fast friends, prompting Nichols to gripe that they were ganging up on him. Carrie viewed herself as "much more neurotic than Meryl. More girlish and creature-like. She is very specifically womanly and more rooted in the world than I am." Meryl, however, thought they shared a "certain cynicism and sense of humor

Shirley, Meryl, and Carrie.

and a willingness to be optimistic and put yourself out there." After more than a decade in the movies, transforming into enigmatic ice queens of another time and place, Meryl lowered her guard to portray someone "closest to me, the way I really look, the way I really sound."

All the same, Meryl hadn't lived Carrie's colorful past—her father, Eddie Fisher, leaving Debbie for Elizabeth Taylor; her *Star Wars* success; her on-off relationship with Paul Simon; her substance abuse, and all the coke she did.

"I had to explain to her what drugs are like because she hadn't really done that," Carrie said. "I do that very well; I have a lot of practice. I didn't know that it was going to turn out to be helping Meryl as research; that's probably what I did it for—as research for Meryl. I had to teach her to be a truant, like a bad girl. I had to teach Meryl bad behavior—and anybody who wants that kind of training, that's my specialty. She understood the notion of it very well."

Meryl shadowed Carrie on the set, and like Carrie, was constantly eating and hovering around craft services. According to actress Barbara Garrick, who had a small role in the movie, when Meryl walked into a room, she was hyperalert to her surroundings and aware of everything happening around her, even if the activity was happening far away. Garrick found this behavior highly unusual.

Meryl connected to this quote from Suzanne: "I can't feel my life. I look around me and I know so much of it is good. But it's like this stuff with my mother. I know that she does these things because she loves me...but I just can't believe it."

Postcards was Suzanne's journey to gain control of her own life, on her own terms, Meryl thought. She begins feeling her life when she stops making choices in reaction to other people. Like her mother.

Meryl kept Shirley MacLaine at a respectful distance. "I never got close to Meryl," Shirley recalled. "I saw that wasn't in the cards right away. We never had dinner, never even had lunch together. But, remember, she becomes the part, so you have to go along with the technique of how she works."

One day, Shirley struck up a conversation on the set.

"Meryl, how do you like California?" she asked.

"You know, I feel sort of guilty, but I love it," Meryl replied. "I love it, I don't know why. It has flowers all the time. I love it—the only thing is, I'm a little bit scared of the earthquakes."

People laughed. But not Shirley. Dead serious, she probed, "How long do you plan on being out here?"

"I don't know—maybe two years at the most."

"Well, you're all right, because there's not going to be a major earthquake until the winter of 1994."

Lo and behold, a magnitude 6.7 earthquake shook LA on January 17, 1994. To Meryl's astonishment, Shirley—always in touch with her spiritual intuition—correctly predicted it.

In her scenes with Shirley, she appears to regress into a young girl living under the roof of a matriarch as sparkly as Mary Streep, who would push insecure, tweenage Meryl to sing for relatives and neighbors. Domineering Doris craves the limelight; Suzanne, passive and reserved, has learned to loiter in the shadows so as not to outshine her mom. At her welcome home party for Suzanne, Doris requests Suzanne perform a song but then steals the show to croon a cabaret-fabulous spin on "I'm Still Here." Suzanne smiles adoringly, happy to bask in Doris's sunshine.

When the roles reverse in "I'm Checkin' Out," Suzanne's grand finale, Doris beams with pride as her daughter owns the stage. It was a tricky day for Meryl. "We did it once and they didn't like the shimmering curtain at the back," she remembered. "Now, I don't have the highest confidence in my performing skills in that area, and I thought I had aced this and gotten away with murder, and I said, 'Well, can you use the track so I can lip sync to that? I'll never be able to sing it again.' And they took the shimmering curtain away, we reshot it and I did it...a little bit better. And we drank a lot of Champagne, and I did a little impromptu concert for the extras, and the word came back from the lab that we had to shoot it again."

Meryl had been bitterly disappointed in the fall of 1989 when a salary dispute, among other studio nonsense, scuttled plans to head-line a big-budget adaptation of *Evita,* a dream role where she could flaunt her singing chops. (I'm sorry I told you about this. Meryl as Eva Perón is a loss from which we may never fully recover.) It wasn't "Don't Cry for Me Argentina," but Meryl appeared to have a blast during the *Postcards* performance. Unfortunately, she was required to loop the song over the visuals in postproduction because ancillary noise ruined the original audio.

The sound editors expected to spend two days with Meryl, loop-ing three minutes of lyrics, frame by frame. Instead, to their amaze-ment, Meryl recorded it seamlessly from beginning to end, somehow matching the music to her lips in the scene. "That's impossible what she did," recalls *Postcards* producer Bob Greenhut. "No one could ever do that again."

Meryl proved herself a technical whiz that day, but her first time acting with special effects would test her patience. The clever script, *Death Becomes Her,* a satire about bitter enemies aging badly, was too tempting to pass up.

Meryl and Carrie's Forgotten Screenplay

The script was called *The Other Woman*, and it never got made. In 1991, Meryl and her new pal, Carrie Fisher, adapted a nineteenth-century play in which the "protagonist, like Madeline Ashton, is a famous actress whose career and marriage have started to fizzle," *Vogue* reported in 1992. "But *The Other Woman* strikes closer to home: the protagonist is Streep's age and cannot resort to face-lifts or magic serums. She has to succeed on pluck." *Parade* magazine described the plot in further detail: the actress, married to an infamous womanizer, "disguises herself and tries to seduce her husband as a way of testing his loyalty."

The collaborators cowrote the dark romantic comedy during the final month of Meryl's pregnancy with her fourth child, Louisa. Universal Pictures acquired the would-be hit, enlisting Meryl to star. "What's the point of killing yourself writing?" she said. "I'm going to write a fabulous part for somebody *else*? I don't *think* so!" At one point, Mike Nichols was reported to be in the running to direct the Streep-Fisher production in a *Postcards from the Edge* reunion. Meryl had planned to move forward with *The Other Woman* following *Death Becomes Her* but was apparently derailed by her roles in *The House of the Spirits*, *The River Wild*, and *The Bridges of Madison County*. Simultaneously, Carrie published two other novels and went on to become a successful script doctor.

The two remained friends until the end. On December 27, 2016, Carrie died unexpectedly of a heart attack; the next day, Carrie's mother, Debbie Reynolds, took her last breath. A week later, Meryl gave the eulogy at their double memorial, singing "Happy Days Are Here Again," a Carrie favorite.

CHAPTER 9

Meryl the Immortal

We have to take care of each other. I'll paint your ass; you paint mine.—Madeline Ashton

(Death Becomes Her, 1992)

In Los Angeles, Meryl ran into actor-comedian Albert Brooks at Carrie Fisher's house. Carrie, a social butterfly, was having a party. Meryl and Brooks got along famously. Afterward, Brooks offered her a role in *Defending Your Life*, a comedy he wrote about a neurotic advertising executive named Daniel Miller who dies in a car accident. The gimmick: Daniel must persuade heaven's gatekeepers that he's learned from past mistakes and deserves to pass through the pearly gates. Brooks was to direct and star, and he was looking for someone to play his love interest, Julia. But he didn't even consider the notion of casting Meryl until encountering her.

"What are you working on?" she had asked Brooks.

"I just finished a movie I'm about to shoot," he replied.

"Is there a part for me?"

They laughed. Driving home later, Albert thought to himself, "Oh my goodness, is there a part for her?"

Without telling Warner Bros., the studio, Brooks sent Meryl the script. "She read it and she loved it," he recalls. "So then I told [Warners], 'Can we get Meryl Streep?' Everybody was...'What?'"

They heard right. Brooks had been surprised by Meryl's naturally fun and easygoing personality. This was the real Meryl? *Who knew?* For Julia, he wanted Meryl to be relaxed—like the charming woman from Carrie's get-together. (An offbeat analogy, but this part reminds me of the time Lady Gaga shed her avant-garde meat dress and began dressing conventionally while hitting the road with unlikely tour-mate Tony Bennett. I realize this makes Meryl the Lady of the Gah and Albert, of the romantic comedy *Broadcast News*, Tony Bennett. Don't @ me.)

Defending Your Life is, at heart, a romantic comedy, featuring Meryl as a Zen pixie dreamgirl who teaches Brooks's hapless Daniel how to let go and take risks. They cross paths in Judgment City, where souls go when they die. The place resembles an airy, soothing Southern California spa: limbo, it turns out, is a wonderful getaway. Julia and Daniel can eat as much as they like without repercussion. Why go back to earth? Ah, but a panel of heavenly tribunals might soon order Daniel's return, reincarnating his soul into another body. An amusing scene at the Past Lives Pavilion, in which Shirley MacLaine makes a self-mocking cameo as a hologram, shows Daniel watching a highlight reel of his former selves, which include a dressmaker and a tribesman running from a lion.

Julia was a whaler, a tailor, and Prince Valiant. The mother of two drowned after hitting her head and falling into the pool: she accepts her death but resents how it happened. "I'm still pissed," she complains. "I was a good swimmer." When attorneys review Julia's life, judging whether she's fit to move on to heaven, the highlights reveal a Meryl-esque model of perfection: she rescues her kids (and a Persian cat) from a house fire! But Daniel's earthly existence reveals trauma. The son of an abusive father, he shrinks through life as a passive bystander, allowing alphas to walk all over him. He never learns to stand up for himself. Hence, the tribunal puts him on the Do-Over Bus, en route to reincarnation, while Julia earns passage to heaven. Showing uncharacteristic bravery, Daniel takes a leap of faith and jumps aboard Julia's bus to follow her into the great unknown. The limbo lawyers nod their approval.

ALL THE TIMES THAT MERYL DIED IN THE MOVIES

It should come as no surprise that La Streep is very, very good at playing dead. She certainly fooled director Héctor Babenco on the set of *Ironweed*, when she laid still for a frightening length of time while filming Helen Archer's final moments. "What's going on? She's not breathing!" a crew member said to Babenco, who went forward with the scene. Meryl remained motionless a full ten minutes after Babenco got his shot. "Now *that* is acting!" the filmmaker enthused. "*That* is an actress!"

She's got the track record to prove it.

Film: *Sophie's Choice*

Cause of death: Unable to live with the loss of her children to the horrors of the Holocaust, Sophie commits suicide by ingesting cyanide alongside her lover Nathan.

Film: *Silkwood*

Cause of death: Officially? A single-vehicle accident. But questions remain as to whether nuclear-facility whistleblower Karen Silkwood was *pushed* off the road en route to meet a journalist.

Film: *Ironweed*

Cause of death: Helen Archer succumbs to illness in a shabby hotel room, frail and alone, a casualty of an unjust society that trapped her in poverty.

Film: *Defending Your Life*

Cause of death: Accidental drowning. In this dramedy about the afterlife by writer-director Albert Brooks, Meryl's character, Julia, perishes after tripping, hitting her head, and falling into a pool.

Film: *Death Becomes Her*

Cause of death: When Madeline Ashton's husband pushes her down the stairs, he believes her to be a goner. But thanks to an age-defying serum, she'll be undead for an eternity.

Film: *The House of the Spirits*

Cause of death: Clara, a saintlike clairvoyant, dies from an apparent heart attack while decorating her home for Christmas. She returns as a ghost to visit her estranged husband.

Film: *The Bridges of Madison County*

Cause of death: Old age or heartbreak? Francesca Johnson, a lonely Iowa housewife, requests her ashes be scattered at the bridge where she fell in love with photographer Robert Kincaid.

Film: *One True Thing*

Cause of death: It seems that Kate Gulden, a devoted wife and mother dying of cancer, kills herself by overdosing on morphine. This just might be Meryl's saddest goodbye.

Film: *The Manchurian Candidate*

Cause of death: With a single bullet, veteran Ben Marco (Denzel Washington) shoots and kills evil Senator Eleanor Prentiss Shaw (Meryl) and her mind-controlled congressman son Raymond (Liev Schreiber).

Film: *Lemony Snicket's A Series of Unfortunate Events*

Cause of death: Although Aunt Josephine lives in constant danger that her house, propped on stilts, will crumble, it's sadistic Count Olaf (Jim Carrey) who leaves her stranded in leech-infested waters.

Film: *Florence Foster Jenkins*

Cause of death: Before heart failure felled her, the New York socialite and wannabe opera diva said, "People may say I couldn't sing, but no one can ever say I didn't sing."

Film: *Mamma Mia! Here We Go Again*

Cause of death: MURDER. The killer: writer-director Richard Curtis, who suggested producers kill off Donna Sheridan in the sequel to the megahit *Mamma Mia!* and explain her backstory with younger actress Lily James.

Unlike other actors with whom Brooks collaborated, Meryl came prepared and ready to work. She never held up the set and said "I don't know how to do this." She'd worked everything out beforehand.

She was open to suggestions, ignoring bad ones. In a 2010 interview with *Vanity Fair*, Meryl quoted Brooks as saying, "'Could you just make it a little sweeter?'—and that's been repeated by other people in the years since then. But I don't listen to it."

She didn't tune out Brooks when he tried to ease her disappointment over *Evita*. The window of opportunity to play a splashy part like that was closing on her as she entered her forties, and the passage of time—and with it, the sting of further rejection—appeared poised to crush her spirit. "You know, Meryl, you could do this and it would be the toughest thing you've ever done in your life. It would be monumental. It would be fantastic. It would be huge. And everyone would say, So what? What else is new?" Brooks rationalized.

She-Devil premiered in December 1989, flopping hard. As the movie's cult status grew over the years, reviews would improve. "I was conscious of needing to work and there was nothing to do," Meryl said in a post-release disclaimer of sorts, adding, "I loved *She-Devil* but in the mix, it didn't work." At the time, she received the best press. "Given the outline of an inherently comic role, and dialogue that doesn't sabotage it, Miss Streep appears to be flying on her own," Vincent Canby wrote. "She has the intelligence and speed of something that passes through sound barriers without a wobble. She is almost worth the price of admission." One critic's trash is another's treasure. Roger Ebert reviewed *She-Devil* with a serious consideration uncommon to his male brethren who often snubbed movies about women and made for women. "If Barr is correctly cast, so is Streep, who has always had a rich vein of comedy bubbling through her personal life—few people are merrier during interviews," observed Ebert, writing of Seidelman, "She has a sure touch for off-center humor, the kind that works not because of setups and punchlines, but because of the screwy logic her characters bring to their dilemmas."

Ebert got it, says Seidelman, pointing out that "some men took offense from the subject matter—maybe took offense that we had the audacity to put an unattractive frumpy housewife as a leading character in the movie."

∘ ∘ ∘ ∘ ∘

Forty-year-old Meryl received offers for three separate witch roles within one year, an insult which she attributed to studios not knowing what to do with actresses who had graduated to middle age—the "most vibrant [time] of a woman's life," she thought. "I think there was, for a long time in the movie business, a period of—when a woman was attractive and marriageable or fuckable, that was it."

On August 1, 1990, Meryl mouthed off in an amazingly sassy—and no doubt cathartic—speech at a Screen Actors Guild women's conference. "In a season where most of the female leads are prostitutes, there's not going to be a lot of work for women over 40. Like hookers, actresses seem to lose their market appeal around that age," she said, referencing a drop in the share of film roles for women to 29 percent. By 2010, she warned, "we will have been eliminated from movies entirely."

Earlier that year, *Pretty Woman*, starring Julia Roberts in her dazzling, breakout role as a hooker with a heart of gold, crossed the $100 million mark within two months. When Meryl delivered her SAG keynote address, the blockbuster fairytale remained high atop theater marquee signs. Speaking to the *LA Times*, Meryl said she was "upset that 15-year-old girls want to go see that four and five times. I know it's the Cinderella thing, but it disturbs me. There are a lot of women screenwriters and a lot of women in development, but I guess because those women want to make it past the glass ceiling, maybe they think they have to say, 'Do *Die Hard II*. Now let me be vice president.'"

Although Meryl might have felt some commercial clout slipping away and that she had nothing to lose, nobody could take away her legendary status. It provided protection of a sort, and credibility:

when she issued a rare public complaint, people paid attention; when she addressed the objectification and unfair treatment of women in Hollywood, it mattered.

"No, I'm not like Jack [Nicholson] with $11 million up front," said Meryl, ripping the industry for paying actresses less than their male counterparts. "I don't feel greedy, but when Rick Moranis makes what Michelle Pfeiffer makes, when he's as big a draw, supposedly—who knows what anybody makes because nobody talks about it, but it is all the way down the line until you hit scale—women make 40 to 60 cents on the male dollar. Now, really, that's all I have to say. I'm not a spokesman. Now I want my brothers in the union to speak up on my behalf. As well as my sisters. I want to hear somebody support us."

Imagine if you were the best in the game, the Serena Williams of your field, but you got paid Rick Moranis money. You might not be happy about that either.

According to a 1989 Screen Actors Guild study, men accounted for 71 percent of movie roles, earning a collective $644 million to women's $296 million. Rachel Abramowitz reported that Meryl, truth-teller, was regarded as "petulant rather than heroic, a Cassandra-like figure spouting verities that no one wanted to hear. Other actresses distanced themselves. They weren't paid equally, but they were paid well." An unnamed agent dismissed Meryl's efforts in the *Los Angeles Times,* saying, "Bottom line, until there is a huge box-office hit with a huge female star as the lead—and there are only [a few] actresses in the country that currently have that kind of clout—nothing will change."

The statement, made by a coward cloaked in anonymity, shifted blame to women rather than hold to account the powerful men who could, if they wanted to, help change the industry from within. Without male allies, it's no surprise that women who lacked Meryl's pedigree felt powerless to say something. Not everyone could afford to challenge the system, though in doing so, Meryl was paving the way for younger actresses who would someday interlock arms and declare, *Time's up.*

A month after Meryl's feisty rant, *Postcards* topped the box office, ultimately raking in $39 million amid strong reviews. Meryl, wrote Hal Hinson of the *Washington Post*, "gives the most fully articulated comic performance of her career, the one she's always hinted at and made us hope for."

On March 25, 1991, she skipped the Oscars for the first and only time as a nominee. Meryl and Don were expecting their fourth child, Louisa, who would arrive in June. Meryl, forty-one, was slated to perform "I'm Checkin' Out," a Best Original Song contender. After she backed out because of her pregnancy, Reba McEntire stepped in to sing it—and sing it 7,000 times better, Meryl thought. She had been up for Best Actress alongside two significant challengers: Julia Roberts, the *Pretty Woman* sensation and male fantasy, and Kathy Bates, the male nightmare, whose terrifying turn in *Misery* scared the living daylights out of men who feared she'd kidnap and torture them like she did James Caan. Bates won. They seemed to prefer a simplified, binary view of women: angel/devil. Nurturing wife material/ psycho single career woman. Julia Roberts/Kathy Bates.

Meryl could not be squeezed into a box. No wonder they didn't know what to do with her.

In May, she made headlines after dropping Sam Cohn and signing with rival agent Bryan Lourd at the powerful Creative Artists Agency. (Back then, Lourd was dating Carrie Fisher.) The move seemed logical on the surface: Meryl and her family had made the giant leap from Connecticut to Los Angeles, where they took up residence in the upscale Brentwood neighborhood. The erstwhile East Coaster, now stationed in the entertainment capital of the world, was closer to her industry's movers and shakers. Cohn pledged allegiance only to New York. But, behind the scenes, he betrayed her trust. Mike Nichols had been planning to make the movie of Kazuo Ishiguro's prize-winning 1989 novel *The Remains of the Day*, which had a plum role for Meryl: Miss Kenton, the housekeeper who harbors feelings for her colleague, a butler married only to his job. Both

Meryl and Jeremy Irons read *Remains* for Nichols, but the filmmaker opted not to cast them in roles later filled by Emma Thompson (ten years Meryl's junior) and Anthony Hopkins (twenty years Emma's senior). Cohn, who was also Nichols's agent, didn't make it clear to Meryl that she was no longer a candidate for Miss Kenton. "I left because of something Mike did that I felt Sam should have protected me from," she told the *New York Times Magazine*. "Mike knows what he did, but unfortunately Sam wears the scar." She eventually absolved Cohn and Nichols, emphasizing that she had "too much of a need for forgiveness in my life."

In her popular gossip column, Liz Smith reported chatter that "Meryl has changed a lot" and quoted a source as saying, "She has gone from being legendary to being difficult."

While *The Remains of the Day* snagged eight Oscar nominations, leaving the 1994 ceremony empty-handed, her next lowbrow film, the campfest *Death Becomes Her*, would outlast the highfalutin, ultimately forgettable prestige drama. It became a cult classic—one that touched on the timeless themes of a woman's desire to stay young (especially in Hollywood) and the zero-sum clash of female rivals for male attention and limited professional breaks. "It was about women and cosmetic surgery and changing yourself, twisting yourself into a contortion," she said. "To be what? A ghastly version of something that used to look like you in your twenties?"

Meryl thought the movie was ahead of its time. Directed by Robert Zemeckis, *Death Becomes Her* costarred Meryl's friend Goldie Hawn in a slapstick battle over Bruce Willis, who minimized his machismo to play meek plastic surgeon Ernest Menville. (The part was originally earmarked for Kevin Kline, a bit of perfect casting that never transpired. Kevin dropped out to join Richard Attenborough's *Chaplin* biopic.)

The hijinks commence after Ernest and his fiancée, Helen Sharp (Goldie), attend a terrible Broadway show starring Helen's frenemy Madeline Ashton (Meryl), a narcissist who heartlessly steals Ernest away from Helen—then marries him. A distraught Helen winds up in a psychiatric hospital. She's bitter, slovenly, and obsessed with revenge. Helen plays the long game. Years later, she publishes a buzzy novel dubbed *Forever Young* and, true to the title, looks as if she's drunk from the fountain of youth. Among the guests at her book party: unhappily married couple Madeline and Ernest. Madeline's star has dimmed with age; Ernest is an alcoholic toiling as a reconstructive mortician. Helen, living her best life in a red body-con gown, seduces Ernest, while a desperate Madeline tries to stop the clock on the aging process. She drinks a potion given to her by the beautiful, ageless Lisle Von Rhuman (Isabella Rossellini), who says she's seventy-one. (She looks thirty-five.)

Madeline regains her youthful bloom but at a cost: she must heed Lisle's advice and disappear from public life after ten years to keep the serum's existence secret. Newly refreshed, Madeline confronts Ernest, taunting him as a "flaccid undertaker," a sick burn. He pushes her down the stairs—and she breaks her neck, loses her pulse, but…she's technically *not dead*. After overhearing Helen insult her in the worst way imaginable ("she was a *bad* actress"), Madeline retaliates by shooting her nemesis in the stomach. Uh oh: Helen rebounds with a gaping hole in her body and eyes like a demented Siberian husky. It so happens that Helen knows all about the secret serum; she's swallowed it, too. Madeline and Helen engage in a violent duel, using shovels to take swipes at one another. "You should know not to compete with me! I always win!" bellows Madeline, in a line made for Meryl.

Ernest wants to wash his hands of both women, yet they persuade him to stay and help reconstruct their damaged bodies. See, without Ernest to constantly maintain them, they'll fall apart. So they scheme to get that serum in his system—and trap Ernest into an eternal life of surgical servitude. But he rejects the elixir, moving on to happily remarry and embrace mortality to its fullest. Thirty-seven years later, Madeline and Helen commiserate in the pews at

Ernest's funeral. They literally start to crack in a grotesque parody of modern-day plastic surgery gone to unsubtle extremes. After the service, the two go all Humpty-Dumpty, tripping down some stairs and losing their heads. Helen's closing one-liner: "Do you remember where you parked the car?"

Meryl, serpentine in a long platinum wig, disliked having to maneuver around Zemeckis's sophisticated special effects, but, naturally, she proved a quick study. The inorganic tedium of technology and prosthetics wasn't for her, though she relished playing a shallow mega-bitch angry at the world. "Madeline Ashton didn't seem to have a drop of kindness or compassion in her body," she said. "I was worried about that. But I was so ready to play someone this vile. I've wanted to play a mean person for a long time. It's fun!"

For Goldie, the effervescent star of the hit comedies *Private Benjamin* and *Bird on a Wire,* playing a villain was doubly fun because she'd been typecast as the lovable, funny girl stretching back to the late-1960s NBC sketch show *Laugh-In.*

♥ ♥ ♥ ♥ ♥ ♥ ♥ ♥ ♥ ♥ 👑 ♥ ♥ ♥ ♥ ♥ ♥ ♥ ♥ ♥ ♥

THE *DEATH BECOMES HER* ENDING THAT NEVER WAS

Director Robert Zemeckis scrapped the original finale after test audiences gave the thumbs-down. In it, Tracey Ullman, Meryl's BFF and *Plenty* costar, appeared as Toni, a bartender who helps Ernest (Bruce Willis) fake his own death so he can escape Madeline (Meryl) and Helen (Goldie). Years later, the undead vixens spy Toni and Ernest, older but happier, holding hands in Switzerland. Goldie recalled the gist of her dialogue with Meryl:

Madeline: "Look at them, they're so old and decrepit."

Helen (welling up): "I wanted that. I wanted a normal life."

> Madeline: "Where do you want to go next? Paris?"
>
> According to Goldie, the scene "was on-theme, but not funny." Zemeckis and the movie's writers rewrote a darker, funnier denouement that nailed the absurdist tone. And so we see the bitter antiheroines trying, and failing, to keep up appearances at Ernest's funeral, in which he's eulogized for living a rich, rewarding life. They proceed to physically crumble—breaking into pieces after tripping on stairs. The sight of their disembodied heads signals to the audience that, this time, the women can't be put back together again. Rather than expressing shock and sadness, Helen deadpans, "Do you remember where you parked the car?"

Goldie first met Meryl through her partner, Kurt Russell, Meryl's *Silkwood* boyfriend. She says Kurt came up with the idea of Helen "getting insanely fat" after Ernest dumps her for Madeline. The dramatic weight gain, achieved via prosthetics and a rubber suit, made Helen's svelte revenge body that much more satisfying. Otherwise, Goldie thought Martin Donovan and David Koepp's script was really good and found it tough to turn down. It was rare to find a movie that featured strong, complicated women. *Thelma & Louise* was a prime example. Meryl and Goldie went out of their way to pitch themselves as the titular outlaws in the 1991 feminist road movie. Meryl would play the controlled Louise to Goldie's flaky Thelma. Director Ridley Scott, who ultimately cast Susan Sarandon and Geena Davis, thought Meryl was "wonderful" but questioned whether she was "tough" enough to tackle a heat-packing badass. Like lots of people, she had a strong opinion on the controversial ending, which involved the women driving off a cliff. According to Becky Aikman, author of the *Thelma & Louise* history aptly named *Off the Cliff,* Meryl posed the idea of altering the script so that Louise heroically pushed Thelma out of the car before taking the plunge, sparing her friend a grisly—and iconic—demise.

Scott didn't think Goldie was right for Thelma. But *Death Becomes Her* offered Goldie another chance to do a movie with her buddy. She and Meryl shared a spontaneous streak. "Just as she wasn't sure what was going to come out of my mouth, I thought the same of her," recalls Goldie, saying of the shovel scene, "It was like we were on the playground together."

Though Meryl balked at going under the knife, she sought to understand the insecurity that drove Madeline to change her appearance. This she-devil wasn't entirely soulless. Meryl persuaded David Koepp, the screenwriter, to make a revision so that Madeline mistakenly believed that her young hunky side piece had genuine feelings for her. An earlier draft showed Madeline wielding the power in the relationship.

It was another case of Meryl advocating for her character and using her clout to tweak the script for the better. Back in her trailer on the Los Angeles set, she played NPR and kept a cappuccino maker as well as framed photos of her children. "I have a sickening feeling they all want to be in the business," she said of her kids.

Henry, now twelve years old, was into hockey and the opposite sex. Once, he asked his mother a question for which she had the wisest nonanswer.

Henry: "Who do you think is the prettiest girl in my class?"

Meryl: "Who cares?"

She would let go of vanity—and prescient dark comedies about aging—for *The River Wild*, which required Meryl to navigate the most dangerous waters of her career.

CHAPTER 10

Meryl the River Goddess

I'm not on anybody's side. I'm on everybody's side. I'm the mother.—Gail Hartman

(*The River Wild*, 1994)

After moving her family from pastoral Connecticut to Los Angeles, that smoggy haven of hustle, Meryl tried to keep life as normal as possible. She switched coasts to film *Postcards* and, in 1990, purchased a $3 million Spanish-style home that boasted a kid-friendly pool. Don kept a studio in beachy, bohemian Venice. Meryl's life in LA revolved around the kids, whom she enlisted in private schools. "We swim. We ride bikes. We go to a lot of hockey games; Henry's team was state champions. We Rollerblade—well, I don't," she confessed. "I'm always afraid I'll get kneecapped."

The superstar was a supermom, her work stamina carrying over into motherhood. Meryl's friends didn't know where she got the energy.

"On weekends, when I would just be collapsing, and having extra nannies, Meryl comes around with a load of 10 kids in a minibus going somewhere, asking if my daughter wants to go along," Tracey Ullman, the mother of two youngsters, told *Vogue* in 1992. Echoed Carrie Fisher, who made Meryl godmother to her daughter, Billie, "She has a great marriage and four children and a nanny who is not live-in, and it's not reflected in her career that she's sacrificed. She does have it all, but she works very hard at it. If I weren't friends with her, though, it would drive me crazy. It upsets other women."

During movie shoots, Meryl and Don—devoted parents, each with a creative, consuming job—recruited a cook to feed the brood. Meryl also kept a personal assistant on her payroll. She wasn't the biggest fan of exercise, having previously attempted Jane Fonda's 1980s-era "feel the burn" workout regime, but braved the tedious treadmill, seven miles a day, to get into shape for *Death Becomes Her*. "If you look back on my career, and checked where I had the babies, then look at my next movie, it's always something like *Ironweed*, where you never have to look at the pooch," she has said.

Though Meryl expressed a queasy mother's intuition that Henry, Mamie, Grace, and Louisa would someday join her in the roller-coaster business of show—she would not be able to deny the power of her maternal influence as the family's major breadwinner. In a town where traditional marriages had been the order of the day, with wives running the household and husbands running studios, Meryl stood apart. Unlike other affluent Angeleno boys his age, Henry bore witness to a strong, feminist working mom who normalized an unconventional upbringing. And her daughters? With front-row seats to Meryl's passion for acting, they absorbed by osmosis her dedication to the craft and her hard work to achieve almost anything she set out to do. The bug bit Mamie, a blonde, blue-eyed Meryl doppelganger, early on. "She really got it," Meryl recalled of Mamie's film debut in *Heartburn*. "They'd say, 'Cut,' and she'd say, 'Go again?' She'd ask for more takes. And she has more energy than 55 locomotives, but when she had to have her hair dyed brown, she'd lie stock-still like at a baptism and wait for the process."

Tongues wagged when Meryl traded New England for California. *She was so not LA. What's up with her?* Never mind that she'd made three movies on location in the City of Angels—her detractors ascribed ulterior motives. On the one hand, ambitious women have always been considered suspicious and calculating; on the other hand, men who desire success are seen as self-starting and industrious. The *New York Times,* which usually had her back, suggested that Meryl relocated to keep her star burning bright. Her blood boiled.

The *Times* "thinks that I stayed there because I was desperate to revive my career that was flagging. Believe me, I don't think about this," she said. "If it was flagging, I didn't know it. No one told me, because I was getting paid a lot of money and I thought they were good movies I was in. Being actors' kids, [my children] have been moved around. My son Henry went to seven schools. He went to prekindergarten in England, prekindergarten in Africa, first grade in Connecticut, second grade in Australia, third grade in Connecticut. Oh, he went to another preschool in Texas. I mean, he's really been jerked around a lot, and by the time he was seven, he said, 'Mom, I don't want to move anymore.' And I really hurt him. Yeah. OK. We're not gonna do that anymore."

Death Becomes Her had a middling run in the summer of 1992, grossing $58 million in North America (roughly the same as the Rick Moranis comedy *Honey, I Blew Up the Kid*) on a $55 million budget. It fared better overseas, collecting a further $90 million to bring the global tally to $149 million. Not too shabby for two divas allegedly past their prime. While opening-night audiences drew a majority of women delighted to watch Meryl and Goldie match wits, film critics winced. "I read somebody said it was misogynistic," Meryl recalled. "Oh, no, no, no. It's the truth!" Like many other reviewers, Janet Maslin thought *Death Becomes Her* suffered from a focus on special effects over story, shining the brightest when it showcased the stars' bitchy repartee. The dialogue is endlessly quotable ("NOW a warning?") and part of the reason *Death Becomes Her* has developed a cult following, particularly in the queer community. It's been embraced at Pride Month viewing parties and on drag show stages. On reality TV, *Death* influenced a *RuPaul's Drag Race* runway contest. For gay male fans, the story is a lowbrow-brilliant catfight with an inspiring narrative: the bad girls boldly hurl themselves in the way of beauty and refuse to go down without a fight. Meryl knew it would resonate, perhaps owing to her sixth sense in choosing eccentric movies that manage to last because they have something to say. It helps, too, if they also appeal to underserved audiences. (Look no further than *Mamma Mia!*)

Meryl's radar for promising material malfunctioned in the instance of her next movie, *The House of the Spirits,* an epic family drama set against the backdrop of political upheaval in Chile and based on Isabel Allende's celebrated novel. But, in her defense, literally *everyone* was after what the *Los Angeles Times* called "the most coveted female part since Catwoman."

The role: Clara, a gentle psychic who marries the despicable Esteban (Jeremy Irons), a wealthy landowner shown raping a peasant woman and kicking his kindly sister (Glenn Close) out of the house because she's grown too attached to Clara. The accent: Spanish. Annette Bening, a new mother, turned it down, as did Michelle Pfeiffer for reasons unknown. (Maybe Michelle is secretly clairvoyant, like Clara, and looked into the future and saw that this film would turn out to be an overwrought mess that lingered too long on the violent rape of Clara's daughter, Blanca, played by Winona Ryder.) The director, Bille August, considered potential Claras including Julia Roberts, Meg Ryan, Nicole Kidman, and Kim Basinger. Forty-five-year-old Glenn Close, whom August judged too old for the part, graciously stepped aside to portray Clara's confidante, Férula. Just two years younger than Close, Meryl exuded an "ephemeral quality" that attracted August. Glenn agreed she "would be a good thing for the movie," according to the *LA Times.*

Truth be told, Meryl and Glenn were just about the *only* good things about the movie. The casting news leaked in September 1992, the same month Meryl departed *The Firm.* The John Grisham book-to-blockbuster thriller was no longer being rewritten to include a woman lawyer character, which Meryl would play. Tom Cruise

Meryl and Joe Mazzello.

now had the movie all to himself. Soon, Meryl was braving strong currents—and a homicidal Kevin Bacon—in the action-adventure nail-biter *The River Wild,* on which Carrie Fisher worked as a script doctor following her split from partner Bryan Lourd. ("That was, not therapeutic, but distracting, at least," Carrie said later.) After wrapping *The House of the Spirits,* which filmed in Denmark and Poland, Meryl reported to Montana and Oregon in the summer of 1993 to play Gail Hartman, a teacher, mama bear, and white-water rafting pro. Gail's rustic family vacation implodes when escaped convicts Wade (Bacon) and Terry (John C. Reilly) hijack the raft she's steering downriver with her ten-year-old son Roarke (Joe Mazzello) and architect-husband Tom (David Strathairn). Wade shoots and kills a handsome park ranger (Benjamin Bratt, gone too soon), a bone-chilling moment that fuels her steely resolve to outmaneuver the sneering sociopath.

Gail and Tom's marriage is on the rocks because of his workaholic ways, but the ordeal brings them closer together. The Hartmans become separated after Tom tries to steal Terry's gun at their riverside campsite; infuriated, Wade runs after Tom and fires at him, believing he's dead. Wade, holding Gail and Roarke hostage, forces the two back into the raft and orders Gail to paddle them through a forbidden series of rapids dubbed the Gauntlet. Gail objects. Although she is only one of three river experts who've survived those rough waters, Gail argues it's too dangerous with Roarke onboard. Nevertheless, she pulls off the impossible. Waiting at the end of the Gauntlet, Tom attacks Terry and frees the gun for Gail to grab and shoot Wade. She kills him in a single shot.

"It's a desperate attempt at something that is fundamentally not achievable," a nameless film executive sneered to *Us* magazine, dismissing Meryl's genuine desire to tackle a new challenge as a shameless play for a box-office smash. With a sarcastic edge, the *Us* source added, "Although I'm looking forward to the raft scenes."

The River Wild allowed Meryl to regain "that old feeling of having climbed a little too high up on the tree—of skating out onto the ice before it's frozen solid enough." She later admitted that, yes, "it was a bit of a midlife crisis." Her preparation involved pumping a lot of iron. She worked out three and a half hours a day for some six months, consuming "900 calories and practically no cooked food," she recalled. "Oh god, it was ridiculous.... And what really amazed me was that I didn't look that different! I did strength training for an hour and a half to two hours and then yoga for an hour, which I still do. Not to sound like I've been in California too long, but it really is very centering."

Arlene Burns, a former river guide in the Himalayas and currently the mayor of Mosier, Oregon, helped Meryl reconnect with her adrenaline-junkie side. Arlene met *The River Wild*'s director, Curtis Hanson, by happenstance while he was scouting filming locations in Idaho. Meryl and son Henry, officially a teenager at age thirteen, joined Arlene in cabins along Oregon's Rogue River, where Arlene showed Meryl how to navigate a raft and swim the rapids without one. The guide, who became Meryl's rafting double during the four-month shoot, soon realized that her trainee was studying her mannerisms.

"It was a trip," Arlene says. "The funny thing was I felt we were like soulmates, and of course we felt like soulmates because she's acting like me—and at least I like myself, you know. I was like, 'Wow I just feel we have so much in common. We had this bond.' Then when I started kind of figuring it out, I noticed that she sat how I sat and she kind of moved her hands the way I moved my hands. That was what she did. I was the person she was mimicking. So that was really funny, but it was just a head trip for me because I would forget that it wasn't just her. It was her acting like me."

They were both roughly the same height, which helped when Meryl, who's 5 feet 6 inches tall, recommended that Arlene be her double on the set. During the shoot on the Kootenai River in Montana, Meryl watched from shore while Arlene demonstrated the technique for a rafting sequence. Next, Arlene would stand behind Meryl on the raft and coach her through the run as many times as it took for her to feel comfortable by herself.

"I felt much closer to her before her entourage arrived," remembers Arlene, calling Roy Helland almost "like her bodyguard.... I kind of backed away when Roy was in close range because he was his own, big person."

Arlene compares Meryl to a Rinpoche, an esteemed spiritual leader in Tibetan Buddhism, and Roy to a follower she had seen during her travels—fiercely loyal to the Rinpoche, though not necessarily warm toward outsiders. Roy, who color-matched Meryl and Arlene's hair, "would listen in on conversations and report to her what people were saying and maybe she wanted it that way," muses Arlene. "God, you want somebody who's doing something like that. Who's making sure you look your very best. He was pretty obsessed with his role. He was the keeper of her, but he was kind of an in-your-face guy." For instance, he would lick his glass and say, "Hey, you wanna sip?" *No thank you.* "What, you think you're gonna get AIDS or something?" Roy would crochet pink Barbie Doll dresses on the set, as if demonstrating to the largely straight, male movie crew: *This is who I am. Deal with it.* "Meryl gave him, in a sense, the power of position to do that and to be as eccentric as he wanted to be," Arlene says. "There was no firing Roy. He was a fixture. Period."

The River Wild was a family-friendly place to work. Meryl brought her daughters and nanny on location. Don and Henry were there some of the time. Kevin's wife, Kyra Sedgwick, and son and daughter stayed with him. David Strathairn, the hippieish father of two sons, chose to live in a trailer near the river. He would pick blackberries and make pies. Joe Mazzello, then starring in the megahit *Jurassic Park,* recalls the experience as one of the best he had as a child actor. Often on movie sets, Joe felt that he wasn't part of the team. "That didn't exist on *River Wild,*" he says. "It was so different, and I credit Meryl. I credit all of them. I mean Kevin and David and John....There was never any condescension, or they never patronized me, or made me feel in any way less than just one of the cast, one of the five people on this boat."

Meryl set a tone of togetherness. According to Joe, "She was incredibly motherly. She made me feel comfortable and happy and kept me engaged, and in a good mood. And we had these long waits. She used to give me head rubs."

Joe describes Curtis, who previously helmed the evil-nanny thriller *The Hand That Rocks the Cradle,* as a "wonderful man" but "so distant," unlike *Jurassic Park* director Steven Spielberg, who liked being around kids, perhaps because he's a kid himself. "Curtis, out of some obligatory mood, would take the time to come down from whatever cliff he was on. It always took, like, 20 minutes for him to get to us. And Kevin, Meryl, all of us would just be doing impressions of Curtis. We'd see him coming and Kevin or somebody would be like, 'Kevin, good. We need one more.' And that was the only thing [Curtis] would ever say. Then, finally, Curtis would show up and say exactly that. He would be, like, 'Meryl, good. We need one more.'"

One time, the group of goofballs, Meryl included, mooned the camera. Joe, embarrassed, didn't participate. "It was just people who really got along, and really had fun together, and just had this sort of wild, really intense experience," he remembers.

The river's unpredictability may have bonded the actors for life. In a death-defying curveball while shooting a scene, a current swept them away into a level-four rapid. The crew watched in horror from the shore. Meryl turned around and said, "Joe, hold on." He wrapped his arms around the rope inside of the raft. The adults got him down the rapid flawlessly. It was incredibly scary and incredibly fun.

One harrowing day, Meryl nearly drowned when she was flung out of her raft toward the end of a long stretch of filming. She disappeared beneath the white water, sending Hanson—who had pushed his tired star to film the scene against her wishes—into a panic as witnesses yelled, "Meryl's gone!" Miraculously, she surfaced, life—and life jacket—intact. A safety kayaker brought her to safety, then Hanson walked down from his remote hill perch to greet the shaken actress. "Fortunately, Meryl agreed—not then, but later—to go back and do it over again," he later recalled. As for Meryl, she reportedly told Hanson that next time he should believe her when she says she can't do something.

The River Wild would be the last of Meryl's athletic adventures for a while, as she turned to a quintessentially female—and epically romantic—role that called for the perpetual student to acquire her first new accent since her '80s heyday. After a rough patch braving the current, Meryl was finally getting back in the game.

Meryl the Environmentalist

In a 1988 press conference promoting *A Cry in the Dark,* a reporter asked Meryl what she'd do if she wasn't an actress. Meryl answered, "I'd probably work with the environmental movement in some way. Just hurl myself at that."

She kind of did anyway. While shooting *A Cry in the Dark* in Australia, Meryl was alarmed by the thinning ozone layer over the country, where residents suffered high levels of melanoma. "We had to cover the children with number-26 sunscreen every time they went outside," she reported. "My dresser there was a girl a few years younger than I was who had had three operations already; half her face had been carved away. So I was barking about this in my kitchen, and finally my friends said, 'Why don't you shut up and do something about it?' So I called the people at the Natural Resources Defense Council." Robert Redford had recommended the environmental advocacy group. They said, "Well, funny you should call, because we have this report about pesticides and children's diets that's going to come out in January [1989]. It is so shocking and upsetting, and we really need a spokesman for it."

Meryl became the public face of the anti-pesticide campaign, leveraging her gravitas to bring awareness to a public health issue that affected children throughout the United States. According to the council's two-year study, millions of preschool kids risked getting cancer from the residues of pesticides discovered on fruits and vegetables. Meryl accompanied the nonprofit to meet with members of Congress in Washington, and a bill that had been in limbo for twelve years finally passed requiring chemical and pesticide companies to register all pesticides on the market.

"Chemicals may be why a lot of women are having trouble getting pregnant, why there's a lot of breast cancer in younger women, and why there is all of this environmental leukemia," she said at the time. "When I thought about it, I remembered that my grandparents lived to be in their 90s, and my mother and father are in great health, *kinehora*. And I realized that when my grandparents and my parents were children, *nothing* they ever touched had *anything* on it."

When she got on the plane from Hartford, Connecticut, to DC, she thought to herself, *You jerk, what are you doing?* "Mrs. Gummer Goes to Washington"? Her sister-in-law told her, "Just remember how *mad* you are."

The biggest threat: daminozide, also known as Alar, a carcinogen that was used on apples. In March 1989, Meryl launched the campaign Mothers and Others for Pesticide Limits and testified against Alar on Capitol Hill, asking, "What's a mother to do?" Government officials sided with the apple industry, so Meryl turned to *People* to plead her case and sing the virtues of organic produce.

"My friends, who are a very motivated group—I'm the laziest among them—organized a symposium in our hometown in Connecticut," she said in a statement clearly intended to mobilize other busy-yet-concerned moms. "About 500 people came, including the managers of the two grocery stores. Within two weeks they both began selling organic fruits and vegetables. They even have a little price war going right now. It's great, because one of our goals is to make these foods affordable."

Three months later, the maker of Alar caved to public outcry and yanked the pesticide off the market. Meryl turned the Mothers and Others crusade into a movement aimed at spreading awareness of eco-friendly consumer products. It encouraged people to shop at farmers markets and avoid buying toxic paints, among other sage advice. Meryl shuttered Mothers and Others in 2001 but reconnected with cofounder Wendy Gordon for an interview a decade later, defending the high grocery bill when we buy organic at, say, Whole Foods (a.k.a. Whole Paycheck).

What if, she posed, "your food budget is a really important thing, maybe as important as your cable budget. Maybe you don't need 20 channels of ESPN. Maybe you spend less over here so you can spend more on healthier, safer foods. Some foods may be more expensive, but they're cheaper in the long run. It's all about the long run, in my view."

Cut to 2019: farmers markets are now a Saturday morning scene, frequented by wholesome parents who have cut the cord on cable TV and *only* buy organic.

CHAPTER 11

Meryl the Romantic

I was acting like another woman, yet I was more myself than
ever before.—Francesca Johnson

(*The Bridges of Madison County,* 1995)

A month before *The River Wild* surged into theaters in September 1994, Meryl and Tracey Ullman took their kids on a rafting trip to "a little bitty river in Massachusetts," said Meryl, recalling that Tracey—whom she's christened her "soulmate"—wanted "me to show off for her so she could make fun of me." The sound of the water made Meryl's heart pulse with a familiar shot of adrenaline and "desire to be there; to do it."

She "emerged from *River Wild* with a lot of metaphors for living," she told the *New York Times Magazine* while doing press for the movie. "Metaphors about taking risks, calculable risks, and being as strong as you can and then just sort of knowing it's all up to fate anyway."

Word-of-mouth momentum was building. An early screening in New York whipped up something of a frenzy, with an audience member standing up to scream, "That's some big woman!" Meryl had been incensed by Universal Pictures' decision to include footage of her wielding a gun in *The River Wild* trailer. "It really made me mad," she said. "I'm always mad, you know, when they say they're going to do one thing and they don't really mean it. They're just saying it to *mollify the woman*. And so they said: 'Oh, it's only two weeks. And we really can't find any other close-up that's as powerful in the whole movie.' And so I—I objected to this being my Christmas gift to America, because they were just gonna run it for two weeks in the theaters at Christmas. Then they got such a great response from the whole trailer that they decided to run it forever."

She refused to be shown with a firearm in the promotional poster. As she explained to *More* magazine in 1999, "Every movie star who stands up and points a gun at America is not only selling the movie—they're selling the gun. The NRA couldn't pay these people enough money to stand there and hold the rifle for their ad— but in the end, they're making that ad and they're making it gratis. I think our profession doesn't take responsibility for the images that we put out in the world."

Even though Universal's marketing team seemingly reinforced the belief that gun imagery sold movies, *The River Wild* glorified neither guns nor violence. Gail killed Wade out of self-defense. Meryl was proud to flip the gender roles in a genre dominated by the usual suspects (see: Cruise, Tom) and, increasingly, unlikely action heroes such as *Speed*'s buzzcut-heartthrob Keanu Reeves.

"I made a movie my girls would be excited to see," she said. "They could put themselves in the hero's role and project it without being a burly man, without having to make the leap girls are used to making. This is not my offering to the male action audience. If they like it, it's great. If they don't, well, we tried."

On August 15, 1994, news hit the trades that Clint Eastwood had cast Meryl in his hotly anticipated adaptation of Robert James Waller's bestseller *The Bridges of Madison County*, which enjoyed effusive praise from Oprah Winfrey even if the coastal literati savaged it as "porn for yuppie women" and "mass dressed up as class." Eastwood would both direct and star as soulful *National Geographic* photographer Robert Kincaid, who romances lonely Italian war bride Francesca Johnson (Meryl) while on assignment shooting Iowa's covered bridges. Jessica Lange, Anjelica Huston, and Cher were among the American actresses vying to play Francesca, but how many could recreate the character's exotic accent? Carrie Fisher gave Meryl's phone number to Eastwood. "He growled, 'I hear you didn't like the book,'" Meryl remembered. "Pause. I said, 'No, no! It's just that I wasn't destroyed by it, like everyone else.'" Eastwood replied, "Read the script. It's good."

Screenwriter Richard LaGravenese had eliminated Waller's purple prose and shifted focus from Kincaid to Francesca. Meryl cried. Then she said yes, turning down Robert Redford's offer to star with him in *Crisis in the Hot Zone* after Jodie Foster dropped out. Redford bolted the project thereafter.

During the *Bridges* casting process, LaGravenese, who wrote the 1991 Robin Williams drama *The Fisher King,* "had heard little ideas of other actresses that were younger, and I remember saying to them, 'You are going to alienate every woman who read this book. Because if she's in her thirties, that's not the same point as a woman who's in her forties who has been married for over 20 years. It's a completely different character.'"

At the time, Eastwood was sixty-four years old and Meryl two decades his junior. But even so, Warner Bros. "felt I was too old to play this character," Meryl recalled. "And so Clint made—I gather— a case for me, which I was glad about."

The Bridges of Madison County was a coup for Meryl, offering proof that *The River Wild* pushed her in the right direction at a pivotal crossroads. Meryl's last major hit was *Out of Africa* in 1985. Afterward, she veered off course. Intriguing, Oscar-bait material like *The Remains of the Day, Thelma & Louise,* and *Evita* passed her by. "She went from being a great classical actress to playing parts in Hollywood that others could have done," said *Sophie's Choice* director Alan J. Pakula. "Sometimes they put her into a picture and it's like having this huge motor on this tiny car."

Meryl, a secretly shrewd businesswoman, seemed ready to level up. In 1994, she hired a new publicity firm, PMK, and cleared her post-*Bridges* schedule for the crime drama *Before and After* with

Liam Neeson. Positive word for *The River Wild* contributed to a salary bump somewhere in the ballpark of $4 to $5 million on the Eastwood production, which also inked a deal to pay Meryl a percentage of the box-office gross. Though stars such as Meg Ryan and Demi Moore had made similar back-end deals, this marked new territory for Meryl. .

While *Bridges* began production in Winterset, Iowa, Meryl—hair dyed Francesca's chestnut brown—took a break to grace the Los Angeles premiere of *The River Wild,* planting her hands in cement outside Mann's Chinese Theatre. A laughing Kevin Bacon, there to witness the event, held her back as she jokingly attempted to smear him with the goopy residue. The movie was a modest success, collecting $94 million worldwide on a $45 million budget; *Speed,* by comparison, netted $350 million, establishing Keanu as the industry's go-to tough guy with a sensitive streak.

When I was thirteen years old and totally obsessed with pop culture, my mother took me to see *The River Wild* at the theater. The first time I watched Meryl on screen felt like a low-key surprise—taut and exciting, with none of the fanfare that accompanied a male-driven spectacle. I distinctly remember feeling confused by the rare instance of a woman action star. Where film critics counted plot holes, I spotted a new role model who pushed through obstacles with dignity and swagger. That year, Winona Ryder's *Little Women* remake blew my mind. It subverted the typical boy's coming-of-age journey to showcase Winona as adventurous girl-hero Jo March, who rejects a proposal of marriage from a dashing neighbor, Laurie (peak Christian Bale), in order to follow her dreams. These films still resonate today. (In 2019, Greta Gerwig remade *Little Women,* with Meryl playing the cantankerous Aunt March to Saoirse Ronan's Jo.) To quote actress-activist Geena Davis: "If she can see it, she can be it."

Like Jo, who tried living the writer's life in New York City only to be pulled back to Orchard House, Meryl returned home to

Connecticut. "I hate being there," she said of LA. "I really require a great deal of privacy. I don't like to be out and dressed up and seen." In an anonymous quote to the *New York Times*, a "prominent director" (undoubtedly Manhattan based, like Alan J. Pakula or Mike Nichols), observed, "You have to keep a distance from there. You've got to stay aloof from the agents and lawyers and gossip. I honestly believe she was looking at career survival and saying to herself, 'Maybe I should join the mainstream more, so I'll listen to my agents.' But she appeared in too much dumb stuff. She listened to voices other than her own."

MERYL'S *SIMPSONS* EPISODE

November 6, 1994: Meryl makes her debut on the wildly popular animated series, voicing Reverend Timothy Lovejoy's daughter, Jessica, in an episode called "Bart's Girlfriend." Her character, even more wicked than Bart, frames him for the crime of stealing collection money from church. (The cash is later discovered underneath her bed.) When Meryl came in to record, Nancy Cartwright, the voice of Bart, was too scared to request her autograph. But, as it happened, Meryl asked for Cartwright's signature. Her kids, like most all children of the '90s, were huge Bart fans.

At forty-five, Meryl was bucking convention while her peers threw in the towel or took what they could get. Jane Fonda abruptly announced her retirement in the early 1990s. Sally Field, forty-seven, had gone from Tom Hanks's love interest (*Punchline*) to his mother (*Forrest Gump*) in the span of six years. Jessica Lange would all but disappear until producer Ryan Murphy cast her comeback in his *American Horror Story* series in 2011.

Meryl dismissed the idea that her choices were part of some calculated strategy. "I don't have a game plan for any of it," she said. "An actor is always dependent on what comes around.... I never aimed for the big hit. I don't have the machine to do that. I'm pretty aware of what I look like. I don't look like Sharon Stone, and I'm not built like her." Years later, she would insist to NPR's Terry Gross that she continued to work into middle age partly because sex appeal "wasn't the first thing about me."

The irony was that Meryl's *Bridges* performance unearths a profound sensuality not yet seen in her work. It flows from her pores, dripping like sweat on a humid August night. Farmer Richard Johnson, kind but dull, hardly seems to notice or appreciate the Sophia Loren thing his wife has going on. But Robert Kincaid does.

Kincaid meets Francesca in 1965 while asking for directions to Roseman Bridge, a deceptively ordinary structure with a rustic beauty that others might overlook. Kincaid deems the bridge good enough for *National Geographic;* his photograph of it later makes the cover. After Francesca's husband and children leave town to enter a prize steer at the Illinois State Fair, Kincaid enters the scene, showing Francesca what she's been missing all these years. Their torrid four-day romance blossoms organically over wistful moonlight walks and long, philosophical dinner-table conversations during which they reveal themselves to one another.

Francesca confesses that Iowa isn't "what I dreamed of as a girl." She'd quit a rewarding job as a teacher because Richard preferred her to stay at home. Unlike her family, with whom she hardly speaks at dinner, Kincaid shows real interest in hearing what she has to say. He tells stories about traveling to far-flung countries she would never visit. He makes her belly-laugh. He even helps in the kitchen! "Men cook," he informs a flustered Francesca. Sensing that she's insecure about being a midwestern housewife, he reassures her, "You're anything but a simple woman."

Clint and Meryl.

Without uttering a word, Meryl vividly conveys Francesca's sexual awakening. The moment she encounters the warm, understated Kincaid, her eyes flicker with attraction and curiosity. She touches her mouth, smooths her dress. She is startled when his arm accidentally brushes her leg in the car en route to the bridge. Kincaid's presence heightens her senses; she often seems on edge, as though consumed by thoughts of touching him. After their first dinner together, she sits alone on the porch reading a book of poetry. Suddenly, she opens her nightgown and flashes the pitch-black sky. In a later scene, she soaks in a tub where Kincaid previously showered, lingering with wordless ecstasy upon the beads of Robert—excuse me, *water*—that drip from the shower head. "Almost everything about Robert Kincaid had begun to seem erotic to me," she declares in voice-over narration.

"In the first half, she managed to portray the balance of being both settled into a life and her dissatisfaction and yearning for something else," LaGravenese said of Meryl. "And then, in the second half, she managed this incredible balance of the attraction and the yearning for him and the conflict that that created."

Sex is inevitable, but, unfortunately for both, it's more than physical: The two are in love. Kincaid asks Francesca to run away with him. She's even packed her bags, but, ultimately, she can't go through with it. Francesca's moral obligation to her kids outweighs destroying their lives to be happy with the love of hers. "This kind of certainty comes but just once in a lifetime," says Kincaid, walking out the door. (He is prone to make poetic statements. OK, fine, here's my favorite: "The old dreams were good dreams; they didn't work out, but glad I had them.")

A few days pass. It's pouring rain. Francesca sits in the truck, waiting for Richard to come out of the store, and spots Kincaid, completely drenched, across the street. She forces a smile; he looks pained. Seconds later, Richard is driving behind Kincaid, and Francesca—tears streaming down her face—watches her lover remove the cross necklace she gave him and wrap it around the rearview mirror. They're at an intersection. The light turns green. Kincaid loiters too long, waiting for Francesca to hop inside. With her palm gripping the door handle, she's ready to make a move. Eastwood stretches the will-she-or-won't-she tension for maximum impact, focusing his camera squarely on Meryl as she chickens out, crying uncontrollably (along with the audience).

In the script, "people are just talking to each other. But then, in the end, the thing people most remember is a visual thing," Meryl said. "It's that hand on the handle. And him in the rain. And her looking out and the traffic lights and the missed opportunity. And I think it has to do with the fact that people don't like to be told what to feel in a movie. They like to have it ambush them and feel it and... they can only do that when there's no talking. And so they have to scream at the screen, 'Open the door!'"

Deep down, we know the bittersweet truth. "Her characterization tells you why she's never gonna leave: She was rooted," explained Meryl, who took inspiration from two Italian women—actress Anna

Magnani as well as a childhood neighbor and Italian war bride from Puglia who married an American GI and moved to New Jersey. *The Bridges of Madison County* is a love story about female sacrifice— namely the choice between familial responsibility and the desire to start a new life. Meryl and Eastwood grounded the drama in naturalism. It was a symbiosis of two artists who understand the importance of restraint—when to pull back, and when to push it.

"Clint shot it like a foreign film almost," said LaGravenese. "He wasn't afraid of the silences. He wasn't afraid of letting the camera just sit and let the performances take over. It was almost like a French film to me."

Eastwood, who won his first Best Director Oscar the year before for *Unforgiven*, didn't spend much time talking to Meryl until they started shooting *Bridges*. He thought their scenes, filmed in continuity, would benefit from the natural awkwardness between strangers and the growing intimacy that developed as they got to know each other. Eastwood's decisive way of working was new to Meryl. After Meryl's first take, he used footage of her rehearsal in the scene. She turned to a group that included cinematographer Jack Green, asking, "Is this how it always is?" About three days later, she said to Green, "I *love* this way of shooting. This is so much fun! I don't have to work up to anything. I can start at the top. I can start right at the highest note."

And, once she cried on cue, it was hard to stop. "No amount of ice could possibly get Meryl's eyes down," Roy Helland told *New York Times Magazine*. "They were so filled with fluid. There's no glycerin with Meryl. When she cries, she cries." Green would wipe away tears when he thought nobody was looking and witness Eastwood do the same. Helland wore a hearing aid because Eastwood was so quiet. Instead of yelling "Action!" he would say, "Well, when you're ready, start."

As Meryl saw it, she and the former *Dirty Harry* star "came from very different genres in film, so there's that attraction of opposites. That helps the magic potion." Eastwood, as vocally conservative as

Meryl is liberal, viewed Kincaid and Francesca as outsiders, and perhaps he shared that in common with Meryl, another industry veteran who lived outside Los Angeles and against whom Pauline Kael, thankfully retired, had harbored a personal vendetta. He set out to befriend Meryl on set. In between takes, the two danced together and had fun.

"It was instant," remembered *Bridges* producer Kathleen Kennedy. "Clint and Meryl were what you always look for in a romance. They had that chemistry on film. You just instantly believed that these two people were deeply in love with one another."

Of course, it was all make-believe. But *The Bridges of Madison County*'s overwhelmingly female fan base considered the Streep-Clintwood rendezvous as real as love at first sight. Meryl accomplished what Robert James Waller did: she gave hope to the hopeless romantics among us. Simultaneously, like a confession told to Betty Friedan for her 1963 game changer *The Feminine Mystique,* Meryl set a match to the myth of the contented midcentury housewife, illuminating the inner turmoil of a woman unfulfilled by motherhood and housework. Francesca, like so many other silent housewives of the era, would never self-actualize beyond her expected domestic duties. Meryl's quietly rebellious performance spoke personally to contemporary women still living the lie that happiness was to be found solely in the home. It was a signal fire for restless souls debating whether to do something different. Meryl, who was rooted but self-actualized, would keep telling their stories.

And because she was drawn to characters who, like she did, resisted conformity in ways that inspired, it was only fitting for Meryl to swoop in and save the day to play the offbeat violin teacher Roberta Guaspari—a role once meant for Madonna.

The Ones That Got Away

Even a queen doesn't get everything she wants, including her pick of movie roles. Behold, four films that evaded Meryl's grasp or weren't offered to her in the first place.

Sweet Dreams:

Meryl has long admired Jessica Lange, an Oscar winner for Best Actress (*Blue Sky*) and Best Supporting Actress (*Tootsie*). Jessica also won the leading role in Dino De Laurentiis's 1976 *King Kong* remake, for which Meryl auditioned but walked out after De Laurentiis criticized her looks. The two actresses were compared in entertainment news stories; as attractive, intelligent blondes who did interesting work, their Venn diagrams intersected. Both scored Best Actress nominations in 1983 (Meryl won) and again three years later, when they lost to Geraldine Page. While Jessica's portrayal of Patsy Cline in *Sweet Dreams* failed to defeat Page, it earned love from Meryl, who wished she'd played the country music legend. "I envied Jessica Lange when she got *Sweet Dreams*," Meryl said. "That was such a great movie; she was beyond wonderful in it." (No, she did not think she could have done it better.)

Evita:

In the late 1980s, Meryl was in talks to play Eva Perón in a big-budget adaptation of the hit stage musical to be directed by an unusual choice: Oliver Stone. She had wanted this part ever since Andrew Lloyd Webber staged *Evita* on Broadway circa 1979, with Mandy Patinkin as Ché and Patti LuPone as Evita, the rags-to-riches wife of Argentine president Juan Perón. A decade later, opportunity struck. Meryl recorded a dub for Stone, and Paula Abdul was going to choreograph the production. "The reason I want to do that thing is because I want to sing," Meryl explained at the time. Bad news for everyone who ever wanted to witness her belt "Don't Cry for Me Argentina": In autumn 1989, Meryl opted to leave the project partly because she was exhausted by the long negotiation process and other studio shenanigans. Stone followed her out the door. "It was a bitter disappointment," she said. "But it's just a movie."

Punchline:

Meryl also craved Sally Fields's role in the 1988 comedy about a housewife and mother who becomes a stand-up comedian with help from a comic played by Tom Hanks. "I would have jumped at that role," she said. "I would have died to do it, died to do it. I have three children. I could have played that part." In a cheeky dispatch, the *Los Angeles Herald-Examiner* wrote, "It's funny to hear Meryl Streep say that she would have liked to have co-starred in *Punchline* but that nobody sent her the script.... Somebody should tell Streep that Sally Field wasn't controlling the property to give it to another actress." All told, can't you imagine Meryl absolutely *owning* the part of a woman escaping the kitchen and rising through the comedy ranks? If naysayers assumed she wasn't funny enough, she'd prove them wrong as a flaxen-haired diva in 1989's *She-Devil* and 1992's *Death Becomes Her.*

The Remains of the Day:

With Mike Nichols behind the 1993 film version of Kazuo Ishiguro's novel *The Remains of the Day,* Meryl had an ally who could help cast her as Miss Kenton, a former housekeeper pining after an emotionally detached butler. Nichols had directed Meryl three times before, in *Silkwood, Heartburn,* and *Postcards from the Edge.* He was one of her biggest cheerleaders. Meryl read *Remains* for Nichols, but he decided she wasn't quite right. When the filmmaker neglected to tell Meryl about the decision, he hurt her feelings. She later got over it, saying, "I was very upset to be upset. I have too much of a need for forgiveness in my life." Emma Thompson scored the part, a casting that accompanied two big changes: Meryl's firing of Sam Cohn, her longtime agent, and her move from Connecticut to Los Angeles.

CHAPTER 12

Mozart Meryl

The board of education and the district attorney think that
music isn't important. But they are wrong! And they're gonna
get a big fight!—Roberta Guaspari

(*Music of the Heart*, 1999)

When Wes Craven, master of the horror genre, suddenly found himself in a filmmaker's nightmare, he didn't panic. Instead, he activated what qualified as a Bat-Signal to reach Meryl Streep: an impassioned letter.

Craven had cast Madonna in *Music of the Heart*, his uncharacteristically earnest drama inspired by the true story of violin teacher Roberta Guaspari, who cofounded the Opus 118 Harlem School of Music and fought for music education funding in New York City. But Madonna turned out to be the wrong fit, so Craven pivoted to Meryl as a replacement. It was the summer of 1998, and Meryl had decided she would not make another movie until after Christmas— nor did she think there was enough time to learn the violin before filming started. Craven's note changed her mind. "This can't fall apart," she recalled him pleading. "I've waited 20 years to make an out-of-genre film. This is my chance and it's something I really care about." Meryl couldn't say no. "I'm a pushover," she explained.

Madonna took voice lessons to expand her range before starring in the 1996 movie musical *Evita*, a role Meryl had yearned to do since the beginning of time. ("I could rip her throat out," Meryl joked of Madge. And, in 1990, amid reports that the pop star was in talks to join *Evita* following Meryl's departure, *Los Angeles Magazine* published a gossipy item relaying that Meryl thought Madonna lacked the vocal range for the role.) For *Music of the Heart,* the Blonde Ambition icon recruited Roberta for private violin lessons at her New York home and also attended a beginner's violin class incognito. Roberta grew to like Madonna. "She was a real workaholic," she recalls. "She was really vulnerable then." The problem: Madonna wanted Pamela Gray's script rewritten to gloss over the reality that two men deserted Roberta: first her husband and then a commitment-phobic love interest played by Aidan Quinn. "Madonna didn't like that," says Roberta. In the end, Craven cut her loose. While Roberta was en route to give her a lesson, Madonna, sobbing, phoned to say she'd been let go. "He fired her because she got too involved trying to run it," Roberta says.

The Miramax production shut down. Feelers were put out to Susan Sarandon and Marisa Tomei. But, they were back in business with Meryl on board. She picked up the violin and went to work.

Three years earlier, in February 1995, Meryl began a streak of somber dramas that lacked the stirring passion of *The Bridges of Madison County.* It started with the bleak, Massachusetts-set prestige drama *Before and After,* the kind of movie you watched only once and never returned to again. The director, Barbet Schroeder, had carved a niche helming slick thrillers such as *Single White Female* and *Kiss of Death;* his moody style suited *Before and After,* which screenwriter Ted Tally adapted from Rosellen Brown's 1992 crime novel of the same name. Meryl played pediatrician Dr. Carolyn Ryan, and Liam Neeson her artist-husband Ben, a role that Robert De Niro had considered three years earlier. The Ryans' blissful existence is turned upside down when their teenage son, Jacob (Edward Furlong), runs away on suspicion that he killed his girlfriend, Martha (Alison Folland). Eventually, Jacob reveals the truth to his parents. According to

Jacob, Martha had blindsided Jacob with a bombshell betrayal: she was pregnant, and Jacob might not be the father. He's stung by the news, yet they sleep together in Jacob's car, which gets snowed in. An argument ensues outside while they try to jack up the vehicle. Jacob slaps Martha and she retaliates by attacking him with a crowbar. He grabs hold of the crowbar and strikes Martha in the head. She falls face-first on the jack.

Ben advises Jacob to lie to authorities, but, during a press conference, Carolyn enrages Ben by subverting their story to tell the real version of events. She won't apologize for doing the right thing, yet her red-rimmed eyes hint at remorse for betraying her kid. Then, Jacob—finding his moral compass—finally confesses to police. He gets sentenced to five years for manslaughter, serving only two; Ben, convicted of destroying evidence, spends less than one year in the slammer. Afterward, the Ryans move to Miami; there's a sense of unease as they canoe down a waterway in the last scene. Though the pro-Jacob narrative attempts to justify Martha's death by smearing her as promiscuous and violent, a young girl is gone because of his actions.

"It interested me because it was like the Hinckley case, this boy who shot President Reagan to get attention and was, from all accounts, from a very happy family. And it destroyed them," Meryl said. "Reality can turn on a dime, and your life is changed forever."

A month into the *Before and After* shoot, Meryl was in talks to star opposite Diane Keaton and Leonardo DiCaprio in *Marvin's Room*, with Jerry Zaks attached to direct and De Niro to produce. The tearjerker was based on Scott McPherson's play about a troubled woman who reconnects with her estranged, terminally ill sister. Both Meryl and Diane reportedly took pay cuts. Despite its distinguished cast, *Marvin's Room*, a Miramax release, was being made with a relatively small budget ($23 million) for an A-list studio picture. Bob and Harvey Weinstein founded Miramax in 1979 and, by the mid-1990s, established the company as the most powerful incubator of independent cinema in Hollywood. Disney acquired Miramax for $60 million in 1993, yet the Weinsteins continued to call the shots at their studio. Their successes included *Sex, Lies and Videotape, The Crying Game,* and *Pulp Fiction,* which transformed writer-director Quentin Tarantino into a household name and indie film into a mainstream event.

Meryl seemed out of place. Though *Pulp Fiction* put John Travolta back on the map in 1994, the clever—and extremely bloody—picture repelled her. "I thought it was very well made," she conceded. "Smart. *Very* smart. And I *hated* it in my soul....And my friends: 'Oh, I loved that!' You can't apply words like love to that movie. Because it doesn't *fit.*"

Like her friend Nora Ephron, director of the sincere '90s romantic comedy *Sleepless in Seattle,* Meryl thought having "edge" was overrated. "All it means to me is depressing," she said, worrying, "It all leaves an imprint on kids who are way too young to be looking at the crap—the stuff—that's out there....Do I want them to page through *Vogue* and see the Nan Goldin models and the heroin look? Or the Calvin Klein downtown porn thing? Is that cool? That's not cool to me, I don't like it."

Writing about Meryl in the *LA Times,* Matthew Gilbert said that, in person, she resembled "an out-and-out soccer mom, minivan with kids waiting outside, an undone load of laundry with her name on it at home." Meryl owned the soccer mom label, telling *People* magazine, "I am, but I don't understand it. They all run up, they all run down. I don't know who is playing what." Like any involved parent, she had strong feelings about PTA meetings: "I hate the PTA. I tend to get too emotional. I'm a wild card, and my friends go, 'Shhh, shhh.'"

Meryl and Tarantino would never work together (imagine that!). She gravitated toward directors who gave her the space to communicate human feelings; she met a solid match in Clint Eastwood, whose later films had a lot of heart and soul (none of which he brought to his baffling empty chair speech at the Republican National Convention in 2012). On June 2, 1995, *The Bridges of Madison County* ranked number two at the box office, behind the family film *Casper,* and went on to make $182 million worldwide. Meryl, a rare *People* cover subject, graced the June 26 issue alongside the headline: "MERYL'S PASSION." Reviews were glowing. *New York Times* critic Janet Maslin wrote, "The movie has leanness and surprising decency, and Meryl Streep has her best role in years." Meryl, noted Maslin, "rises straight out of 'Christina's World' to embody all the loneliness and fierce yearning Andrew Wyeth captured on canvas." *Time's* Richard Corliss called *Bridges* "Eastwood's gift to women: to Francesca, to all the girls he's loved before—and to Streep, who alchemizes literary mawkishness into intelligent movie passion."

One Manhattan movie theater strategically placed a box of tissues for moviegoers walking out of *Bridges.* Meryl, meanwhile, embarked on another emotional film, *Marvin's Room,* which was shot in New York City. She helicoptered in from Connecticut on the regular. "I got very pissy at the end of the day," she said, "if people weren't hustling their butts to finish their work so I could get in the helicopter."

Meryl's character, Lee, is very different from Francesca; her voice is a rich, low alto tinged with cigarette smoke and bitterness. The single mom, a beautician, has buried her emotions to the point where she's incapable of connecting with her two sons, the oldest of whom literally burns down their home to get her attention. When Lee retrieves Hank (a feral, intense DiCaprio) from a mental institution, she barely registers his apology. Earlier she tells a shrink, "Hank is not something I can control, so what's the point of me visiting?"

Turns out that Lee is paralyzed by a past trauma: her abusive ex used to beat Hank when he was a small child. The native Floridian moved Hank and brother Charlie (Hal Scardino) to Ohio, cutting off communication with her sister, Bessie (Diane Keaton), and father, Marvin (the ornery Hume Cronyn), who's bedridden from a stroke two decades earlier. Suddenly, Bessie, his caretaker, receives disappointing news via her socially awkward doctor (a deadpan De Niro) that she has leukemia and requires a bone marrow transplant. She phones Lee, who packs up the kids and drives to the Sunshine State. Hank, unaware that he even *had* an aunt, suspects Bessie is pretending to care about him in case he's a match. While Hank learns to trust adults again, Bessie—patient and compassionate— teaches Lee the value of family and how to listen and let other people in. (Truth: this movie is more earnest than a Sarah McLachlan album—or my teenage self.)

Meryl originally signed on to play Bessie, the dependable sibling, but the role hit too close to home so she switched to Lee. She read Frank J. Sulloway's book on birth order, *Born to Rebel,* and said having two younger brothers influenced her personality. "Being the oldest, and being the only girl, has defined a lot for me," she revealed. "I see it in my son, who is the oldest and has three little sisters. They're allowed to be wild, and he's very responsible."

Meryl agreed to participate in *Marvin's Room* on the condition that Diane be cast in the showiest role. She "wanted somebody I could feel like sisters with, because I never had a sister. So I picked my sister," she said. Diane developed a girl crush on Meryl. "I find her beautiful," she gushed, "and I'm constantly looking at her." When it came time to shoot a scene in which Bessie reveals to Lee that her boys aren't bone marrow matches, Diane insisted upon breaking down in sobs. But director Jerry Zaks pushed back, advising her to go the opposite direction. *Wouldn't Bessie, who always put others first, try to hold it together for Lee's sake? Reassure her that everything's gonna be fine?* "Diane was reluctant to embrace that, which is frustrating, because I'm very spoiled," Zaks says. "I'm used to actors really trusting what I have to say."

Meryl, knowing Zaks was right, helped persuade Diane to let go of her initial idea. "I think he's got a point," she said. As a result,

Diane's affecting performance reflected how Bessie would actually respond to news that her disease will likely kill her. Rather than collapse on the floor, she comforts her weaker sibling.

"Meryl's emotionality is always appropriate," Zaks observes. "And the reason I tell you that is because without Meryl, whom Diane adores, saying what she did, I wasn't able to get the scene the way I wanted. And if you look at that scene now...Diane, she's magnificent. Because she's smiling and yet there are tears in her eyes. She is pulling off the physically impossible act of doing two things at the same time."

When the 1997 Oscar nominations were announced, it was Diane, not Meryl, who received a Best Actress nod. The year earlier, Meryl had been nominated in the category for *The Bridges of Madison County*, conceding defeat to Susan Sarandon of *Dead Man Walking*. And speaking of Susans: perpetual nominee Meryl, who hadn't won since *Sophie's Choice*, was turning into the Susan Lucci of film. Perhaps voters shrugged and said, "Well, she's already got two."

In 1997, Meryl lined up roles in two more dramas: Pat O'Connor's low-budget screen version of the Irish play *Dancing at Lughnasa*, playing the eldest (and fussiest) of five unmarried sisters, and *One True Thing*, Universal Studios' mother-daughter weepie costarring Meryl as a suburban mom dying of cancer and Renée Zellweger as the daughter who's come home to take care of her.

For the former, Meryl took her family on location to Ireland. *Dancing at Lughnasa* filmed in County Wicklow, just south of Dublin, during the month of August. She worried about her accent and dancing skills. An Irish dance teacher near her Connecticut home taught Meryl some steps; she learned the Irish lilt with an assist from Guinness. "I think I made it more difficult than it was and when I relaxed with a pint or two it was fine," she confessed. By far the biggest name on the call sheet, Meryl loved being part of an ensemble filled with British and Irish actors—an experience that fondly recalled her theater days. She hadn't been on stage since

Taken in Marriage at the Public Theater in 1979, when Henry was eighteen months old. "I thought, 'Well, I'm going to have to give this a rest for a while,'" she said. "And then I never imagined I'd have so *many* children. Oh yes, everything is *so* finely calculated!"

Movies checked off more pluses than minuses: they paid more than plays, and she could be with her kids on nights and weekends. She now worked summers or on New York–adjacent fare like *One True Thing*, which kicked off in New Jersey in October 1997. Meryl drove herself back and forth to Connecticut every day. "I understand she drives like a race-car driver," says *One True Thing* director Carl Franklin, whose filmography includes the Denzel Washington noir *Devil in a Blue Dress*. Earlier that year, Franklin had flown out to Ireland to meet Meryl, and the two hung out, drinking Guinness at the pub restaurant. "It was disarming to see her so accessible," he says.

Though Meryl missed the table read and rehearsals due to *Lughnasa,* she arrived on set prepared to shoot her scenes in chronological order so she could authentically chart her character's cancer progression. Meryl had a diet plan to lose weight and even changed her voice and speech pattern as the illness took a toll on Kate Gulden, the latest mother in her repertoire and perhaps the most saintlike. The story, based on Anna Quindlen's 1994 novel, orbits around the relationship between Kate, the unsung glue that holds the family together, and her daughter Ellen, an ambitious journalist. Ellen idealizes her aloof, self-absorbed professor father, George (William Hurt), and resents the sunny, cheerful Kate for leading a domestic life. After Kate's diagnosis, Ellen begins to appreciate her mom and the unconditional love she gave. The two grow very close, and an outing to a town tree-lighting ceremony—when Kate is gravely sick but so happy to be there—tugs at the heartstrings.

"My generation's mothers were the last housewives. And this captures that," Meryl said. "The conflict between the career woman and her mother who bakes. I did relate to it. My mother always worked out of her house. She was a commercial artist, but not really a career woman. Mostly she just took care of me and my two brothers. Still, she was a great role model in many ways."

Though *One True Thing* received positive reviews, Franklin was dismayed by one critic's accusation that the movie, in putting Kate on a pedestal, pushed an insidious message to young women: *get back in the kitchen*. "None of us felt that way, especially not Meryl," Franklin states, emphasizing that Ellen "was going back to work with a greater understanding of that kind of woman."

Meryl balked when Jackie Chan's *Rush Hour* outperformed *One True Thing*, $31 million to $6.6 million, during the movies' opening weekend. *Marvin's Room* completely tanked, collecting just $13 million. Meryl was choosy about which movies she took on—and she publicly stood by her choices, flop or not. But, clearly, commercial success wasn't her sole mission, given the cozy character dramas she favored at the time. "A lot of scripts get sent which my agents no longer even pass on to me," she said. "They're so used to me saying, 'Why do you send me this shit? You know I'm going to give it to the kids to do their crayoning on.'"

Meryl stamped her coveted seal of approval on the Madonna-less *Music of the Heart*. Roberta Guaspari, a big personality with an indomitable spirit, provided plenty of quirks to emulate. According to Roberta's sons, she lacks a filter, spouting whatever comes to mind; that's part of her charm. Although boasting two degrees in music education, she put her career on hold to raise a family and follow her navy-officer husband from post to post. When he asked for a divorce, she jumped back into the workforce. Roberta, armed with nothing but her strong will, talked her way into a gig as a substitute violin teacher at East Harlem's Central Park East School. There, she gained a reputation for inspiring underprivileged and promising young talents, and her success rate allowed her to expand the string program to two additional urban schools. However, ten years later, in 1991, the city eliminated the funds necessary to keep Roberta's efforts going. She lost her job. Down but not out—she'd hit rock bottom before—Roberta gathered the troops and staged a benefit concert featuring her ex-pupils at Carnegie Hall. Joining them: none other than violin virtuosos Itzhak Perlman and Isaac Stern. During the making of *Music of the Heart,* New York poured money into Opus 118, which exists to this day.

Meryl learned the violin from mid-July 1998 through that August, six hours a day for exactly six weeks. Once shooting began, she tried to practice around the schedule, but time was very scarce. Roberta says she gave Meryl one lesson in early September, and Meryl observed a couple of classes, watching her subject in action. The actress-technician sharpened her newfound skills with a violinist from the New York Philharmonic all the way through January, when she was to recreate the climactic Carnegie performance. Character-wise, Meryl nailed Roberta's feisty temperament and New York accent. Roberta assumed she'd seen *Small Wonders,* the Oscar-nominated 1995 documentary on which *Music of the Heart* was based. "She knew how to talk like me, walk like me, she got it down to a science," she says. Her students and their parents noticed, too.

"Playing a real person carries with it a whole other set of responsibilities than you would have when creating a fictional character," Meryl said. "So I did as much research as I could and then I just sort of threw it away, because the real woman is a sizeable phenomenon of energy, inspiration, hard work and irascibility. I tried to capture little parts of her and put it together in the film. But Roberta was around and kind of drove me crazy a bit on the set. I didn't want to make her feel uncomfortable that I wasn't doing it right. But it wasn't a piece of mimicry."

Finally, the moment of truth: not only did Meryl hold her own alongside Stern and Perlman, playing themselves, but she succeeded in impressing the greats with her talent. Everyone was blown away. Meryl would recall being so nervous that Roy Helland held a hair dryer under her armpit.

After *Music of the Heart* premiered in September 1999, Meryl did not release a movie for another three years—well, if you discount her cameo voicing the Blue Fairy in Steven Spielberg's 2001 sci-fi drama, *A.I. Artificial Intelligence.*

Music performed below expectations, grossing $3.7 million its opening weekend and, eventually, $15 million over two months in theaters. Of all her movies, only *Kramer vs. Kramer* surpassed the $100 million mark domestically. Meryl, however, earned wide praise for her salty Roberta Guaspari. "Here you might think she has no accent, unless you've heard her real speaking voice; then you realize that Guaspari's speaking style is no less a particular achievement than Streep's other accents," Ebert wrote. "This is not Streep's voice, but someone else's—with a certain flat quality, as if later education and refinement came after a somewhat unsophisticated childhood."

At fifty years old, Meryl was losing momentum. She had aged gracefully but away from the movies that seemed to capture the zeitgeist. That all changed when she met Spike Jonze.

CHAPTER 13

Meryl the Wallflower

I suppose I do have one unembarrassed passion. I want to know what it feels like to care about something passionately.—Susan Orlean

(Adaptation, 2002)

In the fall of 1999, Meryl received a Gotham Award for Lifetime Achievement at Chelsea Piers in New York. The star-studded gala doubled as a fundraiser for indie filmmakers; Ethan and Joel Coen were there as well as Michael Moore and Darren Aronofsky. Miramax mogul Harvey Weinstein made a dumb joke while presenting her prize: "We co-starred in the original production of *A Streetcar Named Desire*. Boy, was she awful." The next year, she tied with Katharine Hepburn for a record twelve Oscar nominations, arriving to the March 26 ceremony wearing a Mary McFadden power suit in a sea of gowns and tuxedos. Meryl's date: her thirteen-year-old daughter, Grace. Inside the Shrine Auditorium: Hilary Swank was crowned Best Actress for her bravura performance in the indie *Boys Don't Cry*; cynical midlife crisis drama *American Beauty* swept the awards, winning Best Picture and Best Actor for Kevin Spacey, who briefly appeared in *Heartburn* as a stickup man robbing Rachel Samstat's group therapy session. On this glittery night, Spacey was a full-fledged movie star without a glimmer of a notion that his peers would expel him, along with Harvey, amid damaging and credible #MeToo reports in 2017.

Miramax handled international distribution for *The Hours*, one of two acclaimed pictures starring Meryl in 2002. The other was

Sony Pictures' *Adaptation,* an experimental black comedy that cata-
pulted the soccer mom to a level of cool she hadn't projected since
Postcards from the Edge. She credited Sony exec Amy Pascal for insist-
ing she star in the sexy role of Susan Orlean. "At a studio headed
by a man they'd have said, 'Ooh no, why?'" said Meryl. "They don't
want to see their first wife in the movie, and that's what I make them
think of. But Amy wants to see herself."

She also had Spike Jonze to thank for her brand-new hipster
sparkle. The wunderkind, in his early thirties, had transitioned from
directing high-profile music videos to movies; his 1999 debut, the
surreal *Being John Malkovich,* established Jonze as an innovative
young talent who could visualize the words of the gifted, eccentric
screenwriter Charlie Kaufman. The collaborators partnered up again
on *Adaptation,* the riveting product of Kaufman's struggle to adapt
journalist Susan Orlean's *The Orchid Thief* for Columbia Pictures.

Rather than faithfully interpreting the nonfiction bestseller,
Kaufman fictionalized events into a meta-movie: Charlie, a bundle
of nerves and self-loathing, suffers from writer's block. He hits a wall
with his *Orchid Thief* gig and is too scared to talk to Orlean about it.
By comparison, his dopey twin brother, Donald, a well-adjusted ray
of sunshine, writes a shockingly successful script for a psychological
thriller. Donald helps Charlie by pretending to *be* him while meeting Orlean in New York. He senses something off about her, like
she's not telling the full truth.

The siblings follow Orlean to deepest Florida, where they spy her
canoodling and getting high with the subject of *The Orchid Thief:*
the passionate, obsessive, and offbeat-handsome John Laroche. The
outlaw horticulturist has forged a black market career smuggling
the wild ghost orchid *Polyrrhiza lindenii* from a nature preserve.
Pointing a gun, a furious Orlean—whose passion for Laroche has
blossomed into full-fledged mania—forces the Kaufmans to drive
to the swamp, where she intends to kill them. The once-passive
wallflower who studied characters more daring than she is now a

person who might interest a literary journalist scouting her next *New York Times* best seller. Laroche accidentally shoots and kills Donald; karma arrives in the form of an alligator, which drags the orchid thief underwater. Orlean is arrested, and Charlie finally finishes his screenplay, having learned from Donald such valuable lessons as having the guts to believe in your art and put it out into the world.

Donald's contagious positive energy mirrors that of Laroche, both the real man and Kaufman's fictional interpretation. In *The Orchid Thief,* published in 1998, Orlean wrote of Laroche, "One of his greatest assets is optimism—that is, he sees a profitable outcome in practically every life situation, including disastrous ones. Years ago he spilled toxic pesticide into a cut on his hand and suffered permanent heart and liver damage from it. In his opinion, it was all for the best because he was able to sell an article about the experience ('Would You Die for Your Plants?') to a gardening journal." Laroche's orchid fervor rubbed off on Orlean, although the contributing *New Yorker* writer initially objected to Kaufman representing the character of "Susan Orlean" as a twisted, lunatic caricature of herself.

"It was a complete shock," she recalled. "My first reaction was 'Absolutely not!' They had to get my permission and I just said: 'No! Are you kidding? This is going to ruin my career!' Very wisely, they didn't really pressure me. They told me that everybody else had agreed and I somehow got emboldened. It was certainly scary to see the movie for the first time. It took a while for me to get over the idea that I had been insane to agree to it, but I love the movie now."

It helped that Meryl Streep was playing her.

"It was great because she wasn't trying to impersonate me and because she's amazing!" said Orlean. "She created the character just through knowing me from the book. It's actually one of my favorite performances by her. Maybe I'm a little prejudiced, but how could I not be? I really like her portrayal of this strange creature!"

Meryl didn't meet Orlean until the first screening. She felt a "teensy bit guilty for not interviewing her" beforehand but also knew that "we were not doing a docudrama here." She didn't want to be "diverted by the truth." Meryl boarded *Adaptation* in the fall of 2000, joining Nicolas Cage (Charlie/Donald) and Chris Cooper (Laroche); bubbling with ideas and emotion, it was just about the best script she'd ever read. Jonze's efficiency and "cold steel intelligence" impressed Meryl, who no doubt values those aspects of her own personality. "He's so prepared," she said. "I can't tell you what a relief it is for an actor, because it doesn't always happen that way."

At first, she intimidated him. *How much direction would she want or not want? What if he insulted her?* On day one, she made Jonze feel at ease. Meryl could not stop smiling from the moment she started shooting the LA-based movie in the spring of 2001. She would get the giggles, nearly shutting down the set. Her exuberance reached its zenith in a scene where Orlean snorts orchid powder and talks on the phone to Laroche. " 'Well, we got all night. We can just do whatever you want,' " Meryl recalled Jonze saying. "My heart sank. I thought, 'Oh no, I have to invent here.' So I had a ball. It was endless. I was breathing on, and then writing on, a plate glass window with my nose. They didn't put that in. Somewhere there's a nine-act play of me being stoned up in this hotel room."

The part that Jonze kept in is pure joy—with an undercurrent of sadness. Orlean, who wondered what it would be like to have Laroche's passion, asks the flower hunter to join her in harmonizing a dial-tone sound. She's silly yet lonely and yearning to connect to a kindred spirit. Off camera, Meryl made another request of Chris Cooper. "She saw that my acting problem is that I take things too seriously," said Cooper, whom Meryl described as a "volatile" personality (in other words, a perfect Laroche). "During the middle of some takes, I got really frustrated, and she passed by and gently whispered, 'Stop whining.' It was like a great director's single note—that's all I needed, and I'm eternally grateful."

Asked later if she had a Larochian passion, Meryl demurred to *Interview* magazine: "In spurts. And then there's the laziness factor." She had confessed to being lazy in previous interviews, as if to downplay her hard work and ambition to achieve excellence for herself and colleagues like Cooper. Meryl had a big life, filled with obligations, so we might assume the L-word to mean she wasn't purely driven by professional success—that the type B side of her luxuriated in those quiet moments between movie sets, award shows, and media appearances. On *One True Thing*, Carl Franklin was amazed to see Meryl drop character while stepping out of a scene. "It's not a big deal to her," he said. "She's not real precious about it, which I found interesting."

That might be owing to her theater training. On August 13, 2001, Meryl finally returned to the stage in Mike Nichols's Central Park revival of *The Seagull*. It had been twenty long years. She charmed as the fading actress Irina Arkadina opposite a starry cast: Kevin Kline, Christopher Walken, Natalie Portman, and Philip Seymour Hoffman. "Two decades in front of movie cameras haven't diminished her capacity for looming large from a stage, and with a head-to-toe physicality that gives the lie to Pauline Kael's famous suggestion that Ms. Streep acts only from the neck up," wrote the *New York Times'* Ben Brantley, quipping that Meryl "gives expansively to her fellow cast members, feeding them emotional cues that they mostly fail to pick up on."

September was a somber month. A couple of weeks after the Twin Towers fell, Meryl's mother, Mary, died of complications from heart disease at New York Hospital. She was eighty-six. During a magazine interview in September 2002, before the anniversaries of her double heartbreaks, Meryl was feeling fragile. "This just doesn't seem like the right time to be talking about me," she said.

Fame could be rough. She constantly felt tired or deficient, like she wasn't paying attention to the right things, from managing her career to working out. She was so grateful to her family. But she was very, very excited about *Adaptation* and *The Hours*. In December, the movies opened back-to-back in specialty theaters before going wide two months later. The latter film took longer to make, requiring reshoots one year after principal photography ended; director Stephen Daldry had undergone the herculean task of filming three different movies and editing them together into one coherent narrative. Copy that for playwright David Hare, who worked with Meryl on *Plenty* and was tasked with adapting Michael Cunningham's Pulitzer Prize–winning novel, which traces a day in the lives of three women affected by the Virginia Woolf classic *Mrs Dalloway*. Nicole Kidman wore a prosthetic nose to play the suicidal Woolf; Julianne Moore exuded glamour and desperation as Laura Brown, a suburban 1950s housewife who abandons her young son; and Meryl, whom Julianne found "very funny" and "really bossy," channeled a contemporary version of Woolf's Clarissa Dalloway (a married society lady who's planning a party but is preoccupied with memories of former love interests, including a woman she "had not the option" to be with).

Though modern-day Clarissa, an editor in New York, lives openly with partner Sally (Allison Janney), she seems more devoted to caring for her friend and ex-lover, poet Richard Brown (Ed Harris), who's dying of AIDS. She's hosting a shindig to celebrate a big literary award he received and obviously still hung up on what they once had; before the event, Richard commits suicide by jumping out of a window—in front of Clarissa.

Having spent time with Meryl, Hare "realized how powerful the tug is in her between duty and freedom, and that all her greatest performances are about that conflict. My two favorite performances of hers are in *Silkwood*—in which she is amazing [as a] woman [who] gets drawn into realizing what her duty is—and *A Cry in the Dark*. But the same conflict is there, clearly, in *Sophie's Choice*, which is almost like a video game program for the things Meryl does best. One side of her is free-spirited, anarchic, and funny. The other expresses the nobility of duty."

Meryl, he continues, is "so potent in *The Hours* because she's playing to the 'duty' side of her character. She feels she must keep her friend Richard alive and inject into him the love of life that he lacks. She's so heartbreaking because at a certain moment she realizes she has to let go—part of the power of the film is that not even Meryl Streep can keep another human being alive."

Natasha Richardson recommended that Meryl read Cunningham's book, and how could she not? *She was in it.* (Clarissa thinks she sees Meryl filming a movie in downtown Manhattan.) The movie role required her to go to places she would rather not have. "It was a nightmare," she revealed. "And yet, this is why you sign up. You want the challenging work, you search for it, you berate your agent because it doesn't exist. And then when it comes, the night before you're supposed to shoot the scene, you think, Why did I say I would do this?"

In those moments of self-doubt, Don would tell her, "Keep going. Start by starting." Although Meryl at times agonized over decisions, she wasn't like delicate Clarissa, who was fixated in a time of her youth to an unhealthy degree. "Of necessity I live very much in my life, and I think Clarissa lives, in great measure, in the past," she said.

Meryl, meanwhile, had found her way back to New York. The kids were older—aged eleven to twenty-three—and the city offered an artist couple like Meryl and Don access to a cultural scene they didn't have in Connecticut or, for that matter, Los Angeles. "My family and friends are here, I understand life better here," she explained. "I like the street, the action, the seasons."

They lived in a five-story brick townhouse in Greenwich Village, a short subway ride away from Tribeca, where she moved into John Cazale's apartment all those years ago. Back when she could hop on the train or attend a Broadway opening without being recognized. Losing Cazale had been difficult, but his death helped her focus on the important things in life: her loved ones and the arts.

Meryl's experience with loss, and good men dying too young, propelled her to new heights—literally—during a heavenly encounter in *Angels in America*.

CHAPTER 14

Meryl the Shape-Shifter

Stupidity gets me crazy.—Hannah Pitt
(HBO's *Angels in America*, 2003)

When Mike Nichols asked whether she wanted to play three parts in *Angels in America,* his transcendent $60 million HBO adaptation of arguably the greatest play ever written, Meryl answered "Yes!" After she signed her contract, Nichols said, "Would you play a fourth part for free?"

Her four characters: a rabbi presiding over a funeral; the ghost of Ethel Rosenberg, who visits villain Roy Cohn on his deathbed; Hannah Pitt, a Mormon mom who befriends gay AIDS patient Prior Walter in 1980s New York City; and a panelist on a committee of casually dressed angels. The cast featured Al Pacino as the closeted rage-aholic Cohn and Emma Thompson pulling triple duty as a benevolent nurse, a homeless woman, and the Angel who commands Prior to spread the message to humans that social progress must end. While visiting heaven—which resembles San Francisco, according to the brilliant *Angels* playwright Tony Kushner—Prior shuns the prophecy, telling the angel tribunal that humankind will die without progress. "I want more life," he pleads.

Nichols rounded out the boldface names with lesser-known talents, plucking Justin Kirk from relative obscurity (i.e., the short-lived WB series *Jack & Jill*) to be Prior, the center of Kushner's hyper-verbal, hyper-ambitious rebuke to Reagan-era homophobia and ignorance. On Broadway, Kirk earned recognition for his performance in the Tony-winning play *Love! Valour! Compassion!* The thirty-three-year-old had both the stage experience and sardonic humor necessary to portray Prior, but he was very insecure on set with Nichols, who put the fear of God in him during the rehearsal process.

"It's not working," he told Kirk. "I don't know what, but I talked to someone who's worked with you before, and they told me you need a kick in the ass at this stage." Afterward, "it was all I was thinking about," says Kirk. "It's not as though I was half-assing it. I was like, 'What the fuck.' From that point on, I was always freaked out."

On the first day of filming in the spring of 2002, Nichols approached Kirk to say, reassuringly, "This is it, you're the guy. You're doing it."

Meryl, who would later cite the wily, ironic Nichols as an inspiration for Miranda Priestly, skipped rehearsals—which involved lots of talking, not running scenes—but she and the other Big Two, Emma and Al, joined the cast for the big table read. Kirk was dreading their first scene together: Prior's emotional breakdown in his hospital bed and Hannah's surprisingly humane reaction to it. Appearances are deceiving: Hannah, prim and no-nonsense, is an awakening progressive in a conservative's Talbots clothing. She doesn't wince when Prior shows her a lesion on his body. "I wish you would stay true to your demographic profile," he says. "Life is confusing enough."

Although Kirk was anxious, Meryl was "totally chill," he remembers. "She's not in some place where she's deep in the character at all times. She walks in, she does it and then there's 'Cut.' It's all normal. This is not my story, but someone else telling me: They were doing a scene with her, and before each take, she was hunched over with her head down and doing something just as it was leading up to 'Action.' And, finally, the person got the courage to say to her, 'What's happening? Are you preparing? You're doing something.' She looked at him, she's like, 'Oh, no, no. I'm texting my daughter.'"

Smoking was part of Kirk's weight-loss regimen, and Meryl would occasionally bum a cigarette off him. "She was not a full-time smoker, but she was certainly the occasional smoker," he says. "And I remember smoking with her in my tiny little dressing room in Queens."

Otherwise, Meryl could be seen hanging out with Roy Helland between takes or doing the *New York Times* crossword. The mood overall was joyous and "creative," added Trip Cullman, Nichols's assistant on *Angels*, recalling, "Every time Meryl Streep would emerge from her dressing room, it was like, *Who the fuck is that?!*"

The extras hardly noticed Meryl as the bearded, elderly rabbi delivering a eulogy in the opening scene with fake dandruff sprinkled on her shoulders. Nor did *Where the Wild Things Are* author Maurice Sendak, who played one of the rabbis sitting next to Meryl in another scene at a cemetery. According to Nichols, Sendak "almost fainted when the 'old Jewish man' beside him stood up, grew a foot taller and spoke in the voice of a lovely woman" at the end of the day's shooting. Although Nichols was known to tell actors, even the big ones, "Don't act," Meryl and Emma surprised him. The actresses were friends. Mike Haley, Nichols's first assistant director, recalls the two laughing while suspended by wires to film the sequence where Emma sports Victoria's Secret angel wings and kisses Meryl's Hannah in a gesture that sends the devout Christian into orgasmic rapture. Meryl said, "It was hard to kiss midair and not break each other's front teeth."

Emma, a convivial presence, "would move lamps if you wanted her to," says Haley. She helped Kirk work through his nerves. But, when she wrapped her scenes before a break in filming, Nichols forgot to send her off, in grand actors' tradition, with a big to-do on set. So, to honor Emma, Nichols brought in noisy bagpipe musicians. "I'm trying to act here with Meryl Streep," Kirk recalls griping to himself.

Angels in America dominated the 2004 Emmys to win Outstanding Miniseries, Outstanding Lead Actor (Pacino), and Lead Actress (Meryl, besting Emma). "You know, there are some days when I myself think I'm overrated," she joked while accepting her second Emmy statuette. She milked the moment for comic effect. After a ten-second pause, she transformed her deadpan expression into an ecstatic smile, gloating: "But not *todaaaaaaaay*." In a self-deprecating, self-aware performance, Meryl, fifty-five, was letting the audience know that she *knew* what they were thinking. She called Nichols her "king" and poked fun at Emma, haughtily declaring that her friend would "hold a grudge for the rest of her life." More laughs. While reveling in her win, Meryl also managed to preemptively puncture the perception that Emma, absent from the ceremony, might be a sore loser. Gossips love a catfight (see Bette Davis versus Joan Crawford), and Meryl gleefully burst their bubbles.

The awards-season brouhaha, fueled by movie studios pouring money into "For Your Consideration" ad campaigns, alienated the eternal nominee, who told Britain's *Daily Telegraph*, "I find it alarming that all the campaigning for Oscars is getting like a political campaign. It really is distasteful. It won't be long before they start paying for television commercials for best picture, best actor, and all those things."

On March 23, 2003, Meryl—looking regal in a black, off-the-shoulder gown and emerald necklace—brought Don and eleven-year-old Louisa (who wanted to see the celebs) as her dates to the Seventy-Fifth Academy Awards. Nominated in the supporting actress category for *Adaptation,* she lost to *Chicago*'s Catherine Zeta-Jones but surpassed Katharine Hepburn with a record-breaking thirteen Oscar nominations.

The following year, Meryl became only the sixth woman to receive the American Film Institute's lifetime achievement award. A televised Kodak Theatre event resembled the retro series *This Is Your Life,* the Meryl edition. She and her family sat together at a long table laced with flowers. Among the guests: Mike Nichols, Tracey Ullman, Carrie Fisher, Jim Carrey, Claire Danes, Nora Ephron, Kevin Kline, Clint Eastwood, Robert De Niro, Diane Keaton, Jack Nicholson,

Goldie Hawn, Kurt Russell, and Roger and Chaz Ebert. In her hilarious speech, Tracey brought down the house, bellowing, "You're the
only one working! All the rest of us have to show our tits!" Meryl
gave her a standing ovation. Don snapped a photo of Carrey's tribute.
"What are you, man? WHAT ARE YOU?!" said Carrey, pointing at Meryl
from the stage. "SHAPE-SHIFTER! BODY-SNATCHER!"

Roy Helland laughed effusively when Nora took the stage. "I
highly recommend having Meryl Streep play you," remarked the
writer-director-raconteur. "She plays all of us better than we play
ourselves, although it's a little depressing knowing that if you went
to audition to play yourself, you would lose out to her."

Henry put his arm around his mother as Goldie referenced Meryl's late parents. Harry Streep died in July 2003 at the age of ninety-
two. "You were the most devoted and most loving daughter that I
have ever known," Goldie told Meryl, "and your mom and dad are
watching you tonight and taking great joy in this moment."

Now it was Meryl's turn to step up to the podium. The compli-
ment parade had made her exhausted yet deliriously happy. She
thanked Mary and Harry for giving her life, Don for putting up with
so much, and Isaac Mizrahi for her ball gown. "I hope it's not the
end," she said, her voice breathless.

She failed to thank an unpopular American president for starting the unpopular Iraq War. Meryl had always been political, but,
in 2004, she unleashed her opinions as never before. She endorsed
gay marriage at the Golden Globes, eleven years before the Supreme
Court made it legal. She reduced her carbon footprint by driving a
Toyota Prius and wondered why everyone didn't go lean on gaso-
line. She supported Democratic presidential candidate John Kerry's
unsuccessful campaign to unseat Republican incumbent George W.
Bush and lit up Internet forums after repeatedly bashing Bush in
public. She sniped at a Kerry fundraiser, "During Shock and Awe
I wondered which of the megaton bombs Jesus, our president's
personal savior, would have personally dropped on the sleeping

families of Baghdad. I wondered, 'Does Jesus understand collateral damage?'"

When asked what sparked her outrage, Meryl responded, "Name a topic! *Everything* pushed me over the edge! The quiet dismantling of environmental regulations. The phoniness of No Child Left Behind. *Everybody* should be getting up and making a big fat noise. Yes, of course, I always question why anyone would listen to an actor. But it's not your profession so much that defines you as your personhood. I listen to all kinds of people whose qualifications to opine on anything are that they have a radio show or a degree in art history. Our most famous president of late"—Ronald Reagan—"was an actor. You don't jettison your citizenship just because you're famous."

She understood the professional consequences of taking a stand (two words: *Jane Fonda*), but she couldn't resist giving conservative politicians the finger. Ironically, she was playing one in Jonathan Demme's remake of *The Manchurian Candidate*, which opened three months before the Bush-Kerry election. In pearls and pastels, she served death stares as the cunning, sociopathic Senator Eleanor Prentiss Shaw, who allows the evil firm Manchurian Global to implant a microchip inside her son, Raymond (Liev Schreiber), that brainwashes him into believing he's a Gulf War hero—a major selling point in his vice presidential campaign. Only Major Ben Marco (Denzel Washington) knows the truth, but his efforts to warn Raymond, the Manchurian candidate, go nowhere. Eleanor, a power-hungry momager who puts Kris Jenner to shame, mind-controls Marco to assassinate the president-elect so Raymond can assume the nation's highest office. "I will do whatever I can to protect America from anyone who opposes her," she declares with righteous passion.

Another thing about Eleanor: she's the spitting image of Hillary Clinton. The immaculate haircut. The tailored jackets. The self-confidence. Although Meryl acknowledged similarities in appearance—minus the tinted purple art-teacher glasses also seen on *The Hours'* Clarissa—she took inspiration from conservative women like *Wall*

Street Journal columnist Peggy Noonan and Bush advisor Karen Hughes, well known by Meryl the news junkie. It was fun to play someone so *certain*. Willing to bend the rules if that meant making the world her idea of a better place. Certainty, said Meryl, "is just so attractive in people.... [U]nfortunately, it leads to fanaticism."

She loved the description of Eleanor in the screenplay: "ageless with soft curves that conceal razor claws and a titanium backbone." The polished exterior barely hid the dragon within. As Eleanor, Meryl crunches on ice cubes as if they are enemies she intends to snuff out. She gazes at Raymond with a creepy oedipal yearning that raises the question: *Has she already crossed that line?* She emasculates male colleagues like she thinks herself the smartest person in the room. (She is.) "Where are all the *men*, anymore?" hisses Eleanor in a line Meryl wrote.

People are ambivalent about women in power. They don't know what to think, and it's not just men who internalize misogyny. American women have been underrepresented at society's highest levels, denied opportunities to advance professionally, and deprived of role models. A woman achieving success—whether she's a CEO, a senator, or Hillary—is scrutinized more than a man in the same position. Men accustomed to calling the shots resent the woman who doesn't stay in her lane. Their wives might regard the high achiever with a similar level of suspicion: *Who does she think she is? WHAT IS SHE? SHAPE-SHIFTER! BODY-SNATCHER!*

Make no mistake, Eleanor Prentiss Shaw is a monster. But Meryl managed to expose the tragedy of Eleanor's life: no matter how high she climbed, she was never going to be elected president of the United States. She lived vicariously through Raymond to get to the Oval Office—and look how that ended up.

The next villain Meryl played would get the last laugh. Oh yes, Eleanor had nothing on Miranda Priestly.

CHAPTER 15

Meryl the Editrix

Truth is, there is no one that can do what I do.—Miranda Priestly

(*The Devil Wears Prada*, 2006)

Here's how screenwriter Aline Brosh McKenna described Miranda Priestly's grand entrance in her script for *The Devil Wears Prada:* "We see more flashes of MIRANDA...$2,000 crocodile Manolos, Chanel jacket, perfect hair, fabulous Harry Winston earrings...[until] MIRANDA steps out of the elevator and for the first time we see her head-on. MIRANDA PRIESTLY, in all her glory. She is stunning, perfectly put together, a white Hermes scarf around her neck. MIRANDA'S look is so distinctive you can spot her a mile away. She is unlike any other beautiful woman, singularly MIRANDA."

McKenna had observed Meryl hissing Miranda's killer barbs at Anne Hathaway during rehearsals, but nothing could prepare her for the experience of watching the woman transform from Meryl Streep, down-to-earth movie star, to the world's worst best-dressed boss. The makeover was vivid, chilling. McKenna, on set for the big reveal, reflexively threw her arm in front of director David Frankel as if to protect him.

Two years earlier, Paramount Pictures put Denzel, the hero, on the poster for *The Manchurian Candidate*, which earned Meryl high marks for her full-throttle foray into villainy. "She has the Hillary hair and the Karen Hughes attack-dog energy, but the charm, the inspiration, and the constant invention are her own," wrote *San*

Francisco Chronicle critic Mick LaSalle. "She gives us a senator who's a monomaniac, a mad mommy and master politician rolled into one, a woman firing on so many levels that no one can keep up— someone who loves being evil as much as Streep loves acting."

Manchurian grossed $66 million, ranking forty-fifth on the list of 2004's multiplex moneymakers. Franchises reigned supreme, with sequels like *Shrek 2, Spider-Man 2, Harry Potter and the Prisoner of Azkaban,* and *The Bourne Supremacy* collectively crossing the billion-dollar mark. Nobody ever asked Meryl, *Where's the sequel?* Or, *Can we merchandise this?* Except for the fall, when the good stuff came out, there was nothing Meryl really wanted to see. She wished there was wider distribution in non-coastal cities for Americans to catch foreign films. At this rate, would theater owners reject Meryl movies—adult, literate, female focused—in favor of CGI superhero flicks where the women, maybe, get ten lines? Soon, movie stars would be replaced by special effects and skimpy plots in mainstream blockbuster bait intended to reach as broad an audience as possible. Tom Cruise, a Top 40 radio station playing the hits, adapted well to this new era, but Meryl marched to the beat of her own drum. She was a freestyle jazz musician. Look no further than her next three projects:

Lemony Snicket's A Series of Unfortunate Events (2004): an adaptation of Daniel Handler's popular children's novel about orphans escaping an evil guardian, Count Olaf (Jim Carrey), who attempts to murder them for their inheritance. The children briefly seek refuge with Aunt Josephine (Meryl), a neurotic Miss Havisham type who resides in a rickety home that teeters dangerously on the edge of a cliff. She's afraid to cook hot food because the stove might burst into flames. She loves grammar and fears realtors. She fails to resist the charms of a swashbuckling fisherman (Olaf in disguise). Sadly, things don't end well for Josephine, but it's fun to watch Meryl and Carrey—two human shape-shifters—share the screen. "As actors, they instantly found each other like playmates in the sandbox," said director Brad Silberling. "Meryl takes what she's given and gives it back to her scene partner—a Meisner technique."

Prime (2005): In this romantic comedy written and directed by Ben Younger, who was thirty-two years old at the time, Meryl plays an Upper West Side therapist named Lisa who discovers that her twenty-three-year-old son, David (Bryan Greenberg), is dating her thirty-seven-year-old divorced client, Rafi (Uma Thurman, who assumed the role after Sandra Bullock backed out thirteen days before shooting). Lisa approved of the age difference when she didn't know Rafi was describing sex with David, but once she puts two and two together, her reaction is comedy-gold. "Trust me, that was harder for me than it was for you," she tells Rafi of their therapy sessions. "Up until a few weeks ago I didn't even know that my son had a penis." Meryl was originally intrigued by the part when her agent told her *Prime* was about "an older woman and a much younger man." Ooh! Then she learned Lisa was the "older" woman.

A Prairie Home Companion (2006): How do I say this without insulting the late Robert Altman? Unless you're a fan of folksy radio shows that almost nobody listens to, then go right ahead and skip this movie. The saviors of Garrison Keillor's dull, indulgent screenplay are Meryl and Lily Tomlin as the singing Johnson sisters and Lindsay Lohan as Meryl's acerbic daughter who writes poems about suicide. Meryl called Lindsay a "great actress—a game and spirited girl." Like she did with Greenberg, Meryl would improvise a little before a scene, warming up her young costar to get the performance she wanted. Said Lindsay, "She leads you into it." Meryl was maternal toward Lindsay but worried the party-hopping paparazzi magnet was too ubiquitous for her own good.

Outside the *Prairie* set in St. Paul, Minnesota, Lohan's fans congregated, seemingly unaware of the Streepgoddess—as Tony Kushner referred to her—in their midst. "Do you know who this is?" yelled Tomlin. The *Mean Girls* starlet enthusiastically swam in the celebrity fishbowl, paying the salaries of the *Us Weekly* masthead in the process.

She loved being famous. Meryl disapproved. "There's plenty of incredibly wonderful young actresses who have not chosen to be on the cover of everything," she said. "But they're not this other thing that's seen at parties, which is—I don't know what it is, I know it probably limits your ability to be imagined as a lot of different kinds of people."

Lemony Snicket raked in $118 million, though it's been lost to memory alongside *Prime* and *Prairie,* which made a total of $42 million. Meryl appeared destined for a fine late-stage career playing wacky aunts and mothers to Lindsay Lohan, Bryan Greenberg, and whoever graced *People* after selling photos of their triplets for a $6 million payday. Ironically, Meryl's next alter ego, Miranda Priestly, was a cutthroat magazine-maker and Page Six regular. Occupation: editor in chief of *Runway,* the world's most important fashion glossy. Miranda *might* consider making a pay-for-play deal with the Brangelina baby, but clothes ruled her covers. She lived and breathed her work, and she ate assistants for breakfast. If you proved that you could procure the unpublished manuscript of the latest Harry Potter book for her twins, then maybe, just maybe, she'd ease up on you. (Not likely.)

In May 2005, it was reported that Meryl had signed on to star in *The Devil Wears Prada,* with David Frankel (*Miami Rhapsody*) directing and Wendy Finerman (*Forrest Gump*) producing. Fox 2000, a division of 20th Century Fox, had been developing the comedy since 2003. That year, twenty-six-year-old Lauren Weisberger, a former assistant to *Vogue* editor Anna Wintour, then the most powerful and feared woman in the fashion industry, published her dishy roman à clef about a young woman, Andrea "Andy" Sachs, who lands a coveted position assisting Anna, I mean Miranda, at *Runway.* After coming to the conclusion that the demanding editrix is "an empty, shallow, bitter woman who has tons and tons of gorgeous clothes and not much else," Andy tells Miranda to fuck off and promptly gets fired from a job that a *million girls would kill to have.* Her allegiance to friends and family proved stronger than the benefits of remaining tethered to Miranda, who had offered to reach out to the *New Yorker*—Andy's dream employer—for the promising Brown graduate in the future. Still, what might happen if Andy mutated from a nice suburban girl into a dragon she no longer recognized: a mini-Miranda?

Weisberger stayed with *Vogue* only ten months before leaving to join *Departures*, a travel magazine. She wrote *The Devil Wears Prada* under the tutelage of respected writing teacher Charles Salzberg. The book sold to Doubleday within two weeks, netting Weisberger a $250,000 advance, and spent six months on the *New York Times* Best Seller list. It was ignored by the magazine empire Condé Nast, which owns *Vogue,* and savaged in the *New York Times.*

Curiously, the Gray Lady assigned the review to Kate Betts, an ex-*Vogue* staffer with a clear agenda to punish an unknown writer for daring to storm the castle, so to speak. "Having worked at *Vogue* myself for eight years and having been mentored by Anna Wintour, I have to say Weisberger could have learned a few things in the year she sold her soul to the devil of fashion for $32,500," sniped Betts. "She had a ringside seat at one of the great editorial franchises in a business that exerts an enormous influence over women, but she seems to have understood almost nothing about the isolation and pressure of the job her boss was doing, or what it might cost a person like Miranda Priestly to become a character like Miranda Priestly."

All told, Weisberger had created an indelible antiheroine. Elizabeth Gabler, president of Fox 2000, and Carla Hacken, her VP, knew it early on, snapping up the movie rights from Weisberger for $600,000 before the writer even completed the first draft. The studio tapped Peter Hedges to adapt *The Devil Wears Prada* and, after he bowed out, punted it to three male screenwriters without success. Aline Brosh McKenna, who previously wrote the romantic comedy *Laws of Attraction,* was the last scribe to take on Miranda, and it was a match made in heaven—or *Vogue*'s shoe closet.

David Frankel was impressed. He'd rejected a script by another writer as a mean-spirited revenge tale absent likeable characters. In his view, the movie version should focus on a central theme: "the nature of excellence and the sacrifices that have to be made. I was a fan of Anna Wintour and *Vogue* magazine. For me the approach to developing the movie properly was to make Miranda Priestly the heroine, someone to be celebrated sympathetically rather than someone to be reviled. In my view of the world, we should be thrilled to have the people who are excellent at what they do, superior at their jobs. The fact that they are not always nice is irrelevant."

McKenna got it. The New Jersey–born Harvard alumna was smart, funny, fashion-obsessed, and took Miranda seriously as a brilliant businesswoman. She also understood Andy's ambition to break into journalism in New York. McKenna had been there and tried it to no avail. Once, *Glamour* spiked a story she cowrote as a freelancer. In 1991, she moved to Los Angeles to write TV and movies. Gabler and Frankel supported her in making Andy's romantic life secondary to her relationship with Miranda. Unlike other movies targeting women, this passed the Bechdel test. Neither Andy nor Miranda's lives revolved around men. Rather, Andy circled Miranda on tippy-toes, careful not to forget her overlord's steak lunch (the ribeye, medium rare) from Smith & Wollensky. McKenna wrote a new ending that removed gratuitous subplots from Weisberger's book in order to elevate Andy's identity crisis: *What kind of person do I want to become?* She makes her decision while accompanying Miranda to Paris Fashion Week; instead of cursing her out, Andy walks away. Flash-forward to Andy's interview at a shabby-chic newspaper that suits her high-minded sensibility: shockingly, Miranda has written a begrudging letter of recommendation. The rookie had earned her respect.

Meryl was Frankel's first choice to play Miranda. "Whenever I said, 'I'm thinking about doing this thing,' everyone's reaction was, 'Oh, yesss!' Sort of gleeful and venomous," she said. "That interested me very much, the reaction." During the screenwriting process, McKenna and Frankel entertained the possibility that Meryl might do the role. "So, if Meryl's gonna play this, we don't need a line here," McKenna recalls saying. "If it's someone else, we might need a line here, but if it's Meryl, we don't need a line here." After receiving McKenna's script, Meryl met with Frankel and agreed to step into Miranda's Prada heels. McKenna was standing by Larchmont Boulevard when Frankel called to tell her the news. She plunked down on the curb and teared up. "I glimpsed the top of the mountain from there," she says. "I just knew that having Meryl involved took the movie to a completely different place."

Meryl understood she had a hit on her hands, but the salary gave her pause. "The offer was to my mind slightly, if not insulting, not perhaps reflective of my actual value to the project," Meryl later told *Variety*'s Ramin Setoodeh. "There was my 'goodbye moment,' and then they doubled the offer. I was 55, and I had just learned, at a very late date, how to deal on my own behalf." Perhaps taking a cue from Miranda, she negotiated higher pay. (While Gabler recalled paying Meryl "maybe $4 million," Meryl's *Prada* paycheck was also reported to be $5 million.) Fox pushed the green light.

McKenna wore a black Harari kimono top to meet Meryl in the living room of her Manhattan townhome. It was raining outside, and McKenna hadn't made a blowout appointment to smooth her frizzy hair. Should she pile it atop her head, or find a salon a.s.a.p.? "You know what? I don't think she's gonna care," she told herself. McKenna, Frankel, and Wendy Finerman sat with Meryl for four hours while she gave notes on *Prada* the movie. "Meryl is what you want her to be," she says. "She is one of the least disappointing show business people I've ever met. She's incredibly smart in the way you want her to be. Listen, in person, she's absolutely luminously gorgeous." Her skin seemed lit from within. Regarding the notes: none was about Meryl wanting to show off or be the center of attention. What she wanted was to do and say less. To be the calm inside the storm. She identified several McKenna-penned lines she really liked, including "By all means, move at a glacial pace. You know how that thrills me."

The remark, aimed at Andy, was dry, withering, and matter-of-fact, all qualities that helped Meryl locate her inner Miranda. Though the *Prada* team toned down the character's meanness so as to not scare away a big movie star, Meryl said, "No, no. Give her more fangs." She waved her hand at a page where McKenna had written a long monologue for the *Runway* high priestess to give when the fictional designer James Holt presents his less-than-stellar latest collection to her. "I don't need to say all this," she said. As a result, the scene was changed so Miranda simply pursed her lips—the most devastating reaction Holt can imagine.

From a Starbucks in LA, McKenna wrote new dialogue that Frankel sent to Meryl for feedback. Meryl thought McKenna could expand a speech in which Miranda schools Andy—who thinks fashion is irrelevant—on the importance of a blue sweater she's wearing. It was several days before Meryl was to shoot the scene, which McKenna considered cutting. But Meryl wanted more. Said Frankel, "Write as much as you can about it. Write an aria for her." Figuring that Miranda would know the different shades of blue, McKenna gave Meryl the option to choose among three specific hues: lapis, azure, and cerulean. She selected cerulean, a color similar to turquoise (and more fun to pronounce). McKenna fired off a monologue to Frankel, assuming they might not use the whole thing because it was so epic. Meryl uttered every syllable. A mic drop for the ages, Miranda's lecture moves beyond humiliating a clueless employee. It helps skeptical moviegoers grasp high fashion's trickle-down influence in under two minutes. Behold:

"This stuff"? Oh, OK. I see, you think this has nothing to do with you. You go to your closet and you select, I don't know, that lumpy blue sweater, for instance, because you're trying to tell the world that you take yourself too seriously to care about what you put on your back. But what you don't know is that that sweater is not just blue, it's not turquoise, it's not lapis, it's actually cerulean. And you're also blithely unaware of the fact that in 2002, Oscar de la Renta did a collection of cerulean gowns. And then I think it was Yves Saint Laurent, wasn't it, who showed cerulean military jackets?

She goes on to say:

> And then cerulean quickly showed up in the collections of
> eight different designers. And then it filtered down through
> the department stores and then trickled on down into some
> tragic Casual Corner where you, no doubt, fished it out of
> some clearance bin. However, that blue represents millions
> of dollars and countless jobs and it's sort of comical how you
> think that you've made a choice that exempts you from the
> fashion industry when, in fact, you're wearing the sweater
> that was selected for you by the people in this room. From a
> pile of "stuff."

Meryl thought it was crucial to show Miranda in everyday work
mode, whether it be picking the right cerulean belt to put on a *Runway*
model or terrifying staffers at a meeting. ("Florals? For spring? Groundbreaking.") Finerman compiled two large folders of information on first
jobs, clothing designers, and Anna Wintour. To the producer's surprise,
she not only read the clippings—Meryl asked for more. She wasn't interested in impersonating Wintour, nor did she want to meet the stylish
Brit, who favored ladylike floral dresses, wearing sunglasses indoors,
and never changing her immaculate chin-length haircut that Anna
wannabes mostly failed to emulate. "Embedded" within Weisberger's
book, said Meryl, "is what the perceived deficits are of women in a leadership position. Chief among them is to expect women to be endlessly
empathetic, a sense of employees' discomfiture that she doesn't give a
shit, all the things that they would not ask of a male boss....It interested
me that Anna Wintour was expected to be smilier, nicer, sweeter...
what we wish women to be is nicer."

Leaving *nice* out of it, Meryl wondered, "Well, hell, what is her
job? What does she have to do? What are her deadlines? What do
we have very little time for, even though the dress and heels have to
have the outward accoutrements of being appealing, womanly?"

Anne Hathaway pursued Andy Sachs with admirable gusto. Fox's first choice, Rachel McAdams, breakout star of *Mean Girls* and *The Notebook*, repeatedly declined the part because she wanted to put the brakes on mainstream movie roles. The studio powers-that-be underestimated the size of Anne's fan base coming from the wholesome teen fairytales *The Princess Diaries* and *Ella Enchanted*. Following a meeting with Carla Hacken, Anne wrote "Hire me" in the sand on Hacken's desk Zen garden so the executive would see it. She didn't have to audition. Frankel liked her, and so did McKenna, who said the then-twenty-two-year-old "gets across that sense of a super-smart books/art person, which is a difficult thing to fake. She nailed the smugness, that slight you feel when you come out of the school world which was your oyster because you got A's in college."

Rounding out the cast: newcomer Emily Blunt as Miranda's most senior assistant, Emily, who charmed Frankel with her irreverent humor and clipped British accent, and Stanley Tucci as Nigel, the second-in-command whose snark is worse than his bite. The Tooch, a character actor with a long list of film credits (*Big Night, Road to Perdition, Maid in Manhattan*), joined *Prada* several weeks into the New York shoot unfolding in the fall of 2005. Barney's creative director Simon Doonan and E! fashion correspondent Robert Verdi auditioned for Nigel, as did BBC personality Graham Norton. (Doonan complained that Tucci, who is straight, was given the part of a gay man.) "I felt like I met every actor in New York," Frankel says. "I met a lot of non-actors...famous literati in town. I thought maybe they can act. I was trying to give the role some more authenticity. But in the end, we just needed a great actor. The minute I met Stanley, all right, genius."

When the company assembled for the table read, Blunt heard Meryl—wearing a madras blazer and khaki pants, her hair in a ponytail—laugh throatily. Then, roughly ten minutes later, Miranda showed up. "I think we all had an idea of what Miranda would sound like," said Anne. "It was a strident, bossy, barking voice. So when Meryl opened her mouth and basically whispered, everybody in the room drew a collective gasp. It was so unexpected and so brilliant."

MIRANDA THE INSULT COMIC

"When I was growing up, I was a huge fan of Don Rickles, as was my father," says *Prada* screenwriter Aline Brosh McKenna. "I love insult comedians, and I always have, and it always makes me laugh. And Miranda Priestly is an A-plus insult comedian. Like, if you asked me right now to write 10 pages of dialogue in Miranda's voice, I could." Just a few of Miranda's most vicious lines:

"Details of your incompetence do not interest me."

"Is there some reason that my coffee isn't here? Has she died or something?"

"I said to myself, go ahead. Take a chance. Hire the smart, fat girl."

"By all means, move at a glacial pace. You know how that thrills me."

"Also, I need to see all the things that Nigel has pulled for Gwyneth's second cover try. I wonder if she's lost any of that weight yet."

"Florals? For spring? Groundbreaking."

There to observe, Elizabeth Gabler noticed Meryl, in character, serving Anne looks that read "You little dimwit." For Miranda, Meryl used men as models; there weren't enough women in power to mimic. "The voice I got from Clint Eastwood," she explained. "He never, ever, ever raises his voice and everyone has to lean in to listen, and he is automatically the most powerful person in the room. But he is not funny. That I stole from Mike Nichols. The way the cruelest cutting remark, if it is delivered with a tiny self-amused curlicue of irony, is the most effective instruction, the most memorable correction, because everyone laughs, even the target. The walk, I'm afraid, is mine."

At the end of the read-through, they released all the actors except

Meryl and Anne. An exec asked Meryl, "Do you have notes for Aline?... She'll do whatever you want." Turning to McKenna, Meryl said, "I have nothing but praise for you, darling." McKenna thought this was Meryl's way of letting the studio know that she wanted to keep the writer around. Anne, following Meryl's lead, had no notes.

During a second table read, Meryl looked at McKenna before changing a line in the climactic scene when Miranda and Andy are being driven to a Paris fashion show. Instead of proclaiming, "Everybody wants to be me," she said, "Everybody wants to be *us*." She explained to McKenna that Miranda doesn't care about anyone wanting to be like her. She cares about people aspiring to be like *them*—the magazine, and what it represents.

Meryl and Roy collaborated on Miranda's distinctive white wig with dark roots at the back, drawing from silver-haired septuagenarian model Carmen Dell'Orefice and elegant French politician Christine Lagarde. Costume designer Patricia Field, who created Carrie Bradshaw's trendsetting *Sex and the City* look, loved the idea. The studio? Not so much. Execs worried Meryl would look old, but seeing the wig in person changed minds; Meryl glowed. And thanks to Roy and Field, Miranda had A Look. All iconic fashion editors needed one.

Although the $35 million ode to haute couture offered designers the best publicity money couldn't buy, not everyone leaped at the opportunity to dress Meryl Streep. They feared offending Wintour, who could make—and break—careers. Finerman and Valentino Garavani had a personal relationship from when the sartorial star lent clothes to the 1998 Julia Roberts dramedy *Stepmom*, which Finerman produced. Valentino, who outfitted Miranda in that glam black gown for the gala at the Met, took a risk by agreeing to a cameo where he greets the doyenne backstage at a faux fashion show. In the process, he opened the door to get other VIPs on board. Heidi Klum, host of the cult reality competition *Project Runway*, appeared alongside Valentino, and supermodel Gisele played a larger role as one of

Miranda's underlings after McKenna approached her on a flight that was delayed to offer a part in the movie. Gisele's agent "tensed up," recalls McKenna, so "I just kept saying the words 'Meryl Streep,' over and over again, because I thought that would make them know that it was a real thing and it was safe." Sold, Gisele said, "OK, I don't want to play myself, and I want to play a bitch."

Field, restricted by a meager $100,000 budget, called upon her fashionista friends for help. She thought of Anne as a "Chanel girl" as opposed to a "Versace" girl. The French fashion house, overseen by Karl Lagerfeld, provided Andy's jaw-dropping makeover ensemble: the black skirt suit and thigh-high boots that made Emily and Miranda do double takes. Andy also wore Dolce and Gabbana and Calvin Klein. For Meryl, Field sourced timeless separates from Donna Karan's 1987 archives and Michael Vollbracht for Bill Blass; these pieces wouldn't be instantly recognizable, thereby rendering Miranda a bold original impervious to trends. Or animal rights activists' red paint. The costumer called upon a local Russian furrier with a New York showroom to lend fur coats that Miranda could fling at Andy's desk.

In Field's estimate, some one hundred designers loaned clothing worth a whopping $1 million—that was more than Anne's *Prada* salary. Many were on edge. *What would Anna think?*

ZAC POSEN ON WHAT *PRADA* GETS RIGHT ABOUT THE FASHION INDUSTRY

"That it's tough, that there's a grind. That this is about excellence. That you have to work really hard to succeed and it's relentless. And it never ends. I think that's the reality of the gift and honor to be working in a rare field that combines art and commerce."

Meryl couldn't believe that one handbag cost $12,000. She preferred Andy's "tragic blue sweater and her scruples about all of it." But when Miranda stepped out of the elevator in a black coat and gray bag, both by Prada, the ferocity was real. The transformation startled McKenna and Frankel. At a group meeting on the first day of shooting, some studio people were overstepping with opinions on what Meryl should wear. "I don't make my decision by committee," Wendy Finerman recalled her saying. She deferred to the producer. "Wendy, which earrings should I wear?" "Wendy, which belt should I wear?" "Wendy, you can stay."

She purposely kept Anne and Emily at a distance, telling Anne that her frostiness wasn't personal. "She was always Meryl in rehearsals—warm smile, nicknames, hugs, 'what's going on?'" said Anne. "But once she was Miranda, she didn't care about those things, because Miranda didn't care about those things."

Meryl would never use the word "starlet" to describe Anne, said Frankel, "but it was just sort of 'Yeah, we're both starring in a movie, and you might even have a bigger part than me, but we're not equals.'"

Anne was nervous to film opposite Meryl in a scene where they get out of a car. To get the shot, the two had to circle the block, take after take. She forced herself to seize the day and talk to Meryl but felt pressure to impress her cultured costar rather than attempt a normal conversation.

"Meryl, have you ever heard the Nick Drake album *Pink Moon*?... I can bring you a copy if you want?"

That would be lovely, Annie.

"Meryl, by any chance, have you read the Jeffrey Eugenides book?"

No, I haven't.

"Meryl, by any chance did you see *The Daily Show with Jon Stewart* last night? He's just so brilliant. I think he's saving America."

Meryl said nothing. The silence panicked Anne, who sought the woman's approval. Finally, Meryl responded: "No, I don't think Jon Stewart is going to save America. I think Stephen Colbert is."

According to Angel De Angelis, a hairstylist on *The Devil Wears Prada,* Anne would arrive to "work late, in front of Meryl. How could you do that to Meryl? She's such a professional." Then again, "she was young and she was dating this guy who would go out at night.... Meryl was great. She was just very patient with her, and let her know in her very Meryl way that you got to know your lines." Anne, says De Angelis, "got better by the end." The actress was twenty-one when Italian real estate developer Raffaello Follieri swept her off her feet. Follieri accompanied Anne to red carpet events and showed her a jet-set, luxury lifestyle that included yacht vacations on the Mediterranean. They were celebrity magazine fixtures. But unbeknownst to Anne, Follieri was defrauding investors out of millions of dollars. She dumped him nearly three years later, in June 2008, shortly before he was arrested and charged with wire fraud, money laundering, and conspiracy. He pleaded guilty and served four and a half years in prison before being deported to Italy in 2012.

"The days were long," Frankel said. "Annie was very emotional. She was living with a guy who was a felon and embezzler. He didn't want her to be working at all; he hated that she worked nights. She was always fragile when we shot late."

Anne was also experiencing health problems related to a cyst. Although others suggested she lose weight for *Prada,* Meryl advised her not to listen. Anne had gained ten pounds following a surgery, and, when she went to her first costume fitting, "couture didn't fit," she recalled. "So then I had to lose the 10 pounds again. Yeah, there were tears." (Anne's ordeal lent a nugget of truth to Blunt's one-liner, "I'm just one stomach flu away from my goal weight.")

Meryl, meanwhile, dropped seven pounds during the shoot. "It killed me," she said. Her costars were a fun-loving crew, Tucci and Blunt especially, and Meryl—who loved to joke around and be social—was feeling the strain of self-imposed isolation. She attributed the weight loss to anxiety. "There was a lot of anxiety in this character," she said. "Everybody says: 'Was it fun to play a villain?' No. It was not fun to be in this person's body, it just wasn't at all. So, maybe I took the pressures that she felt, too much to heart. But I felt that was in the plot. I read the script and I read that there was pressure to replace her in her job as editor. And I know how replaceable middle-aged women are in our society and I felt that and so it wasn't enjoyable to be her. It was hard work dressing like that too, I felt like I was wearing or putting on underwater gear. I guess a normal woman would find it extremely enjoyable to wear those clothes. For me, I didn't enjoy it. It felt like a straitjacket."

Meryl went makeup-free for the scene where Miranda tearfully lets down her guard and informs Andy that her husband has filed for divorce. Predicting tabloid schadenfreude, she says, "Rupert Murdoch should cut me a check for all the papers I sell for him. Anyway, I don't really care what anybody writes about me. But my girls... it's just so unfair to the girls."

Throughout her fleeting moment of vulnerability, Miranda keeps it callous. *By all means, move at a glacial pace.* Andy, apparently suffering from Stockholm syndrome, shrugs off the insult. Though Meryl steered clear of Anne off camera, her doe-eyed costar became very close friends to Blunt. "They would gird each other's loins for dealing with Meryl," says Frankel. "They really carried each other along."

Whereas Anne played the straight man, Blunt got to flaunt her masterful comic timing. McKenna added an extra scene at the end when Andy calls Emily to say she's sending over designer hand-me-downs from Paris. Emily sounds stern and high-strung over the phone, but the audience sees her eyes well up with emotion.

After Blunt wrapped her role, Meryl—ditching Miranda's wig and the Prada for a puffy jacket—ran out of her trailer to say goodbye. "You were so great!" she exclaimed. Blunt started to weep for real. She hadn't realized how much Meryl's praise would mean to her.

The Devil Wears Prada did more than give Meryl her grandest success in decades. It broadened her appeal as an actress while enhancing the mystique of Streep. Was Meryl as ferocious and uncompromising as Miranda? Did she eat ingenues for breakfast? Amy Adams would soon find out on the set of *Doubt*.

The Devil Wears Prada *Career Bump*

The movie, which became an instant classic, minted new stars, and Meryl deserves a lot of the credit.

Anne Hathaway: She went on to win an Oscar for her devastating portrayal of Fantine in *Les Misérables* and pile up prestige credits in *Rachel Getting Married*, *The Dark Knight Rises,* and *Interstellar.* Like Meryl, she uses her platform to support humanitarian causes.

Stanley Tucci: The dynamic actor is beloved among *Prada* fans as Miranda's witty, competent art director, Nigel. He reunited with Meryl in *Julie & Julia,* playing supportive husband Paul Child, and La Streep even attended his wedding celebration to Felicity Blunt (yep, Emily's sister!).

Aline Brosh McKenna: Taking a chance on the clever writer paid off for Meryl, director David Frankel, and 20th Century Fox. McKenna has continued her success writing *27 Dresses* and creating the beloved TV comedy *Crazy Ex-Girlfriend.*

Emily Blunt: After her star-making turn in *Prada,* Blunt graduated to leading roles in *Edge of Tomorrow, The Girl on the Train,* and *A Quiet Place.* Plus: *Into the Woods* and *Mary Poppins Returns,* both opposite Meryl. And, like Meryl, she deftly balances comedy and drama.

CHAPTER 16

Meryl the Nun

I have doubts. I have such doubts!—*Sister Aloysius*
(Doubt, 2008)

After all the hullabaloo and fashion designers' fears over partici-
pating, Meryl finally came face-to-face with her *Devil Wears Prada*
alter ego, whom she could no longer avoid. In a power move, Anna
Wintour, displaying good sportsmanship, actually *showed up* to the
movie's New York premiere on June 19, 2006, in a black-and-white
Prada dress. Her arrival outshone the actors on the red carpet, giving media gossips their top headline of the night. Rather than run
toward the exits when they were introduced, Meryl found Wintour to
be "very, very cordial."

The following day, Wintour's spokesperson released this statement to the press: "She thought it was very entertaining. It was satire. What's not to like?" The movie made her famous outside fashion
and publishing circles. Though her persona was now entwined with
Miranda, that turned out not to be a bad thing: Wintour got shit
done, and nobody else could do what she did. After *Prada*, she was
admired for her toughness. Later that year, Barbara Walters included
Wintour among her ten most fascinating people of 2006, wherein
the editor extolled the virtues of decisive leadership, conceding that
"if Meryl seemed somewhat strong, I respect that."

The love letter to fashion exceeded expectations, collecting $326 million at the global box office. It was the biggest commercial hit of Meryl's storied career. And it surprised no one that Meryl owned the part, scoring Oscar nomination number fourteen. A lesser actor might turn Miranda into a shallow cartoon villain, but as the *New York Times'* A. O. Scott marveled, "No longer simply the incarnation of evil, she is now a vision of aristocratic, purposeful, and surprisingly human grace."

Meryl had done her job. Nobody else could do what she did. But she hadn't expected men—men!—to identify with her corporate queen.

Meryl told NPR:

When I made *The Devil Wears Prada*, it was the first time in my life that a man came up and said, "I know how you felt. I have a job like that." First time.... For men, the favorite character that I've ever played is Linda in *The Deer Hunter*, without question. The heterosexual men that I've spoken to over the years, they say, "That's my favorite thing you've ever done."

Or Sophie. And they were a particular kind of feminine, recessive personalities. No question that this person was not going to dominate the conversation at a dinner party. So they fell in love with her, but they didn't feel the story through her body. It took [me until] *The Devil Wears Prada* to play someone tough, who had to make hard decisions, who was running an organization, [where] a certain type of man [would be able] to empathize and feel the story through her. That's the first time anyone has ever said that they felt that way.

The movie would go on to infiltrate the culture in ways the cast and crew could not anticipate. It's been referenced on TV, as when Steve Carell's hapless Michael Scott imitates Miranda in *The Office*, and Kris Jenner dresses as the *Runway* chief in *Keeping Up with the Kardashians*. The zeitgeisty *Prada* captured a growing public fascination with the personalities behind luxury labels and the front row at Fashion Week. In 2006, *Project Runway* was a cultural phenomenon boasting its own catchphrases ("Make it work!"). The Swedish fast-fashion trend factory H&M had moved into American shopping centers, offering designer looks at discount prices. Wintour capitalized on her steely image to make the Met Gala the hottest runway in the world. And Meryl became an Internet meme, her brutal bons mots endlessly quoted online. Miranda remains her most popular role ever.

The Devil Wears Prada was a tough act to follow. Over the next two years, Meryl starred in an assortment of meh movies that her presence could not improve. She voiced a computer-animated insect queen in *The Ant Bully*, a box-office flop, and, in the low-budget drama *Dark Matter*, based on actual events, she apparently raided a Chico's (no shame) to play a kindly bougie-bohemian philanthropist who tries to help a brilliant Chinese student adapt to an American university until he snaps and goes on a shooting spree. Meryl, nobody wants to see that! (And you hate guns!) Then, in 2007, she made an all-too-brief appearance as an older version of daughter Mamie Gummer in *Evening*, which marked the twenty-three-year-old's debut as a leading lady. After graduating from Northwestern University with a theater degree, Mamie starred in the off-Broadway plays *Mr. Marmalade* and *The Water's Edge*, earning awards for both. The plodding, overwrought *Evening*, directed by Lajos Koltai, wasted Mamie's Streepian talents alongside those of Vanessa Redgrave, Natasha Richardson, Glenn Close, Claire Danes, and Toni Collette. Tanked by bad reviews, it lasted only a month in theaters. The poster, however, deserves to claim wall space in the Streep household forever. It features Mamie and Meryl's names next to one another.

One year before Barack Obama's historic, hope-fueled election victory, Meryl returned to overtly political cinema. The thriller *Rendition* was inspired by the true story of Khalid El-Masri, a German and Lebanese citizen whom the CIA wrongfully arrested and tortured. Jake Gyllenhaal played an intelligence agent with a moral compass, and Meryl a senior spy without one. Her accent: southern, slightly Reese Witherspoon.

Under the direction of Robert Redford, *Lions for Lambs* was an unusual, intellectually challenging war drama costarring Redford, Meryl, and Tom Cruise. As liberal TV journalist Janine Roth, Meryl dons black-frame glasses and a notepad to interview wild-eyed, charismatic Senator Jasper Irving (Cruise) about his idea for a new strategic operation in Afghanistan. He hopes it will unite the country and be a win for Republicans. Because Janine once wrote that Jasper was the future of the GOP, he thought she might give his plan positive coverage. She doesn't take the bait, prompting Jasper to scold the news media as hypocrites complicit with the government in selling the war in Iraq.

Back in the office, Janine excitedly recaps the intense meeting to a male editor who tells her to "calm down" and write Jasper's one-sided story even though she's morally opposed to it. The blowhard reminds her that she's fifty-seven years old, sniping, "What other network is gonna snag you up after this, OK?" Janine stands her ground. At least she can walk away with a clear conscience. To Meryl, *Lions for Lambs* was about "the difficulty of standing up and saying what you think." She argued that "every movie is political. It's political in what it doesn't say, what it chooses to ignore."

It turned out that moviegoers longed to escape from depressing reminders of an uncertain, post-9/11 world. They avoided *Rendition* and *Lions*, which together pulled in a dismal $25 million in North America.

Really, the only way to follow up back-to-back, ripped-from-the-headlines downers is to make a big-budget jukebox musical featuring ABBA's bubblegum pop songbook. Naysayers snickered when

Meryl agreed to headline Universal Pictures' *Mamma Mia!*, an adaptation of the Broadway sensation being produced by Judy Craymer in tandem with Tom Hanks, Rita Wilson, and ABBA songsmiths Benny Andersson and Bjorn Ulvaeus. The studio tapped Phyllida Lloyd to direct. Craymer's stage production had been packing theaters around the world since launching in London in 1999. It's the ninth-longest-running show on the Great White Way, with more than $2 billion in worldwide ticket sales. Unlike the snobbiest of high-culture consumers, Meryl loved *Mamma Mia!* and wrote Craymer a letter to say so. She'd brought Louisa and six of her daughter's friends to see it just after September 11. They wound up dancing in the aisles. The joy! The music! The love! Wasn't that what life was all about?

Meryl's note, said Craymer, is why she dared ask her to consider the part of Donna Sheridan, a single mom who runs a botique hotel on a picturesque Greek island. Meryl's agent assumed she would pass. *Are you kidding?* She was like, Say *yes!*

"I couldn't believe that they wanted me to do this part, and I was so thrilled," Meryl recalled. "I kept asking, are you sure, are you sure?"

Amanda Seyfried signed on to play Donna's bride-to-be daughter, Sophie, who wants her father to walk her down the aisle. The problem: she doesn't know his identity. Sophie mails wedding invites to three of her mother's former lovers, portrayed by Pierce Brosnan, Colin Firth, and Stellan Skarsgård. Donna is horrified when all three handsome rakes show up for the big day, dredging up memories of her glory days as a freewheeling hippie. Brosnan can't carry a tune, but he still makes her heart flutter. Meryl strapped on overalls, a staple of her Yale Drama School wardrobe, to dance and sing the hell out of the title song as well as "The Winner Takes It All" on location in Skopelos, Greece. In the exuberant finale, Donna, not Sophie, gets hitched. The groom: Brosnan, a fantasy come true for women living vicariously through Meryl, a beacon of hope that it is never too late to find your soul mate. Though it was ambitious and audacious, nothing about *Mamma Mia!* screamed *cool* to straight male movie critics who dominated big-league newspapers and magazines. Many were quick to write off a picture that wasn't made with *them* in mind. "In press screenings, there are murmurs that to be singing karaoke [ABBA] songs in a relentlessly cheerful musical is a terrible career misstep," relayed the *Guardian*. "After all, Streep is renowned for much more substantial roles."

Rumors of Meryl's death by ABBA were greatly exaggerated.

Opening in July 2008, two months before Meryl and Don celebrated thirty years of marriage, *Mamma Mia!* grossed a staggering $609 million worldwide. On a $52 million budget. "It's so gratifying because it's the audience that nobody really gives a shit about," Meryl said. She told the *Los Angeles Times,* "Nobody wanted to make that. The smart guys banked on *Hellboy* to carry them throughout the year. The *Mamma Mia!* wagon is pulling all those movies that didn't have any problem getting made." As for the negative criticism, she could not care less. "I knew it would make lots of people happy… and when the bad reviews came out, the blogosphere just exploded with women empowered to say, 'These people are crazy! What's the matter with you? Life-hating, life-sucking, desiccated old farts.'"

Once again, Meryl was proving to patriarchal Tinseltown that making movies about women and for women was a bankable business. Declared Mike Nichols, "She broke the glass ceiling of an older woman being a big star—it has never, never happened before."

She continued to immerse herself in new identities. On Christmas Day, Miramax released *Doubt,* costarring Meryl as an austere Catholic nun and Philip Seymour Hoffman as the progressive priest who she believes sexually abused an altar boy. John Patrick Shanley directed and adapted the gripping drama from his Pulitzer-winning play. Meryl's character, Sister Aloysius Beauvier, is a parish school principal in a working-class Bronx neighborhood. She has a thick

New York accent, a black-and-white worldview, and no sense of humor.

It's 1964 and times are changing. She doesn't know what to make of the liberal, gregarious Father Brendan Flynn, who's new to St. Nicholas of Tolentine Catholic Church and has taken special interest in the school's only African American student, Donald Miller (Joseph Foster). Her suspicions grow when the sweet, innocent Sister James (Amy Adams) reports that Father Flynn requested Donald meet him in the rectory; later, she notices that Donald is upset and smells alcohol on his breath. Flynn insists that Donald had been caught drinking church wine. Sister Aloysius smells a lie.

Producer Scott Rudin arranged for Shanley and Meryl to have lunch. When Shanley handed Meryl the script, she said, "I know you know this, but a film is different than a play."

"Yeah, I know," he replied. "Actually, one of the things that I'm thinking of doing is making the wind a character in the [film]—sort of the winds of something new, which could either be perceived to be disturbing or refreshing, depending on your point of view."

"Oh, I love the wind!" said Meryl.

That's when he knew she was going to star in the movie version. Meryl researched the role by talking to nuns, including Shanley's first-grade teacher, Sister Peggy, who taught the Bronx-born playwright how to read. "Nuns are easy comedy, so we have made fun of them from Monty Python to Chris Durang, but I think there's something that's confounding to the outside world about women who reject all the things that most women build their entire lives around, which is getting a man, getting the husband and the children and looking good," she said. "And they just jettison all of that, and there's great liberation in that, I think."

Shanley had considered Tom Cruise for Father Flynn, but cast the enigmatic Hoffman instead. Seven years earlier, Hoffman had starred with Meryl in Nichols's Central Park revival of *The Seagull*, and he had since won an Academy Award for *Capote*. He special-ized in playing weirdos on the margins of society and making them likeable despite their quirks. There was no better choice to convey Flynn's ambiguous combination of charisma and creepiness. Is the fun priest actually a pedophile, or has buzzkill Sister Aloysius overreacted?

"Phil sort of viewed [Meryl] as a relative, and a somewhat tor-menting relative," says Shanley. "From his point of view, she would try to get in his head. So, they'd be offstage—I think it was *The Seagull*—and she'd be whispering stuff in his ear about his char-acter that he didn't want to hear. And he would have to sort of keep her out of his head." Before filming a take in one of their dialogue-heavy *Doubt* showdowns, "she would be muttering 'I'm going to kick your ass.' And Phil is just ruefully smiling and shaking his head, muttering something along the lines of 'Go ahead and try it.' Then they'd go into the scene and they'd have this amazing ability to go up against each other and feed each other at the same time."

Shanley told this anecdote at a panel discussion with Meryl and Hoffman in the run-up to the Oscars. Laughing, Meryl denied say-ing "I'm going to kick your ass," to which Hoffman replied, "Oh, yes, you did."

And Shanley will never forget what transpired during a scene in Sister Aloysius's office. "Meryl was going off, and she gestured vio-lently with her hand, and there was a lamp—a standing lamp—and she shattered it," he recalls. "I was kind of amazed at how she didn't seem to give a shit. She's like 'Yeah, I do that sometimes.' It wasn't like, 'Oh my God, I broke the set.' It was sort of like, 'Eh, you'd better get another one.'"

There were times when Shanley witnessed Meryl struggling with doubts of her own. When Sister Aloysius dismisses "Frosty the Snowman" as heresy, Meryl didn't seem to believe that her character would think that.

"Is she serious?" she asked Shanley.

"She's dead serious," he replied, to which he remembers her saying, "I'm not sure how to do this."

On a day of reshoots, "I saw suddenly her vulnerability about the role, how deeply she cared, how worried she was that we got it," Shanley told the LA Times. "She was like a young girl, very vulnerable and very shaky."

Before their scenes, Meryl and Amy Adams would sit side by side on the set, knitting quietly and wearing all black. Around Meryl, Amy's naturally ebullient mood became subdued. There's a sequence in Doubt that shows the gender divide at St. Nicholas: while Father Flynn and members of the male clergy are having a raucous, boozy dinner, Sisters Aloysius and James eat in spartan silence with the women. Though Aloysius manages to force Flynn to quit his post, the church—predisposed to believe men over women—ignores her warning and transfers him to a bigger parish, thereby exposing more children to his inappropriate behavior. She has battled the patriarchy and lost. She seems to have lost faith in an institution to which she's devoted her life, and it's jarring to watch this confident woman break down. "I have doubts," she confesses to Sister James through tears. "I have such doubts!"

Shanley wouldn't tell me what happened in the rectory, but I have an idea. I believe the nuns.

For her next role, Meryl hung up Sister Aloysius's bonnet and slipped on a chef's jacket to enter the joyful consciousness of Julia Child, who found salvation in French cooking.

Viola's Breakthrough

Viola Davis graduated from Juilliard's elite acting program, but nothing prepared the rising talent for her major scene with Meryl Streep in *Doubt*. She was terrified.

In anticipation, Viola wrote a character biography of more than fifty pages for the embattled Mrs. Miller. Although Viola had a small but pivotal role (think Dame Judi Dench's eight-minute *Shakespeare in Love* performance), she wanted to understand it better. It was tricky: Sister Aloysius (Meryl) believes that Mrs. Miller's young son, Donald, is the victim of sexual abuse at a Bronx parochial school. The alleged perpetrator: Father Flynn, who's taken Donald under his wing. The boy is troubled; his father beats him because he's different. He is the only African American student in his class. Sister Aloysius tracks down Mrs. Miller outside of her home in the Bronx projects and tries to persuade her of Flynn's misdeeds to no avail. For Mrs. Miller, protecting Donald means remaining in denial about an abuser who could help him advance in society.

"I have to tell you, I see her as being kind of the same as Sister Aloysius," said Viola. "A woman of limited choices...which feeds the desperation of the scene. She is a woman who is being the advocate for her son and is loving her son in extraordinary circumstances."

According to *Doubt* writer-director John Patrick Shanley, Viola was "antsy" coming into the production two-thirds of the way through filming. She and Meryl rehearsed their outdoor confrontation indoors, which made Viola feel confined. "I'm locked up," she told Shanley. Her husband, Julius Tennon, encouraged Viola to tell Meryl how much she meant to her. "You've been waiting all your life to work with this woman! Say something," he advised. She never said anything. Instead, Viola poured her nervous energy into the scene and Streeped it up, creating unexpected sympathy for a woman content to exist in life's gray areas if that meant Donald could have a better life. *Doubt* was Viola's big break, launching a career that included an Oscar (the 2016 drama *Fences*), an Emmy (the Shondaland series *How to Get Away with Murder*), and another Tony (*Fences* on Broadway, to join the trophy she received for the 2001 play *King Hedley II*).

In 2017, Viola presented Meryl with a Lifetime Achievement Award at the Golden Globes, gushing, "You make me proud to be an artist. You make me feel that what I have in me—my body, my face, my age—is enough."

The following year, Viola expressed frustration about the racial barriers that held her back from the perks given to Meryl and Julianne Moore on the basis of their skin color. "I'm nowhere near them in terms of money, job opportunities—nowhere close to them," she said. If people dubbed her the "black Meryl Streep," then "pay me what I'm worth." Meryl would give a standing ovation in agreement.

CHAPTER 17

Meryl Masters the Art of French Cooking

Bon appetit!—*Julia Child*

(*Julie & Julia*, 2009)

Three out of four kids were out of the house. Meryl's eldest, known professionally as Henry Wolfe, was a musician and actor living in LA, with credits ranging from big budget (*The Good Shepherd*) to experimental (*Lying*, *The Wait*). Like Meryl, Mamie balanced drama (Sally Adams in HBO's *John Adams* miniseries) and comedy (her recurring character, the loopy-brilliant attorney Nancy Crozier, on CBS's *The Good Wife*). In October 2009, Mamie would announce her engagement to actor Benjamin Walker, with whom she starred on Broadway in *Les liaisons dangereuses*. "My mom loves him!" she gushed. At twenty-two, Grace Gummer, who briefly appeared as a younger version of Meryl in 1993's *The House of the Spirits*, had graduated from Vassar with degrees in art history and Italian. But acting was in her DNA. Grace would conquer stage and screen, including roles opposite Greta Gerwig in the indie gem *Frances Ha* and portraying Nora Ephron in the cult Amazon series *Good Girls Revolt*. Louisa, her youngest, would soon enroll at Vassar College. Victoria Edel went to high school in Brooklyn with Louisa, and both were involved in theater. Victoria remembers Meryl sewing a button on her costume. "And most iconically, one time my mom ran into this lady she knew who said, very rudely, 'Ohh I didn't know your kids were smart enough to go here,' and Meryl said, loudly, 'Wow, some people are so rude,' or something like that."

Meryl could finally exhale. She came across lighter, on camera and off.

"I think she's very happy," Nichols told *Vanity Fair* in 2010. "Anybody raising four children has worries, but they turned out so great, and you begin to relax a little bit. I think you're seeing her freedom and her relief, to have brought four kids all the way through into hot careers of their own and happy love relationships. You still have them invisibly connected to you, but she's free. At last you're not thinking, 'I have to run home,' and things happen out of that freedom that are, if not new, deeper."

Was Nichols referring to her pockets? Between June 2008 and June 2009, the month she turned sixty years old, Meryl had grown wealthier, with earnings of $24 million, ranking third on *Forbes'* list of the best-paid actresses. Angelina Jolie, thirty-four, and Jennifer Aniston, forty, claimed the top spots, yet all three earned significantly less than their male counterparts. Harrison Ford pocketed $65 million to Angelina's $27 million. Collectively, the top ten money-making actors made it rain $393 million during that period, compared with $183 million for actresses. Given those cringe-inducing statistics, it's something of a miracle that Meryl had not been placed on a shelf in the grande dame cupboard with Julie Andrews.

MERYL'S BARNARD COLLEGE COMMENCEMENT

On May 17, 2010, Meryl addressed graduates of the private women's liberal arts institution in Manhattan, dropping poignant pearls of wisdom and personal insights. A few of her best, and most revealing, quotes:

- "I gave a speech at Vassar twenty-seven years ago. It was a really big hit. Everybody loved it, really. Tom Brokaw said it was the very best commencement speech he had ever heard—and of course, I believed this. And, you know, it was much, much easier to construct than this one. It came out pretty easily because, back then, I knew *so much!* I was a new mother, I had [two] Academy Awards, and it was all coming together so nicely.... But now, I feel like I know about one-sixteenth of what that young woman knew. Things don't seem as certain today."

- "Women are better at acting than men. Why? Because we have to be. If successfully convincing someone bigger than you are of something he doesn't want to know is a survival skill, this is how women have survived through the millennia. Pretending is not just play. Pretending is imagined possibility. Pretending, or acting, is a very valuable life skill and we all do it."

- "I can assure you that awards have very little bearing on my own personal happiness, my own sense of well-being and purpose in the world. That comes from studying the world, feelingly, with empathy in my work."

- "No matter what you see me or hear me saying when I'm on your TV, holding a statuette and spewing—that's acting. Being a celebrity has taught me to hide. But being an actor has opened my soul."

- "You know, you don't have to be famous. You just have to make your mother and father proud of you, and you already have."

As Meryl broke barriers for women of a certain age, she claimed no credit for her achievements. Instead, she gave props to the women in power pulling the strings. At an October 2009 event in Toronto, film critic Johanna Schneller asked whether she was actively choosing projects that were more fun. "I really don't get a choice; I don't produce my own movies. So, I'm sort of like the girl at the dance who waits to be asked," she replied. "I think what you're referring to is something that only happens now because there are more women in decision-making positions who are able to greenlight movies." In another interview with the *LA Times,* she conjured the sad, faintly defeatist image of waiting for the phone to ring.

That said, Nora Ephron didn't think her movie about Julia Child would have been made without Meryl's participation. Nora had been in movie jail after directing the early-aughts flops *Lucky Numbers,* an off-brand black comedy, and a clever but critically savaged remake of *Bewitched* starring Nicole Kidman and Will Ferrell. But Nora's failures couldn't erase her legacy as one of the most successful female filmmakers to get behind the camera. She was best known for directing the Tom Hanks–Meg Ryan romantic comedies *Sleepless in Seattle* and *You've Got Mail,* in addition to writing the sleeper hit *When Harry Met Sally,* which elevated the love genre to ubiquity during the 1990s and 2000s. Following *Bewitched,* Nora fired her agent and stepped away from movies to focus on writing plays.

Later, Amy Pascal, cochair at Sony Pictures, recruited super-foodie Nora to direct and adapt Julie Powell's bestselling memoir *Julie & Julia.* Remember blogs? Back when blogs were exciting and new, thirty-year-old Powell—a disillusioned office secretary—cooked up the Julie/Julia Project, giving herself one year to re-create all 524 recipes from Julia Child's *Mastering the Art of French Cooking.* Her ambitious efforts paid off. The blog attracted a cult following as well as the attention of a publisher, Little, Brown and Company, culminating in her 2005 ode to the culinary queen. Nora wasn't sure she could stretch Julie's story into a two-hour movie, but then Pascal suggested combining Julie's and Julia's stories into a parallel structure. *That's brilliant,* Nora thought.

Around this time, Meryl ran into Nora at a funeral and asked what she was up to, recalls *Julie & Julia* producer Larry Mark. Nora's response: "Funny you should ask."

Meryl and Amy Adams officially joined the cast in November 2007, one month before going full-on nun to shoot *Doubt* in New

York. They fit the mentor-mentee dynamic perfectly on both films. Amy, thirty-three, was a seasoned actor who considered quitting before her breakthrough role in the 2005 indie drama *Junebug.* Despite her experience, she projected an everygirl innocence that counterbalanced Meryl's worldliness. If the two were wines, Amy would be a bubbly prosecco and Meryl a rich, complex cabernet.

Julie & Julia is about women gourmands reinventing themselves. At fifty-one, Julia debuted her groundbreaking cooking show, *The French Chef,* in 1963. She was an atypical TV star, taller than average with a high-pitched, singsong voice. A human sunbeam, she exuded joie de vivre and popularized excellence in the form of fine cuisine that tickled taste buds over bland American recipes defining mediocrity. Viewers found Julia irresistible, and, thanks to her, roasting a chicken seemed less intimidating. Above all, the movie pays rare tribute to a happy marriage. Paul Child worshipped Julia and watched proudly as her dreams came true.

"What's liberating about these characters," mused Meryl, "is that there's this huge throbbing love between two people who don't look like our normal package of lovers. It made it more real and intimate because somehow those concerns were thrown away. If you've been married for a long time you love without looking. I don't assess how my husband looks every single day and think, *Is he cute enough* or whatever? And I sure hope he doesn't do it to me!"

She suggested Stanley Tucci to play Paul. The two shared history and an easy rapport. They genuinely liked each other. Beyond that, Stanley knew his way around the kitchen, so he would certainly appreciate Julia's contributions to society. (Yes, I own *The Tucci Cookbook.* Try the lasagna made with polenta and gorgonzola cheese.)

Meryl called herself a "horrible cook," but she was her own worst critic. "I made a soufflé and Meryl showed me a better way to separate the eggs," Carrie Fisher once said. David Frankel remembered her "baking for everyone" on set. For *Julia,* she mostly learned how

Nora, Meryl, and Tucci.

to use cooking equipment ("You need a very good pan") and useful tips such as the best way to remove the smell from your fingers after chopping garlic and onion ("dip your hands in salt and then rinse them in cool water").

Nora told Meryl, "You're not really Julia Child, you're Julie's idea of Julia Child." That insight freed her to harness Julia's boundless joy rather than do a clinical impersonation. It was the perfect moment for Meryl to honor her late mother, Mary, "who was sort of that person in my life," she said. "She was someone who turned the lights on when she came into a room. I have a much more reserved side. But I've always wanted to be more like her, so playing Julia gave me the chance."

Meryl studied old tapes of the chef before the shoot. Mimicking her mannerisms? Doable. But Julia was six foot two, which Meryl couldn't fake. Still, she *had* to be six foot two. The crew used camera angles, risers, and high heels to pull off the optical illusion. She bubbled with giddiness—like Julia, or Mary Wilkinson Streep—en route from her trailer to the set in the morning. "She finds acting this wonderful adventure. It's never an assignment. It's never a gig," says Larry Mark. "In a way, it's similar to Spielberg. He seems to have this childlike exuberance about directing."

The critics melted like butter on a very good pan. "By now this actress has exhausted every superlative that exists and to suggest that she has outdone herself is only to say that she's done it again," wrote A. O. Scott.

> Her performance goes beyond physical imitation, though she has the rounded shoulders and the fluting voice down perfectly. Often when gifted actors impersonate real, familiar people, they overshadow the originals, so that, for example, you can't think of Ray Charles without seeing Jamie Foxx, or Truman Capote without envisioning Philip Seymour Hoffman. But Ms. Streep's incarnation of Julia Child has the opposite effect, making the real Julia, who died in 2004, more vivid, more alive, than ever.

Several months after Meryl wrapped *Julia*, she was in negotiations to topline the romantic comedy *It's Complicated,* about a middle-aged divorcée in a love triangle with two suitors. Nancy Meyers, Meryl's third woman director in two years, wrote the character of Jane Adler *for* Meryl. "Even though I'd never met her, I never thought of anybody else, and when I would think about her in the part it made me more brave as a writer, because I could imagine her doing these things. It would really push me into a great place," recalled Meyers, who wrote and directed the upscale dreams *The Holiday* and *Something's Gotta Give,* the latter pairing Jack Nicholson and Diane Keaton to the tune of $125 million.

Honestly, it seemed as if Meyers spent her entire production budgets on luxurious locations and home decor for rich white ladies, from a drool-worthy Hamptons beach escape in *Something's Gotta Give* to Jane's serene Santa Barbara sanctuary (actual venue: upstate New York). It's a wonder she didn't cast Ina "Barefoot Contessa" Garten and her lucky devil of a spouse, Jeffrey. Instead she turned to Meryl, who responded well to the screenplay. (According to the *LA Times,* she was now commanding a salary in the ballpark of $7 to $8 million.) With the most important asset in place, Meyers installed Alec Baldwin as Jane's swaggering ex-husband, Jake, who tries to win her back, and Steve Martin as Adam, the gallant architect remodeling her cozy kitchen. Jane, a successful baker, is a fantasy woman not unlike the Food Network's Garten: if you crack her inner circle, she'll serve you an open-faced croque monsieur at midnight while wearing an elegant blouse in a tasteful neutral color. More importantly, she knew how to let loose. Meryl's best scenes are her sexiest: flirting it up with Alec at a fancy hotel bar or dissolving into hysterics while she and Steve smoke pot on a date.

Through Meyers's lens, Meryl shattered the sexless, grandmotherly image that long defined women of a certain age in the movies. Jake left Jane, with whom he had three children, to remarry the much-younger Agness, a stern, judgmental marketing executive played by an amusingly brittle Lake Bell, not yet thirty. On Lake's first day reporting to *It's Complicated,* she was to film the party scene where Agness gets wise to Jake's unresolved feelings for Jane, at whom he gazes adoringly while she's high as a kite and having the time of her life with Adam. *Why did he ever leave this lovely creature?*

Meanwhile, Agness brings down the vibe. "I didn't get it together," Lake recalls. "I was, like, way too excited. I was just like amateur hour shenanigans. Just all over the place. So Nancy had to pull me aside and be like, 'What's going on?' And she's like, 'Yeah, so get it together and stop wooing, fawning over them all.'" Finally, she affected Agness's bored demeanor in a way that puts Jane's warmth in movingly bold relief. For Jake, it's too little too late. He blew it. Karma is a bespectacled architect.

Lake found Meryl disarmingly kind, and that was intimidating in its own way. She witnessed Meryl going off-book to improvise weed euphoria, which made her feel comfortable riffing during rehearsals. The script supervisor warned Lake not to try improvising dialogue (a no-no on a Nancy Meyers movie), to which Lake responded that she was following Meryl's lead. Script supervisor: *I'll give Meryl a note.* Lake: *No. Fine. She wasn't improvising. It's fine.* Inside her head, Lake panicked: "Oh my God, I accidentally just told on Meryl."

It's Complicated, which cost $85 million to make, premiered on Christmas 2009, grossing $113 million over fourteen weeks. The summer before, *Julie & Julia*, made for $40 million, accumulated $94 million in domestic ticket sales during roughly the same length of time. While *Avatar* reigned supreme ($749 million), Meryl offered a grounding alternative to James Cameron's 3-D sci-fi epic, which featured her Yale classmate Sigourney Weaver. When the Oscars rolled around in March 2010, Meryl snagged her sixteenth nomination (for *Julia*), losing Best Actress to *The Blind Side* dynamo Sandra Bullock. "I'm just really happy to be here. I am," she said on the red carpet, looking the best she's ever looked in a low-cut ivory Chris March gown. Meryl's plus-one: brother Harry.

Later that night, she partied at the Governors Ball with Harry and her agent, CAA's Kevin Huvane. Surprising a CNN reporter, she actually stopped for an on-camera interview. She was feeling good. She burst into a rendition of "Sixteen Candles" (the number of her Academy Award nods). "That's how much I had to drink," she joked. In response to a question about being "simply the best," she laughed, saying, "I don't think there is such a thing as the best. I really don't. I didn't think there was such a thing in high school because the Most Likely to Succeed wasn't *me*."

In the ensuing months, news leaked to the press that Sony had picked up a mother-daughter comedy called *Mommy & Me,* costarring Meryl and Tina Fey. Stanley Tucci was to direct. Then word broke that Meryl was attached to star alongside Bullock and Oprah in another comedy, this one staged behind the scenes at a home-shopping cable channel. These movies never got past the development process. Meryl's next film, *The Iron Lady,* had been fast-tracked. It was most definitely *not* a comedy. She would go incognito as Margaret Thatcher, the controversial former prime minister of the United Kingdom. Love her or loathe her, Thatcher wasn't afraid to be hated.

CHAPTER 18

Meryl the Stateswoman

*With all due respect, sir, I have done battle every single day
of my life, and many men have underestimated me before.*
—Margaret Thatcher

(*The Iron Lady*, 2011)

Becoming Margaret Thatcher took a small village. Meryl flew to London three times to meet prosthetics expert Mark Coulier, who crafted an uncanny disguise that could fool anyone into believing she was the British stateswoman from middle age to her eighties. She would joke that, when she looked in the mirror, she saw her father instead. Beyond the audience, she most desired to fake out her fellow actors so they saw a person and not a mask. The voice was another factor. While running for prime minister on the Conservative ticket, Thatcher worked with a coach to alter the way she sounded so that voters (and male colleagues) would pay attention—and respect.

"She already had whatever the stentorian tones [were] that she acquired over time—they were all lying in wait there, within her arsenal," Meryl said. "She had...a plummy kind of aspirant, upper-middle-class voice, and so what the voice coach did was enable her to expand her breath, deepen her voice, bring it to a place where men could listen to it in its most emphatic tones."

Thatcher's primary goal was to "win the argument," she explained. Her approach "had to do with bringing out a word that you *didn't* normally think was the most important word in the sentence. And she also had a way, like a railroad train, of taking a breath quite quietly and making a point in a way that you don't realize that this point is going to be made through several examples, and there will not be a break in the speaking voice at any point, and if you think you're going to interrupt her, you're not going to have the opportunity, because she's just got capacity."

That infinite lung power left Meryl breathless. She couldn't keep pace. The production, helmed by *Mamma Mia!* director Phyllida Lloyd, commenced in the winter of 2011, with Manchester Town Hall representing Parliament. In January, Meryl observed Conservative prime minister David Cameron debate Labour leader Ed Miliband as part of her research. Thatcher, in office from 1979 to 1990, addressed members of Parliament, or MPs, twice weekly. Presiding over a resurgent economy in the 1980s, she was the UK's equivalent of Ronald Reagan. *Iron Lady* dramatizes her decision to declare war on Argentina after its invasion of the Falkland Islands, a British colony, in 1982. She won that battle, but, on the home front, her detractors deeply resented policies that reduced government spending for education and housing. When the IRA bombed a Brighton hotel during the 1984 Conservative Party convention, Thatcher and husband Denis (played by Jim Broadbent) were nearly killed.

It goes without saying that Meryl was extraordinary, notably in scenes where elderly, widowed Margaret battles dementia. Outraged British politicos accused the movie of exploiting Thatcher's mental decline while she was still alive. Thatcher died of a stroke in April 2013 at the age of eighty-seven; neither she nor her children saw *Iron Lady* when it premiered the year before, drawing mixed reviews but near-unanimous praise for Meryl's performance. Roger Ebert bestowed two out of four stars for what he protested was Lloyd's wishy-washy take on the divisive figure. The *Chicago Sun-Times* critic once witnessed Thatcher at a gathering of bigwigs in the Windy City. "Invisible psychic threads of respect and yearning extended toward her from the men," he recalled. "When she spoke, they fell silent. No one interrupted. No one disagreed. Her pronouncements were issued as recitals of fact. It was the most remarkable display of personal authority I have ever seen. *The Iron Lady* suggests that only indirectly." He goes on to assess that "Streep is flawless, but the film, like a great many people at the time, is uncertain how to approach her."

Finding herself at the helm of a rare biopic about a woman politician, perhaps Meryl felt obligated to present Thatcher in a somewhat neutral, unclouded way, placing the burden on the audience to form an opinion. The outspoken liberal didn't match Thatcher politically but admired "her personal strength and grit. To have come up, legitimately, through the ranks of the British political system, class bound and gender-phobic as it was, in the time that she did and the way that she did, was a formidable achievement. To have won it, not because she inherited position as the daughter of a great man, or the widow of an important man, but by dint of her own striving.... I see that as evidence of some kind of greatness, worthy for the argument of history to settle."

During her *Iron Lady* media blitz, Meryl pledged $1 million toward the establishment of the National Women's History Museum in Washington. She wanted to support an institution where women's place in history, relegated to sidebars in textbooks, could be collected, archived, and publicized to showcase "incredible stories that we don't know anything about."

Iron Lady, a Weinstein Company release, did a respectable $30 million in North America and scored Meryl her seventeenth Oscar nomination and third win. It had been awhile—twenty-nine years, to be exact. The cherry on top: Roy Helland finally won an Academy Award, sharing the Best Makeup prize with Coulier.

"When they called my name I had this feeling I could hear half of America going, 'Oh no! Oh, c'mon why? Her? Again?' You know? But, whatever," she said, choking up as she thanked Don and her "other partner," Roy.

Winning top honors at the Golden Globes one month earlier, Meryl credited Harvey Weinstein in an acceptance speech that later came back to haunt her. Somewhat begrudgingly, she called him "God" and "the punisher, Old Testament, I guess." Michelle Williams, forced to sit next to Harvey, laughed as the power broker shook his head during the televised ceremony. Williams won Best Actress, Musical or Comedy, for *My Week with Marilyn*, which Harvey produced. Another producer on the biopic later recalled "creepy, stalkerish" Harvey showing up unannounced when Williams filmed nude scenes. For Williams, standing up to a notorious bully could have severe consequences. Harvey used his clout to intimidate and silence women, and to destroy their reputations when they rejected his casting-couch overtures. By contrast, Meryl appeared to have a Thatcher-esque effect on Harvey. He treated her as an equal. Maybe he feared her, too.

After Margaret, Meryl worked nonstop playing eight roles over four years. First, she joined Tommy Lee Jones in the David Frankel dramedy *Hope Springs*, a sobering portrait of a long-married Nebraska couple undergoing counseling to rekindle the flame. Kay is a lonely, traditional wife who cooks and cleans up after her cantankerous husband, Arnold, who barely acknowledges that she's there. They sleep in separate bedrooms. When Kay, who works at a Coldwater Creek store, spends her savings on therapy sessions, Arnold puts up a fight. According to Arnold, marriage "means we have a marriage license and I pay all the bills." He finally agrees to do the work of repairing the relationship because the thought of losing Kay is too much. Who else will do the dishes? Fold the laundry? Make the meals? Tell me why she doesn't divorce his ass?

Again, Meryl was attempting to restore dignity to an invisible woman we've met before and might not fully appreciate. But it's maddening to see Meryl hobbled by a power imbalance that favors an obnoxious man. Jones, who was in awe of his costar, fit the role like a well-worn glove. At the August 2012 premiere, Meryl told me, "I heard somebody describe him in this movie as '50 Shades of Grumpy'! And I *loved it*. I said, 'I'm stealing that!' So I'm letting you have it." She hoped other husbands would learn from Arnold's example and open themselves up to change.

Two years later, Meryl did Jones a solid by taking a super-small role in *The Homesman*, his directorial debut. The 1850s period drama stars the actor as a drifter driving three sick pioneer women back home to Iowa; Grace Gummer played a catatonic nineteen-year-old who's lost three children to diphtheria. Unlike *Evening*, featuring Mamie and Meryl in separate scenes, Grace got to share screen time with her mother, who played a kindly minister's wife offering shelter to the passengers. *The Homesman* might have benefited from more Meryl: it grossed $2.4 million to *Hope Springs'* $64 million.

In other dreary dramas: please see Meryl's turn as a cruel matriarch terrorizing her dysfunctional family. *August: Osage County*, filmed near Tulsa, Oklahoma, in the fall of 2012, was based on Tracy Letts's Pulitzer Prize–winning play of the same name. Violet Weston, who suffers from mouth cancer and prescription drug addiction, needles daughter Barbara (Julia Roberts) and pretty much everyone else. Meryl and Julia, who voiced animated insects in *Ant Bully*, are electric in their first live-action movie together. Cue the scene where Barbara wrests Violet's pills away, screaming, "I run things now!" The best line, however, is Barbara scolding Violet at dinner: "Eat the fish, bitch!" (Perhaps this was retribution for Meryl's anti–*Pretty Woman* remarks in the early '90s.)

Meryl resisted the part many times. "I didn't want to play this woman who is afflicted by her past and by cancer and by her own self," she recalled. "She is detested by her children and quite rightly so. I didn't want to imagine all that and to have to experience it." But her agent pushed her to do it, saying, "We have to make this happen." She changed her mind when a friend said, "You have to do this role for me and for every girl who has a bad mother." She hardly enjoyed the experience. Neither did Julia, who was homesick for her family in California. "It was hard for Julia to get in that skin because the real Julia is so warm and engaging," Meryl revealed. "You immediately connect with her, while Barbara is disappointed with all the doors in her life that are closing. It can be unpleasant to be inside the skins of certain characters."

To re-create the ensemble feel of *August: Osage County*'s original Steppenwolf Theatre Company production, Meryl insisted her costars—Julia, Chris Cooper, and Abigail Breslin, among others— live together in a condo village behind a Toyota dealership. At the end of the day, the group would gather in Meryl's apartment to eat and rehearse dialogue-heavy scenes. She would cook chicken, ribs, and chili topped with Fritos. "Thank God we had a contentious election happening at the same time," she said. "I would unwind by going home and shouting at the news! That was my only relief."

That October, reports surfaced that Meryl, in talks to headline Disney's *Into the Woods,* was on the verge of accepting a character she long avoided: the Witch. But, oh, what a role it was. She would get to perform scenery-chewing songs from the classic Sondheim musical opposite Johnny Depp, James Corden, her *Devil Wears Prada* costar Emily Blunt, and her close friend Tracey Ullman. In the ensuing months, Disney assembled the rest of the cast and set a September 2013 start date to shoot in England. Before jetting across the pond, Meryl joined Jeff Bridges in *The Giver,* a Harvey-backed futuristic parable based on Lois Lowry's acclaimed dystopian YA novel. She was to play the authoritarian Chief Elder, who outlaws the expression of emotion in her quest to form a perfect society. Harvey's daughters reportedly grew up reading the book.

The Weinstein Company, which distributed *Osage County,* aimed to sell the catfight quotient between two major actresses. When the poster was revealed in October 2013, it showed Julia pushing Meryl to the ground, and, weeks before the movie's December 27 release, the *National Enquirer* published a curious report that quoted an anonymous "Hollywood insider" alleging that Meryl never wanted to work with Julia again. Julia's purported crime: suggesting that director John Wells change the ending to focus on Barbara driving away from home rather than the sad image of Violet alone, which test audiences panned. The popular blog Lainey Gossip called BS. "It's possible for two powerful women of stature to co-exist perfectly amiably," said writer Sarah Marrs. "Maybe Meryl and Julia won't be exchanging Christmas cards, I don't know. But any changes made to *August* aren't because of girl sh*t, it's just Harvey Weinstein being an asshole and thinking people can't handle a sad movie."

Although Meryl and Julia scored Oscar nods—Best Actress and Best Supporting Actress, respectively—it's worth noting that Julia never worked with Harvey again. Nor did Meryl following *The Giver.* She began to draw more public attention to sexism in the entertainment industry, even coming for Walt Disney. In January 2014, Meryl blasted the sainted studio and theme park mogul during her fiery, funny, F-bomb-laden speech honoring Emma Thompson at a National Board of Review dinner. Thompson had just played *Mary Poppins* author P. L. Travers in Disney's *Saving Mr. Banks,* which chronicled efforts by Disney (Tom Hanks) to obtain the rights to her stories about the resourceful governess. Disney's daughters grew up reading them. Meryl was courted for the role but passed.

Onstage to toast Thompson, she shed light on why. "Disney, who brought joy, arguably, to billions of people, was perhaps, or had some...racist proclivities," said Meryl. "He formed and supported an anti-Semitic industry lobby. And he was certainly, on the evidence of his company's policies, a gender bigot." To back her claim, she presented a 1938 rejection letter from Walt Disney Studio to an aspiring cartoonist named Mary Ford. "And I'm going to read it here in Emma's tribute because I know it will tickle our honoree, because she's also a rabid, man-eating feminist, like I am." An excerpt from the aforementioned letter: *Women do not do any of the creative work in connection with preparing the cartoons for the screen, as that task is performed entirely by young men. For this reason, girls are not considered for the training school.*

Watching *Mr. Banks*, "I could just imagine Walt Disney's chagrin at having to cultivate P. L. Travers' favor for [the] 20 years that it took to secure the rights to her work. It must have killed him to encounter, in a woman, an equally disdainful and superior creature, a person dismissive of his own, considerable gifts and prodigious output and imagination."

Meryl's attack on the beloved cultural icon made headlines. Disney defenders disputed the charges. His grandniece, Abigail Disney, however, gave Meryl her stamp of approval, posting on Facebook: "Anti-Semite? Check. Misogynist? OF COURSE!! Racist? C'mon he made a film (*Jungle Book*) about how you should 'stay with your own kind' at the height of the fight over segregation!... But damn, he was hella good at making films and his work has made billions of people happy. There's no denying it. So there ya go. Mixed feelings up the wazoo."

Soon after, Meryl lined up Fox's *Suffragette*, playing British activist Emmeline Pankhurst, and TriStar Pictures' *Ricki and the Flash*, picking up the guitar in a juicy role written by Diablo Cody. The *Suffragette* shoot kicked off in London in February. Meryl boasted little screen time in comparison to Carey Mulligan and Helena Bonham Carter, yet her gravitas overshadows the entire film—and rightfully so. Pankhurst, the godmother of the women's suffrage movement in turn-of-the-century England, inspired legions of activists to break windows, set fires, and wreak havoc to get men in power to change laws that made women second-class citizens. When Meryl, channeling Pankhurst, comes out of hiding to fire up Mulligan and other suffragettes, it's hard not to become radicalized by her passion and powers of persuasion.

"We have been left with no alternative but to defy this government!" she intones. "If we must go to prison to obtain the vote, let it be the windows of government, not the bodies of women, that shall be broken! I incite this meeting and all the women in Britain to rebellion! I would rather be a rebel than a slave!" She advises Mulligan, "Never surrender. Never give up the fight."

In the fall of 2015, Meryl and Mulligan found themselves the subjects of controversy over a *Time Out London* photoshoot that featured the costars wearing T-shirts with the slogan "I'd rather be a rebel than a slave," inspired by a speech Pankhurst gave in 1913. The images, meant to promote *Suffragette,* backfired on American social media, generating complaints about insensitivity and ignorance of the quote's reference to slavery. The writer Ijeoma Oluo tweeted, "No matter how well-intentioned, educated, liberal, when [there's] only white people in the room, shit like this happens."

Responding, *Time Out* said it had invited the actresses to appear in the shoot, calling the message tees "a rallying cry, and absolutely not intended to [criticize] those who have no choice but to submit to oppression."

Meryl stayed mum. She wasn't immune to making mistakes, such as the unwittingly tone-deaf decision, as a white woman, to sport the shirt in the first place—yet another sign, critics argued, that intersectional feminism was still a concept, and not even close to reality.

If Meryl didn't know better then, she's certainly removed her privileged blinders today. When Meryl joined the Time's Up campaign against sexual harassment in January 2018, she and fellow wealthy and famous power players Reese Witherspoon and Shonda Rhimes each donated $500,000 to establish a legal defense fund for victims of workplace misconduct in industries such as food services and construction. According to the National Women's Law Center, which oversees the fund, 40 percent of the women seeking help in October 2018 were women of color, and 65 percent were low income. Earlier that year, Meryl brought Ai-jen Poo, director of the National

Domestic Workers Alliance, as her date to the Golden Globe Awards. She ceded the spotlight to the Taiwanese American labor activist during a joint red-carpet interview with Ryan Seacrest. "This is a movement where there's space for everyone and there's a role for everyone," said Poo.

Rewinding back to 2015 and that *Time Out* feature. Meryl also drew ire for her response to the magazine's question, "Are you a feminist?" She said, "I'm a humanist, I am for nice, easy balance." The comment confused many of her fans, given Meryl's feminist bona fides and work that year urging Congress to support the long-dormant equal rights amendment. In 1990, the year of her gutsy SAG keynote, a male reporter asked whether she was a feminist. "It's a dull subject," she answered. "I'm definitely a humanist and I believe in women's rights."

All told, when Meryl became famous, she had no qualms declaring in public arenas from the *Washington Post* to the Oscars press room that, yes, she's a feminist. Perhaps, as she got older, she grew tired of even having to answer the question.

Let's be clear: Meryl's next character wouldn't be caught dead at a Pankhurst rally. Ricki and her band, the Flash, play to near-empty bars in Tarzana, California. With boyfriend Greg (Rick Springfield!) on guitar, the raspy-voiced singer covers "American Girl," "Bad Romance," and "I Still Haven't Found What I'm Looking For." She doesn't seem especially introspective or informed. She cracks jokes about Obama and twice voted for Dubya because she supports the troops. Meryl reached deep down into her lower register to make the rock chick sound like Cher or Chrissie Hynde.

Ricki abandoned her family years ago to pursue rock stardom (or lack thereof) out West. She gets a reality check when ex-husband Peter (Kevin Kline) summons her home to Indianapolis to reconnect with their daughter Julie (Mamie), who attempted suicide. Julie is divorcing an unfaithful husband. (Ricki didn't even go to the wedding.)

A parallel to real life: Mamie split from Benjamin Walker in March 2013 after less than two years of marriage. "It's very amicable," the twenty-nine-year-old's rep said at the time. Weeks earlier, The CW pulled the plug on Mamie's short-lived medical drama, *Emily Owens, M.D.* After the uncoupling announcement, she and Meryl were spotted hanging out in Vancouver, and, one year later, Mamie snapped up a two-bedroom bachelorette pad in Manhattan's Chelsea neighborhood. Though she was moving on, the ordeal doubtless triggered pain when filming *Ricki and the Flash* alongside Meryl in suburban New York. Julie is a ball of anger and grief; Ricki is an unexpected oasis of calm. Ricki goes with the flow, unlike Julie's devoted, tightly wound stepmother (Audra McDonald). She motivates Julie to muster the courage to attend her brother's wedding, even if it conjures memories of happier times. "Don't run away," she says. "Walk on."

Ricki is among my favorite Meryl roles precisely because nobody saw her coming. Director Jonathan Demme, a music buff, requested live performances, so sixty-five-year-old Meryl spent months learning to shred. Her acoustic solo of Ricki's original song "Cold One" is sublime. For fans of *A Star Is Born* crooner Jackson Maine: this is Meryl's "Maybe It's Time."

She wasn't ready to stop singing. She planned to jump from Ricki to opera legend Maria Callas in an HBO movie directed by Mike Nichols. The project, based on Terrence McNally's play *Master Class*, never came to fruition. Nichols, eighty-three, died of cardiac arrest on November 20, 2014. In a statement, Meryl eulogized her collaborator as an "inspiration and joy to know, a director who cried when he laughed, a friend without whom, well, we can't imagine our world, an indelible irreplaceable man."

Meryl plunged into a new role that would make Nichols laugh through tears. Instead of hitting the high notes as a world-renowned soprano, she screeched arias with abandon to play the most infamous opera singer in history. Afterward, she would go to bat for the First Amendment.

INTERMISSION

⚬ ⚬ ⚬ ⚬ ⚬ ⚬ ⚬

Celebrity Streepers

Kelly Clarkson: The Grammy-winning pop star is a Meryl superfan. She first encountered Meryl on the red carpet at the 2018 Golden Globes, yelling, "I've adored you since I was, like, 8!" What she didn't tell her idol: that she owns a cardboard cutout of Meryl. "She traveled with me to New York," Clarkson said of the likeness. "We put her on the plane, just carrying her like it's normal."

Mindy Kaling: The writer, actress, and creator of *The Mindy Project* centered an episode of her Hulu comedy around her characters' Meryl Streep costume party. The cast donned ensembles inspired by Meryl movies from *The Devil Wears Prada* to *A Cry in the Dark*. Mindy dressed up as Julia Child in *Julie & Julia*. In 2018, Mindy referenced Meryl while defending the all-girl heist movie *Ocean's 8* from critical backlash on Rotten Tomatoes. "Meryl was talking about this, she had a great point of view about it," she said. "She made movies for women but they are reviewed by men who don't necessarily value it or don't look at it in the same point of view as a woman doing it, but it just seems unfair."

Billy Eichner: The actor and comedian, who rose to fame on the game show *Billy on the Street,* met Meryl in 2012 when both appeared on Bravo's *Watch What Happens Live.* Five years later, he saw her speak at a Planned Parenthood benefit, and she imparted some words of wisdom. "We talked about *Billy on the Street* and as she walked away, she said, 'stay mad,'" he recalled.

Jennifer Lawrence: Stars, they're just like us! Not even Lawrence, who won the Oscar for Best Actress in 2013, is impervious to experiencing panic at the sight of Queen Meryl. "One time someone was introducing me to Bill Maher, and I saw Meryl Streep walk into the room, and I literally put my hand right in Bill Maher's face and said, 'Not now, Bill!,' and I just stared at Meryl Streep." Well, did she speak to her? "Of course not. I just creepily stared at her."

Zoe Kravitz: "I'm still having a really hard time casually saying [Meryl's] first name," she told *Entertainment Tonight* following news that Meryl was joining Kravitz, Reese Witherspoon, and Nicole Kidman for the second season of HBO's *Big Little Lies*. "I had lunch with the cast and Meryl, and I still can't do it. Meryl Streep, you guys. Meryl f—king Streep!"

CHAPTER 19

Meryl the Superhero

My decision stands, and I'm going to bed.—Katharine Graham
(The Post, 2017)

Long ago, in the January 1980 edition of *Cue* magazine, Meryl confessed, "Usually I think I can play anything. I have great faith in myself. If I felt that I wanted to go sing *Norma* at the Met my friends might say, 'No, no. Not for you.'"

She was referring to Vincenzo Bellini's 1831 opera, sung many times by Maria Callas post–World War II. It had been decades since Meryl took singing lessons with Estelle Liebling before deciding opera wasn't her thing. But she clearly respected the endangered art form and the talented artists, such as Callas, who mastered it. She also admired the chutzpah of Florence Foster Jenkins, the wealthy New York socialite whose unlikely foray into soprano divadom turned her into a laughingstock.

"People may say I can't sing, but no one can ever say I didn't sing," Florence declared of her critics. By popular demand, the seventy-six-year-old, who performed privately for decades, gave her first public concert at Carnegie Hall on October 25, 1944. The next morning, she opened newspapers to find blistering, ego-bruising reviews. The *New York Post* dubbed the performance "one of the weirdest mass jokes New York has ever seen." Five days later, Florence suffered a heart attack. She held on for a month. Though an *LA Times* obituary claimed she died of a broken heart, Stephen Temperley, whose play about Florence's life debuted on Broadway in 2005, argued that "she may have been shocked but I daresay had she lived she would've got over it."

A prestige biopic of the chanteuse—who cornered the "so bad it's good" market well before the cult crowd-pleaser *The Room* sold out midnight screenings—proved catnip to Meryl. Also onboard: director Stephen Frears (*The Queen*) and Hugh Grant as Florence's dapper partner, St. Clair Bayfield. The shoot was set to begin May 2015 in London.

Ignoring Meryl's Walt dis, Disney chose to prominently feature the vindictive Witch, not Johnny Depp's pervy Wolf, on the promotional poster for *Into the Woods*. The dark, twisted musical, which cleverly deconstructs Brothers Grimm fairy tales, wrangled $128 million in North America and rave reviews for Meryl. "Streep is quite wonderful, delivering something far richer than her karaoke turn in the clunky *Mamma Mia!* . . . She reinvents this role from scratch, bringing powerful vocals, mischievous comedic instincts, bold physicality and raw feeling to the Witch," wrote the *Hollywood Reporter's* David Rooney in a backhanded compliment. Right on cue, she earned a Best Supporting Actress nomination, competing against Patricia Arquette (*Boyhood*), Emma Stone (*Birdman*), Keira Knightley (*The Imitation Game*) and Laura Dern (*Wild*).

And the winner was . . . Arquette, the no-nonsense single mom and unsung hero in Richard Linklater's coming-of-age drama. I'll never forget her speech on February 22, 2015. It was the beginning of something, even if Arquette chose her words poorly. After thanking colleagues and family, Arquette closed with a rousing declaration: "To every woman who gave birth to every taxpayer and citizen of this nation, we have fought for everybody else's equal rights, it's our time to have wage equality once and for all, and equal rights for women in the United States of America." Arquette brought significant attention to gender inequality and the wage gap, although she undercut her message by overlooking the fact that gay people and people of color also battle pay discrimination. The camera panned to Meryl as she cheered from the audience. Her spirited reaction produced an instant classic go-to GIF to signify approval on Twitter threads.

Feminism was in the air, infiltrating actresses' awards-show speeches in a bold, new way. A major studio actually decided to take *Suffragette* mainstream. Outrage brewed after hackers leaked Sony Pictures' emails in December 2014, revealing that Jennifer Lawrence, a megastar, was making less money on *American Hustle* than male costars including Jeremy Renner.

On April 15, 2015, Hillary Clinton announced she was running for president. Her supporters were emboldened. If Hillary cracked the highest glass ceiling and wound up making history as the first woman to occupy the Oval Office, then women wouldn't have to put up with bullshit anymore. On that note, a week after Hillary's announcement, an anonymous Tumblr page, Shit People Say to Women Directors, landed online, sharing horror stories of Hollywood misogyny. "There was a cultural ennui where everyone was so used to the status quo that the notion of questioning it seemed almost, if I may say, unnecessary," Cathy Schulman, president emerita of Women in Film Los Angeles, told me at the time. "And there was this kind of…acceptance of this unusual lack of parity given that we're living in the year 2015."

Meryl had been raising her voice since 1990. Now she was putting her anger into action. On April 19, news spread that she had funded an annual four-day script development lab for women screenwriters over forty in partnership with New York Women in Film and Television. The first year, established woman writers, directors, and producers descended upon a rustic upstate New York retreat to mentor a small group of winning applicants. Meryl laid low, careful not to disrupt the newbies, but her presence was felt.

Once more, she flew to Great Britain on location—this time inhabiting a shameless heiress with an unlimited supply of outrageous costumes and ornate tiaras. The *Florence Foster Jenkins* crew used Liverpool's stately Drury Lane to replicate 1940s Central Park West. As for mimicking the off-key Florence, Meryl worked with a voice coach; she butchered "Queen of the Night" in multiple takes, at Frears's request. "It was way, way more fun, but it was more terrifying," said Meryl, who originally thought she would lip-sync to her own terrible recordings. "That made us very alive because it changed each time."

Donald Trump, a former reality TV host with a history of appalling behavior toward women, would have bullied Florence to death. He entered the presidential race June 16, eventually becoming the Republican nominee. His dark, divisive campaign broke norms. With unhinged glee, Trump maliciously attacked immigrants, journalists, and war hero John McCain, among countless other targets. Of GOP candidate Carly Fiorina, he said, "*Look* at that face! Would anyone *vote* for that? Can you imagine that, the face of our next *president*?!"

Trump's goal was to strengthen his power by sowing discord. At rallies, his racism encouraged white supremacists to spew hatred and threaten violence toward the Other. He led them in chants of "Lock Her Up," "Build That Wall," and "All Lives Matter." What a clown. But what did you expect from the racist who spread a hoax about President Obama's birth certificate?

Thank goodness Hillary was going to win. Soon, Trump would retire to Mar-a-Lago, and things could go back to normal. For now, Meryl was stumping for Hillary at the Democratic National Convention.

"What does it take to be the first female anything?" she declared, wearing a flag-print dress to deliver her July 26 speech. "It takes grit and it takes grace.... Hillary Clinton has taken some fire over 40 years of her fight for families and children. How does she do it? That's what I want to know."

As Mamie and Grace clapped from the stands, Meryl predicted that Hillary "will be our first woman president! And she will be a great president!"

The next month, Paramount—aiming to position both Meryl and *Florence* for Oscars—released the movie stateside, echoing the *Julie & Julia* strategy: arrive early to the crowded awards-circuit party, drop the mic, and build an aura of inevitability around Meryl's nomination. "I hope the movie does some decent business, because it's a nice movie, with some great performances and a resonant chord of melancholy running throughout," wrote *Vanity Fair* critic Richard Lawson, noting its lackluster sales in the UK and France. "It's yet another of Streep's increasingly same-y grande dame roles, sure, but she plays this one a little more subtly than she did, say, Margaret Thatcher."

In a flashback to the 1980s, Meryl's serial disguises had begun to irritate movie critics who wanted to see the master technician tone down the flamboyance and get real. *Florence,* argued Sheri Linden in the *Hollywood Reporter,* is "a signed, sealed and delivered tribute that doesn't want to dig too deep or give much room to character aspects that are unflattering or disturbing. It's Streep's dexterity that lets in the shadows and light. There's something both touching and freeing in watching a performer known for her technical rigor hit the wrong notes with such gusto. Her ability to convey self-importance, vulnerability, yearning, and delusion in a single tortured melody is exhilarating. It makes you wish she'd bring that fluency to something in a minor or more intimate key, a story that strips away the bells and whistles."

Florence bowed October 27 after two months and $27 million. Twelve days later, Donald Trump was elected President of the United States.

Oh, shit.

♦ ♦ ♦ ♦ ♦

Steven Spielberg felt a sense of urgency. The filmmaker had been immersed in preproduction on a passion project, *The Kidnapping of*

Edgardo Mortara, but put it on hold after blowing through a thrilling script written by Liz Hannah about *Washington Post* publisher Katharine "Kay" Graham's brave decision to defy President Richard Nixon. In 1971, Graham risked the newspaper's future when she went against the grain and published the Pentagon Papers, a top-secret government study on the hugely unpopular Vietnam War. Whistleblowing military analyst Daniel Ellsberg leaked the classified documents to the *New York Times,* which reported excerpts from the study. The president fired back with a court order. Ben Bradlee, the *Post's* swashbuckling editor, lobbied Graham to pick up where the *Times* left off. After hesitating, she finally pushed the button, instigating other media to follow her lead.

"There was an undeniable relevance to what happened in 1971 with the Nixon administration trying to stop the free press from printing a story which was not flattering to him or his administration, and all the obvious parallels with today," Spielberg recalled. On March 3, 2017, he called Amy Pascal, who was producing *The Post,* and said he wanted to direct it immediately with Meryl as Graham and Tom Hanks as Bradlee. By May 30, Spielberg—gathering the troops and going to war against the Trump administration—had begun principal photography in New York. He had never assembled a movie faster.

Meryl and Tom earned equal paychecks, according to Spielberg. The director didn't know Meryl well, although the two were close to Carrie Fisher. Like Tom, Meryl had a strong moral center that filtered through the characters she played on screen. She was not afraid to criticize the president-elect in front of millions of viewers at January's Golden Globes, two weeks before Trump's apocalyptic inauguration ceremony where he vowed, chillingly, to end "American carnage." While accepting the Cecil B. DeMille Award, she admonished Trump for mocking disabled reporter Serge Kovaleski on the campaign trail and invited people to join her in supporting the Committee to Protect Journalists.

"This instinct to humiliate, when it's modeled by someone in the public platform, by someone powerful, it filters down into everybody's life, because it kinda gives permission for other people to do the same thing," she warned. "Disrespect invites disrespect, violence incites violence. And when the powerful use their position to bully others, we all lose."

In closing, she referenced Carrie: "As my friend, the dear departed Princess Leia, said to me once, take your broken heart, make it into art."

The room burst into applause. Conservative pundits watching remotely seized the opportunity to smear a truth-telling actor as another out-of-touch Hollywood liberal whose politics further antagonize Trump's followers. Inevitably, the thin-skinned Trump lashed out on Twitter. "Meryl Streep, one of the most overrated actresses in Hollywood, doesn't know me but attacked last night at the Golden Globes. She is a Hillary flunky who lost big," he tweeted, denying he had ridiculed Kovaleski.

But of course he had. Kovaleski has arthrogryposis, impairing the movement of his arms. He happened to write a story Trump didn't like, which made him a target. "You've got to see this guy," Trump told supporters at a South Carolina rally, shaking his arms in an impression of the journalist.

Meryl's fans and allies rallied to her defense. According to documentarian Ken Burns, she "said if she ended up in the East River I would know whodunit. But they're too scared of her to do anything, especially when she reminds us constantly when the emperors of the world have no clothes." Jimmy Kimmel, hosting the 2017 Academy Awards, joked, "From her mediocre early work in *The Deer Hunter* and *Out of Africa,* to her underwhelming performances in *Kramer vs. Kramer* and *Sophie's Choice,* Meryl Streep has phoned it in for more than 50 films over the course of her lackluster career. This is Meryl's 20th Oscar nomination, made even more amazing considering the fact that she wasn't even in a movie this year—we just wrote her name down out of habit."

On October 5, 2017, the *New York Times* published damning reports of sexual harassment against Harvey Weinstein, expanding the #MeToo movement founded by activist Tarana Burke in 2006. For decades, Harvey, an aggressive dealmaker and Oscar campaigner, had leveraged his power to harass and abuse women, including the actresses who starred in his films. Gwyneth Paltrow was twenty-two years old when he appointed her to star in the Miramax adaptation of Jane Austen's *Emma,* an exciting role that would lead to an Academy Award nomination. She told the *Times* that, before filming began, Weinstein requested she visit his hotel room at the Peninsula Beverly Hills, where he placed his hands on her and proposed they go into the bedroom for massages. She declined. After Paltrow's then-boyfriend, Brad Pitt, had words with Weinstein, telling the producer, "If you ever make her feel uncomfortable again, I'll kill you," Weinstein warned Paltrow to keep quiet about his advances. "I was a kid, I was signed up, I was petrified," she later said, recalling, "I thought he was going to fire me."

Meryl, seemingly sheltered by her own power, said she had no idea this was happening. "I don't know where Harvey lives, nor has he ever been to my home," she stated that December, defending herself from accusations of complicity. "I have never in my life been invited to his hotel room." She'd been to his office just one time to meet with Wes Craven about *Music of the Heart* in 1998. Abusers like Weinstein are adept at lying and covering their tracks; that includes hiding behavior from a respected icon such as Meryl. "I don't think she'd have stood for it," says Carl Franklin, her *One True Thing* director. "She's been fighting the fight for a long time."

⦿ ⦾ ⦿ ⦿ ⦾

What does it take to be the first female anything? It takes grit and it takes grace. Kay Graham's husband, Philip, inherited the *Post* from her father. After Philip's suicide, the Washington socialite took over the company in 1963, becoming the first woman publisher of a prominent American newspaper. She confronted sexism and her own self-doubt and insecurities to preside over a journalistic golden age that peaked in the *Post*'s hard-nosed coverage of the Watergate scandal that brought down Nixon.

It was Graham's handling of the Pentagon Papers that marked a major turning point in her life and career. It showed the world, and Graham herself, that she had what it took to lead. Meryl honored her memory with a subtle, nuanced performance that effectively portrayed the interior life of a woman learning to feel comfortable with her power. It's a struggle to which many women can relate. Spielberg and Tom, newly minted members of the elite, humbling "I've worked with Meryl club," marveled at her wizardry, as did critics catching early screenings of *The Post*, which Spielberg, a magician in his own right, managed to turn around for a December release. On the Internet, the extraordinary caftan that Meryl wore in the movie—costume designer Ann Roth sourced the shimmering gold fabric in New Jersey—ignited a torrent of tributes online.

Like almost everything she did, *The Post* was a manifestation of Meryl's civic duty. That included skewering ignorant fools. On June 6, 2016, David Hare, who wrote *Plenty* and *The Hours*, witnessed his favorite Meryl characterization in recent years at a Public Theater gala in Central Park. She emerged onstage looking grotesque in an ill-fitting suit with loads of padding underneath and orange makeup smeared across her face to sing "Brush Up Your Shakespeare," from Cole Porter's *Kiss Me Kate*, with Christine Baranski. In the classic musical, the song is a duet between gangsters bragging about how quoting the Bard works wonders on women. Sample lyric: "If she says your behavior is heinous / kick her right in the Coriolanus / Brush up your Shakespeare / And they'll all kow-tow."

"It was authentic genius, which made the hairs stand up on the back of my neck," Hare recalls. "I wish Brecht could have been present because she was doing exactly what he wanted from an actor—she was both totally inside the part, inside the ridiculous idea of

Trump singing Cole Porter, but at the same time standing beside her own performance, and commenting on it, as if to say 'Isn't this the stupidest thing you ever saw in your life?' It was anarchy incarnate, but under the tightest possible technical control—like seeing Laurence Olivier play Archie Rice."

Meryl treated theater as a sacred playground to experiment and entertain, give voice to the voiceless, and lampoon depraved would-be tyrants. This time, she went for laughs, missing the pre-show dinner to get ready backstage, where she pinned her own hair into a golden bouffant. She was born to be bold. She was born to be brave. She was born to be a light in the darkness.

A Streeping Genius

In drama school, Meryl considered acting a silly, frivolous profession, all ego gratification. Shouldn't she be doing something worthwhile with her life, like saving the planet? Obviously, Meryl's thinking changed. She once attended a dinner for artists in Washington, DC, where Alexander Haig, a career Republican serving under Presidents Reagan, Nixon, and Ford, delivered a message that surprised her. "What a strange choice for a speaker, I thought, and he was really more than half in the bag and sort of reeling a little bit," Meryl said during a 1988 press conference to promote *A Cry in the Dark*. "And he said, you know, 'Nobody remembers the armies that anybody held or the bridges built or the railroads built. People are remembered for their artists and we have to support the arts.'"

By then, Meryl and Haig, the "unlikely mouthpiece," were in full agreement. She was proud to be an actor and didn't take her success for granted. She chose movie roles responsibly, intertwining activism and art to dignify stories about women who are misunderstood and in need of some compassion. While honoring Emma Thompson at the 2014 National Board of Review awards, Meryl appeared to draw subtextual parallels to herself. "Emma considers, carefully, what the fuck she is putting into the culture," she stated. "Emma thinks: Is this helpful? Not: Will it build my brand? Not: Will it give me billions? Not: Does this express me? Me! Me! My unique and fabulous self, into all eternity in every universe for all time? Will I get a sequel out of it, or a boat? Or, a perfume contract?"

Ironically, Meryl made a fortune expressing herself as the rare character actor who attained leading lady status into her seventies. She's come a long way since playing Robert De Niro's *Deer Hunter* girlfriend—or Dustin Hoffman's slap victim on *Kramer vs. Kramer*. More than forty years and twenty-one Oscar nominations later, Meryl has transcended both. Even De Niro, a mere footnote in her epic résumé, is today just another subject laying flowers at the feet of the queen.

Meryl, ever self-deprecating, might insist she makes an awkward movie star, yet nothing could be further from the truth. Always destined for bigger things, she's had that razzle-dazzle stretching back to Bernards High School. Character actors simply don't break Academy Award records unless they are movie stars. And a movie star has to want it. Meryl so clearly did. She worked hard and she fought hard, navigating the bumpy *River Wild* rapids of her career to reach *The Devil Wears Prada* and *The Post*. Along the way, she and Don raised four well-adjusted children away from the spotlight while keeping one of Hollywood's longest-running marriages intact.

When Meryl studied at Yale, an instructor asked the class for their thoughts on how to play a king. "And everybody said, 'Oh you are assertive,' and people would say, 'Oh you speak in a slightly deeper voice.' And the teacher said, 'Wrong. The way to be king is to have everybody in the room quiet when you come in.' The atmosphere changes. It's all up to everybody else to make you king. I thought that was really powerful information," she recalled a decade ago. It was a story she liked to tell—not to mention a revealing insight into how *she* managed to graduate from stressed-out student to Queen Meryl, American royalty.

"She kicks against all the people she loves—because she wants them to be better—but at the same time she's 100 percent loyal," observes David Hare. "You can say she's like Katharine Hepburn, because she's done everything on her own terms. But you have to take on the fact that she's also a far, far more gifted actor. She also has done something truly admirable. [She's] knowingly used her power to get things made. *Plenty* wouldn't have happened without her, nor would *Silkwood,* nor would *A Cry in the Dark*. Part of what audiences respond to in her performances is what she is as a person. An unallotted force for good."

Human rights. Climate change. The freedom of the press. The Time's Up movement in response to #MeToo. Name a noble cause—there's a pretty good chance Meryl supports it. She is an undeniable leader in the anti-Trump Resistance but wary of being its public face.

"I don't want to be that," she said in December 2017, nearly one year after her galvanizing Globes speech and the Women's March, when protesters were spotted brandishing signs that read "What Meryl Said" and "Meryl Streep for President."

"I'm a really private person, and like a lot of people in show business, I'm actually shy so it's hard for me to do all this stuff," she demurred.

Meryl was guarding her privacy. A dissident as famous and controversial as she risks everything to stand up to a Manchurian candidate who instigates acolytes to commit violence against political opponents. In these messy, uncertain times, she continued protesting through pop culture. Following Kay Graham and the Pentagon Papers, Meryl joined Steven Soderbergh's *The Laundromat,* a thriller based on a real-life journalistic investigation that linked the Panama Papers to international politicos using offshore bank accounts to dodge taxes.

Look, she's a serious woman. But, like any cultural phenomenon, Meryl skirts the line between highbrow class and lowbrow camp. She is an Internet meme whose priceless reactions on camera at televised events, ranging from the Oscars' *Moonlight* mix-up to a US Open tennis match, dart across social media with warp speed. It's not like she needs a celebrity Instagram account to remain relevant, though it would be absolutely delightful if she posted whimsical slice-of-life photos à la Candice Bergen. (Come on, Meryl, show us your aspirational kitchen!) To compensate, numerous fan Instas have popped up, none more absurdly funny than Taste of Streep,

which photoshops images of Miranda Priestly peering out of a can-
noli and Mary Fisher atop a pink donut, among other hilarity.

Onstage, the all-male *Streep Tease* revue sold out shows in Los
Angeles, with the cast performing monologues such as *Prada*'s
cerulean smackdown. Mindy Kaling, creator of TV's *The Mindy
Project*, wrote an episode wherein she and her castmates dressed as
Meryl movie characters like Karen Blixen, Sister Aloysius, and (ha!)
Lindy Chamberlain.

Of Meryl's fans, called Streepers, "I'm a little alarmed," she has
said. "I'm grateful that I've had a sort of renaissance of interest in my
career. It's wonderful, it really is. Celebrity has become a very odd
thing in our culture. I don't have a Twitter account but apparently
I have five. But they're not me. I'm not on Facebook, but yes, apparently, I am. They're a little scary to me, but everyone needs a hobby."

It's my cue to quote Miranda! For all the fans:

That's all.

ACKNOWLEDGMENTS

Thirteen years ago, when I was working as an arts and entertainment reporter at the Associated Press in New York City, I saw *The Devil Wears Prada* for the first time in advance of a press junket interview with Anne Hathaway. I was utterly captivated by the story of a young woman navigating her first job in media while sporting Chanel. *Prada* felt fresh, original, empowering. However, as I got older, my admiration shifted from Anne's Andy Sachs to Meryl's Miranda Priestly—her competence, her grace under pressure, her chic, white bob.

Writing this book has been a thrill. I could not have crossed the finish line without my amazing research assistant Caroline Jorgenson, whose organizational skills are unmatched, and transcriber extraordinaire Crystal Duan. Thank you to my forever reader, Jennifer Keishin Armstrong, the Miranda/Meryl of pop-culture nonfiction. I thank everyone who took the time to discuss Meryl and her movies. People like Goldie Hawn, John Patrick Shanley, David Frankel, Aline Brosh McKenna, Robert Benton, Wendy Finerman, David Hare, Susan Seidelman, Fred Schepisi, Justin Kirk, Joe Mazzello, Albert Brooks, Lake Bell, Sarah Jones, Carl Franklin, Vanessa Taylor, Jerry Zaks, Arlene Burns, Albert Wolsky, Buzz Hirsch, Larry Mark, Bob Greenhut, Stephen Goldblatt, and Mark Livolsi, among many other gracious individuals. Another round of thanks is due to the publicists, managers, and agents who connected me with sources and to the invaluable archives at the Margaret Herrick Library in LA and the Paley Center for Media in New York.

I am eternally grateful to my agent, Daniel Greenberg, for having my back and to Brant Rumble, my talented editor at Hachette Books, for his exceptional skill, patience, and humor. Justin Teodoro, your gorgeous illustrations capture Meryl's dynamic, joyful artistry.

Last but not least, much love to my parents, family and friends, and especially Dave Beeman, the Paul Child to my Julia.

SOURCE NOTES

A journalist never reveals her sources. OK, fine.

Introduction: Gird Your Loins!

Abramowitz, Rachel, *Is That a Gun in Your Pocket? Women's Experience of Power in Hollywood*, Random House, New York, 2000.
Meryl Streep interview, *Fresh Air*, NPR, February 6, 2012.

Chapter 1: From Geek to Streep

Booth, John Michael, "Meryl & Me," *Us*, August 25, 1986.
Britten, Nick, "Baftas: Meryl Streep's British Ancestor 'Helped Start War with Native Americans,'" *Daily Telegraph*, February 14, 2002.
Burns, Ken, "Meryl Streep," *USA Weekend*, November 29 to December 1, 2002.
Commentary in Richard Shepard's John Cazale documentary *I Knew It Was You*, HBO Films, 2009.
Current Biography, August 1980.
De Vries, Hilary, "Meryl Acts Up," *Los Angeles Times Magazine*, September 9, 1990.
Garey, Juliann, "Meryl Streep," *Us*, October 1994.
Goodman, Joan, "Keeping It in the Family," *Sunday Times*, January 20, 1991.
Good Morning America, ABC, February 17, 1983.
The Graham Norton Show, BBC One, October 9, 2015.
Gray, Paul, "A Mother Finds Herself," *Time*, December 3, 1979.
Greene, Bob, "Streep," *Esquire*, December 1984.
Gussow, Mel, "The Rising Star of Meryl Streep," *New York Times Magazine*, February 4, 1979.
Haddad-Garcia, George, "Mysterious Meryl," *Antonio Light*, October 1981.
Kaplan, James, "I Chose Family," *Parade*, May 28, 2006.

Kroll, Jack, "A Star for the '80s," *Newsweek*, January 7, 1980.

"Mary W. Streep, 86, Artist, Volunteer," newjerseyhills.com, October 4, 2001.

"Meryl Streep: 'I'm Not Always Happy,' " *Talks*, July 13, 2011.

Miller, Julie, "Here's Where Meryl Streep Found the Confidence to Become an Actress," June 19, 2015.

Proudfit, Scott, "Behind the Magic," *Back Stage West*, February 18 to February 24, 1999.

Rosenthal, David, "Meryl Streep Stepping In and Out of Roles," *Rolling Stone*, October 15, 1981.

Schulman, Michael, *Her Again*, HarperCollins, New York, 2016.

Skow, John, "What Makes Meryl Magic," *Time*, September 7, 1981.

Streep, Meryl, appearance in *Faces of America*, PBS, aired February to March 2010.

Streep, Meryl, speeches to graduates of Barnard College in New York City on May 17, 2010, and of Vassar College in Poughkeepsie, New York, on May 23, 1983.

Streep, Meryl, "2006 (79th) Academy Awards: Nominee Questionnaire," undated.

Winters, Laura, "Master Class," *Vogue*, December 2002.

Intermission: When Meryl Met Roy

Barton, Robert, and Annie McGregor, *Theatre in Your Life*, 3rd ed., Cengage Learning, Stamford, CT, 2014.

Karger, Dave, "Oscars 2012: Love Story," *Entertainment Weekly*, March 2, 2012.

Chapter 2: Runaway Meryl

Abramowitz, Rachel, *Is That a Gun in Your Pocket? Women's Experience of Power in Hollywood*, Random House, New York, 2000.

AFI Tribute to Jane Fonda, TNT, June 14, 2014.

Buckley, Cara, "Meryl Streep and Tom Hanks on the #MeToo Moment and 'The Post,' " *New York Times*, January 3, 2018.

Commentary in Michael Arick's *Finding the Truth: The Making of 'Kramer vs. Kramer,'* distributed by Columbia TriStar Home Video, 2001.

De Dubovay, Diane, "Meryl Streep," *Ladies' Home Journal*, March 1980.

"Don Gummer," http://www.imagogalleries.com/bios/Don_Gummer_Biography.pdf.

Dreifus, Claudia, "Meryl Streep: Why I've Taken a Year Off for Motherhood," *Ladies' Home Journal*, April 1984.

Good Morning America, ABC, February 17, 1983.

Graham, Ruth, "Meryl Streep Once Said Dustin Hoffman Groped Her Breast the First Time They Met," slate.com, November 2, 2017.

Gray, Paul, "A Mother Finds Herself," *Time*, December 3, 1979.

Gussow, Mel, "The Rising Star of Meryl Streep," *New York Times Magazine*, February 4, 1979.

Interview with Robert Benton.

Interview with Robert Greenhut.

Kennedy, Dana, "Meryl, Revealed," *More*, December 2002 / January 2003.

Kimball Kent, Ruth, "Actress Meryl Streep: Her Own Woman," *Plain Dealer*, 1978.

Kroll, Jack, "A Star for the '80s," *Newsweek*, January 7, 1980.

Kummer, Corby, "Streep vs. Streep," *Cue*, January 5, 1980.

Longworth, Karina, *Meryl Streep: Anatomy of an Actor*, Phaidon Press, London, UK, 2014.

Rosenthal, David, "Meryl Streep Stepping In and Out of Roles," *Rolling Stone*, October 15, 1981.

Schulman, Michael, *Her Again*, HarperCollins, New York, 2016.

Shalit, Gene, "What's Happening," *Ladies' Home Journal*, December 1979.

Watch What Happens, Bravo, August 9, 2012.

White, Lesley, "Her Significant Others," *Sunday Times*, October 31, 2004.

Williams, Christian, "Scenes from the Battle of the Sexes," *Washington Post*, December 17, 1982.

Winters, Laura, "Master Class," *Vogue*, December 2002.

"Young Actresses: Meryl, Tovah, Jill & Swoosie," *Horizon*, August 1978.

Chapter 3: Mother Meryl

Bandler, Michael, "Streep," *American Way*, December 1982.

Behind-the-scenes material, *Sophie's Choice*, DVD, Lions Gate, 1998.

Bennetts, Leslie, "About Meryl," *Vanity Fair*, January 2010.

Biskind, Peter, "The Vietnam Oscars," *Vanity Fair*, March 2008.

Burns, Ken, "Meryl Streep," *USA Weekend*, November 29 to December 1, 2002.

Champlin, Charles, "Meryl Streep as Silkwood and Herself," *Los Angeles Times*, December 18, 1983.

Darrach, Brad, "Enchanting, Colorless, Glacial, Fearless, Sneaky, Seductive, Manipulative, Magical Meryl," *Life*, December 1987.

De Dubovay, Diane, "Meryl Streep," *Ladies' Home Journal*, March 1980.

Deeley, Michael, *Blade Runners, Deer Hunters, and Blowing the Bloody Doors Off: My Life in Cult Movies*, Pegasus Books, New York, 2009.

Ebert, Robert, "Kramer vs. Kramer," *Chicago Sun-Times,* December 1, 1979.

Forster, Evan, "Meryl Streep: A Star in Any Language," *Biography Magazine,* September 1998.

Gittelson, Natalie, "Meryl Streep: Surprising Superstar," *McCall's,* March 1983.

Good Morning America, ABC, February 17, 1983.

The Graham Norton Show, BBC One, April 15, 2016.

Harmetz, Aljean, "Miss Streep and Kline Cast in Movie 'Sophie,'" *New York Times,* July 22, 1981.

Harmetz, Aljean, "Oscar-Winning 'Deer Hunter' Is Under Attack as 'Racist' Film," *New York Times,* April 26, 1979.

Harris, Radie, "Broadway Ballyhoo," *Hollywood Reporter,* August 11, 1980.

Hinson, Hal, "Streep and Irons Make a Big-Time Movie Twosome," *Los Angeles Herald-Examiner,* September 15, 1981.

Interview with Robert Benton.

Item about United Artists offering a studio for Don Gummer on location of *The French Lieutenant's Woman, People,* May 12, 1980.

Kaplan, James, "I Chose Family," *Parade,* May 28, 2006.

Kasindorf, Jeanie, "A Man's Place Is in the Movies," *New West,* January 22, 1980.

Kennedy, Dana, "Meryl, Revealed," *More,* December 2002 / January 2003.

Kroll, Jack, "A Star for the '80s," *Newsweek,* January 7, 1980.

"Jaffe, Benton, Hoffman and Streep Talk About New Films," *Hollywood Reporter,* March 25, 1980.

Jimmy Kimmel Live!, ABC, January 13, 2012.

Jimmy Kimmel Live!, ABC, January 15, 2014.

Maslin, Janet, "At the Movies," *New York Times,* August 24, 1979.

Maychick, Diana, *Meryl Streep: The Reluctant Superstar,* St. Martin's Press, New York, 1984.

"Meryl Streep and Sophie's Choice," *Us,* April 29, 1980.

"Meryl Streep Says She Is Proud to Be Acting 'on Behalf of...Old Broads,'" *Telegraph,* February 2, 2009.

"Nathan" casting list, Alan J. Pakula collection at Margaret Herrick Library in Los Angeles, June 1980.

Pakula, Hannah, "Meryl, Unrehearsed," *More,* October 1999.

Rea, Steven, "Meryl Streep Talks About 'Sophie's Choice,' Acting & Other Things," *Movie Magazine,* Winter 1983.

Rosenthal, David, "Meryl Streep Stepping In and Out of Roles," *Rolling Stone,* October 15, 1981.

Saltzman, Barbara, item detailing Justin Henry's encounter with Queen Elizabeth II, *Los Angeles Times*, March 26, 1980.

Schulman, Michael, *Her Again*, HarperCollins, New York, 2016.

Shalit, Gene, "What's Happening," *Ladies' Home Journal*, December 1979.

Shoard, Catherine, "Meryl Streep: 'I Wasn't Happy with *The French Lieutenant's Woman*,'" theguardian.com, April 18, 2016.

Skow, John, "What Makes Meryl Magic," *Time*, September 7, 1981.

Sternbergh, Adam, "Why Was *Kramer vs. Kramer* the Top-Grossing Movie of 1979?," vulture.com, October 3, 2014.

Weinraub, Bernard, "Her Peculiar Career," *New York Times Magazine*, September 18, 1994.

White, Lesley, "Her Significant Others," *Sunday Times*, October 31, 2004.

Williams, Christian, "Scenes from the Battle of the Sexes," *Washington Post*, December 17, 1982.

"Young Actresses: Meryl, Tovah, Jill & Swoosie," *Horizon*, August 1978.

Chapter 4: Meryl Goes Nuclear

Abramowitz, Rachel, *Is That a Gun in Your Pocket? Women's Experience of Power in Hollywood*, Random House, New York, 2000.

AFI Tribute to Meryl Streep, USA Network, June 21, 2004.

Alexis Fisher, Lauren, "An Ode to Cher's Unbeatable Oscars Style," harpersbazaar.com, February 23, 2017.

Anthony, George, "Meryl Streep & Cher Get Together in *Silkwood*," *Marquee*, December 1983.

Bennetts, Leslie, "About Meryl," *Vanity Fair*, January 2010.

Champlin, Charles, "Meryl Streep as Silkwood and Herself," *Los Angeles Times*, December 18, 1983.

Cher, *The First Time*, Simon & Schuster, New York, 1998.

"The Devil Wore Prada, but Meryl Wore...," *People*, February 24, 2007.

Dreifus, Claudia, "Meryl Streep: Why I've Taken a Year Off for Motherhood," *Ladies' Home Journal*, April 1984.

Ginsberg, Steven, "ABC Pix Begins Work on Third Feature Sept. 7," *Variety*, September 3, 1982.

Gittelson, Natalie, "Meryl Streep: Surprising Superstar," *McCall's*, March 1983.

Gordon, Wendy, "Role of a Lifetime: Meryl Streep as Eco-Activist Mom," marias farmcountrykitchen.com, February 28, 2012.

Harmon, Katherine, "Fukushima Absorbed: How Plutonium Poisons the Body," blogs.scientificamerican.com, June 26, 2011.

Interview with Buzz Hirsch.

Interview with Albert Wolsky.

"The Karen Silkwood Story," *Los Alamos Science No. 23*, 1995.

Kleiner, Diana J., "Silkwood, Karen Gay," *Handbook of Texas Online*, tshaonline .org/handbook/articles/fsi35, November 23, 2010.

Kohn, Howard, "Karen Silkwood Was Right in Plutonium Scandal," *Rolling Stone*, October 20, 1977.

Kroll, Jack, "The Reluctant Superstar," *Ladies' Home Journal*, May 1985.

Krupp, Charla, "How Close to the Real Story?," *Glamour*, January 1984.

Latson, Jennifer, "The Nuclear-Safety Activist Whose Mysterious Death Inspired a Movie," *Time*, November 13, 2014.

Luscombe, Belinda, "7 Myths About Meryl," *Time*, June 19, 2006.

Maychick, Diana, *Meryl Streep: The Reluctant Superstar*, St. Martin's Press, New York, 1984.

Mizoguchi, Karen, "Having the Time of Their Lives! Meryl Streep & Cher Share a Kiss at *Mamma Mia* Premiere in London," people.com, July 16, 2018.

Montgomery, Paul L., "Throngs Fill Manhattan to Protest Nuclear Weapons," *New York Times*, June 13, 1982.

"Nation: Poisoned by Plutonium," *Time*, March 19, 1979.

Passafiume, Andrea, "Behind the Camera on Silkwood," tcm.com, undated.

Rashke, Richard L., *The Killing of Karen Silkwood*, Houghton Mifflin, Boston, 1981.

Stogsdill, Sheila, "Forty Years Later, Silkwood's Children Reflect," tulsaworld.com, November 10, 2014.

Watch What Happens, Bravo, August 9, 2012.

Weaver, Hilary, "Cher and Meryl Streep's Friendship: A History," vanityfair.com, July 17, 2018.

Intermission: Meryl's Antinuke Crusade

Carasik Dion, Diane, "Catching Up with Meryl Streep," *Dial*, July 1984.

Green, Jesse, "What, Meryl Worry?," *New York Times*, July 25, 2004.

Kimball, Daryl G., "Looking Back: The Nuclear Arms Control Legacy of Ronald Reagan," armscontrol.org, July 8, 2004.

Kroll, Jack, "The Reluctant Superstar," *Ladies' Home Journal*, May 1985.

Lebow, Richard Ned, and Janice Gross Stein, "Reagan and the Russians," *Atlantic*, February 1994.

Montgomery, Paul L., "Throngs Fill Manhattan to Protest Nuclear Weapons," *New York Times*, June 13, 1982.

Schell, Jonathan, "The Spirit of June 12," *Nation*, July 2, 2007.

Skow, John, "What Makes Meryl Magic," *Time*, September 7, 1981.

Streep, Meryl, speech to Vassar College grads in Poughkeepsie, New York, on May 23, 1983.

"Streep Throat," *Los Angeles Herald-Examiner*, August 28, 1984.

Chapter 5: Meryl the Lion

AFI Tribute to Meryl Streep, USA Network, June 21, 2004.

Capshaw, Kate, note to Sydney Pollack, dated June 16, 1984, courtesy of Margaret Herrick Library special collections.

Champlin, Charles, "Meryl Streep as Silkwood and Herself," *Los Angeles Times*, December 18, 1983.

Charles Dance's quotes about Meryl Streep and Shirley MacLaine, IMDb.com.

Commentary by Meryl Streep and Sydney Pollack, *Out of Africa*, DVD, Universal Pictures, February 29, 2000.

Darrach, Brad, "Enchanting, Colorless, Glacial, Fearless, Sneaky, Seductive, Manipulative, Magical Meryl," *Life*, December 1987.

Dinesen, Isak, *Out of Africa*, Modern Library ed., Random House, New York, 1992.

Dreifus, Claudia, "Meryl Streep: Why I've Taken a Year Off for Motherhood," *Ladies' Home Journal*, April 1984.

Ebert, Roger, "Silkwood," *Chicago Sun-Times*, December 14, 1983.

Goodman, Joan, "Keeping It in the Family," *Sunday Times*, January 20, 1991.

Greene, Bob, "Streep," *Esquire*, December 1984.

Haskell, Molly, "Who'll Get Oscar?," *Vogue*, February 1983.

Interview with Ian Baker.

Interview with David Hare.

Interview with Ed Pressman.

Interview with Fred Schepisi.

"Isak Dinesen," *Encyclopedia Britannica*, 2016.

Kael, Pauline, "Tootsie, Gandhi, and Sophie," *New Yorker*, December 27, 1982.

Longworth, Karina, *Meryl Streep: Anatomy of an Actor*, Phaidon Press, London, UK, 2014.

Mamie Gummer birth announcement, *Time,* August 29, 1983.

Maslin, Janet, "Styron's 'Sophie's Choice,'" *New York Times,* December 10, 1982.

Maychick, Diana, *Meryl Streep: The Reluctant Superstar,* St. Martin's Press, New York, 1984.

Palmer, Martyn, "Meryl Up Close," *Good Housekeeping,* August 2008.

Passafiume, Andrea, "The Critics' Corner: *Silkwood,*" tcm.com, undated.

"Oscar-Winning Artists Share Stories at New Yorker Festival," makeupmag.com, October 19, 2014.

Rea, Steven, "Meryl Streep, Acting Funny," *Home Viewer,* November 1986.

Rovin, Jeff, "I Want It All—But in Manageable Proportions," *Los Angeles Herald-Examiner,* August 17, 1986.

Schneider, Wolf, "Don't Stop Talking," *Hollywood Reporter,* June 10, 2004.

Schneider, Wolf, "Power," *Hollywood Reporter,* June 10, 2004.

Siskel, Gene, "Meryl Streep Not Looking for a Role as American Icon," *Chicago Tribune,* July 20, 1986.

Skow, John, "What Makes Meryl Magic," *Time,* September 7, 1981.

Streep, Meryl, speech to Vassar College grads in Poughkeepsie, New York, on May 23, 1983.

Transcript from 1988 Hollywood Foreign Press Association conference for *A Cry in the Dark,* courtesy of Margaret Herrick Library special collections.

Watch What Happens, Bravo, August 9, 2012.

Intermission: The Meryl Effect

Bradley, Ryan, "The Accent Whisperers of Hollywood," *New York Times Magazine,* July 20, 2017.

Interview with Diane Kamp.

Interview with Rocio Rocier.

Mann, Roderick, "Seymour Loses One, Wins One," *Los Angeles Times,* December 21, 1985.

Wilkinson, Alec, "Talk This Way," *New Yorker,* November 9, 2009.

Chapter 6: Meryl the Heartbreaker

Attanassio, Paul, "Meryl Streep & the Human Resonance," *Washington Post,* July 25, 1986.

Audience feedback to *Out of Africa* by Universal Studios analyst David Saunders, dated August 28, 1985, Margaret Herrick Library special collections.

Brown, Scott. "Streep at the Top," *Hollywood Reporter*, November 1983.

Campbell, Virginia, "Beloved Neurotic," *Movieline*, October 18 to October 24, 1985.

Canby, Vincent, "Screen: 'Out of Africa,' Starring Meryl Streep," *New York Times*, December 18, 1985.

Carlson, Erin, *I'll Have What She's Having*, Hachette Books, New York, 2017. (Why yes, I cited myself!)

Conconi, Chuck, "Divorce with a Heartburn Cause," *Washington Post*, June 28, 1985.

Ebert, Roger, "Heartburn," *Chicago Sun-Times*, July 25, 1986.

Eliot, Marc, *Nicholson*, Three Rivers Press, New York, 2013.

Haskell, Molly, "Hiding in the Spotlight," *Ms.*, December 1988.

Interview with Robert Greenhut.

Item about Meryl requesting Jack Nicholson do "equally sexually explicit" in *The Postman Always Rings Twice*, *People*, February 18, 1980.

Item about Meryl (then pregnant with her third child), saying she did not plan to work for another year, *Variety*, March 25, 1986.

Kroll, Jack, "The Reluctant Superstar," *Ladies' Home Journal*, May 1985.

Letter from African cast and crew members of *Out of Africa* to the editor of the *Kenyu Times*, dated February 12, 1985, Margaret Herrick Library special collections.

Longworth, Karina, *Meryl Streep: Anatomy of an Actor*, Phaidon Press, London, UK, 2014.

Rea, Steven, "Meryl Streep, Acting Funny," *Home Viewer*, November 1986.

Schneider, Wolf, "Don't Stop Talking," *Hollywood Reporter*, June 10, 2004.

Siskel, Gene, "Meryl Streep not Looking for a Role as American Icon," *Chicago Tribune*, July 20, 1986.

"Sounds Like Heartburn," an item reporting Meryl's $3.5 million salary in 1986, *People*, September 8, 1986.

Witchel, Alex, "Mandy Patinkin: 'I Behaved Abominably,'" *New York Times Magazine*, August 21, 2013.

Chapter 7: Meryl the Martyr

A Cry in the Dark, boxofficemojo.com.

Abramowitz, Rachel, *Is That a Gun in Your Pocket? Women's Experience of Power in Hollywood*, Random House, New York, 2000.

AFI Tribute to Meryl Streep, USA Network, June 21, 2004.

Attanassio, Paul, "Meryl Streep & the Human Resonance," *Washington Post*, July 25, 1986.

Chamberlain, Lindy, on receiving $1.3 million in compensation following her exoneration, lindychamberlain.com/files/Compensation.pdf.

De Vries, Hilary, "Meryl Acts Up," *Los Angeles Times Magazine*, September 9, 1990.

Ebert, Roger, "A Cry in the Dark," *Chicago Sun-Times*, November 11, 1988.

Eliot, Marc, *Nicholson*, Three Rivers Press, New York, 2013.

Fink, Mitchell, "Happy Birthday, Jack," *Los Angeles Herald-Examiner*, April 22, 1987.

Hammer, Mike, "Why Meryl Takes Chances," *Ladies' Home Journal*, October 1988.

Handelman, David, "Winning Streep," *Vogue*, April 1992.

Haskell, Molly, "Hiding in the Spotlight," *Ms.*, December 1988.

" 'Heartburn' Heat?," *Press-Telegram*, August 31, 1986.

Interview with Ian Baker.

Interview with Fred Schepisi.

"Ironweed: Miscellaneous Notes," tcm.com.

Item about Meryl's reported $4 million salary for *A Cry in the Dark*, *Variety*, April 20, 1987.

Kempley, Rita, "A Cry in the Dark," *Washington Post*, November 11, 1988.

Transcript from 1988 Hollywood Foreign Press Association conference for *A Cry in the Dark*, courtesy of Margaret Herrick Library special collections.

Wasserstein, Wendy, "Streeping Beauty," *Interview*, December 1988.

Chapter 8: Middle-Aged Meryl

Abramowitz, Rachel, *Is That a Gun in Your Pocket? Women's Experience of Power in Hollywood*, Random House, New York, 2000.

Bennetts, Leslie, "About Meryl," *Vanity Fair*, January 2010.

Denby, David, "Meryl Streep Is Madonna and Siren as *The French Lieutenant's Woman*," New York, September 21, 1981.

De Vries, Hilary, "Meryl Acts Up," *Los Angeles Times Magazine*, September 9, 1990.

Garey, Juliann, "Meryl Streep," *Us*, October 1994.

Goodman, Joan, "Keeping It in the Family," *Sunday Times*, January 20, 1991.

Handelman, David, "Winning Streep," *Vogue*, April 1992.

Hopler, Robert, "Meryl as Co-star and Coach," *Variety*, April 14, 2008.

Interview with Robert Greenhut.

Interview with Susan Seidelman.

Plaskin, Glenn, "Reflections from the Edge," *Press-Telegram*, September 16, 1990.

Schneider, Wolf, "Power," *Hollywood Reporter,* June 10, 2004.

See, Carolyn, "Heartfelt, Original Outtakes from the Life of an Actress," *Los Angeles Times,* July 27, 1987.

Intermission: Meryl and Carrie's Forgotten Screenplay

Boboltz, Sara, "Meryl Streep Sings Carrie Fisher's Favorite Song at Memorial with Billie Lourd," huffingtonpost.com, January 6, 2017.

Handelman, David, "Winning Streep," *Vogue,* April 1992.

King, Andrea, "Fisher-Streep Pic May Go to Nichols," *Hollywood Reporter,* August 16, 1991.

Scott, Walter, "Personality Parade," *Parade,* February 12, 1995.

Chapter 9: Meryl the Immortal

Abramowitz, Rachel, *Is That a Gun in Your Pocket? Women's Experience of Power in Hollywood,* Random House, New York, 2000.

Aikman, Becky, *Off the Cliff,* Penguin Press, New York, 2017.

Archerd, Army, "Just for Variety," *Variety,* April 7, 1992.

Bennetts, Leslie, "About Meryl," *Vanity Fair,* January 2010.

Canby, Vincent, "Streep Spars with Barr in a Comedy of Revenge," *New York Times,* December 8, 1989.

Darrach, Brad, "Enchanting, Colorless, Glacial, Fearless, Sneaky, Seductive, Manipulative, Magical Meryl," *Life,* December 1987.

Easton, Nina J., "Meryl's Latest Accent Is a Laugh," *Los Angeles Times,* December 10, 1989.

Ebert, Roger, "She-Devil," *Chicago Sun-Times,* December 8, 1989.

De Vries, Hilary, "Meryl Acts Up," *Los Angeles Times Magazine,* September 9, 1990.

Dutka, Elaine, "Meryl Streep Attacks Hollywood's Gender Gap at SAG Conference," *Los Angeles Times,* August 3, 1990.

Handelman, David, "Winning Streep," *Vogue,* April 1992.

Hinson, Hal, "Postcards from the Edge," *Washington Post,* September 14, 1990.

Interview with Albert Brooks.

Interview with Goldie Hawn.

Item about Kevin Kline dropping out of *Death Becomes Her, Screen International,* October 11, 1991.

Item about Meryl backing out of an Oscars performance due to her pregnancy, *Variety*, March 25, 1991.

Longworth, Karina, *Meryl Streep: Anatomy of an Actor*, Phaidon Press, London, UK, 2014.

McHenry, Justin, "The Reasoning Behind Meryl's *Mamma Mia! Here We Go Again* Plotline," vulture.com, July 19, 2018.

Meryl Streep interview, *Fresh Air*, NPR, February 6, 2012.

Rosen, Marjorie, "Who's So Vain?," *People*, August 24, 1992.

She-Devil, boxofficemojo.com.

Smith, Liz, "Streep's Losing Streak," *Los Angeles Times*, May 20, 1991.

Travers, Peter, "Meryl Streep," *Rolling Stone*, November 15, 2007.

Voland, John, "Streep Switching to CAA from ICM," *Hollywood Reporter*, May 15, 1991.

Weinraub, Bernard, "Her Peculiar Career," *New York Times Magazine*, September 18, 1994.

Chapter 10: Meryl the River Goddess

Abramowitz, Rachel, *Is That a Gun in Your Pocket? Women's Experience of Power in Hollywood*, Random House, New York, 2000.

Adams, Sam, "Interview: Carrie Fisher," avclub.com, August 13, 2011.

Azzopardi, Chris, "A Candid Meryl Streep Opens Up About Being 'in Love' with Gay People and Her Iconic LGBT Roles," pridesource.com, August 9, 2016.

Case, Brian, "Hidden Depths," *Time Out London*, February 22 to March 1, 1995.

Elder, Sean, "Getting In on the Action," *Vogue*, July 1994.

Eller, Claudia, "Streep Getting into 'Spirits,'" *Variety*, September 10, 1992.

Garey, Juliann, "Meryl Streep," *Us*, October 1994.

Gittelson, Natalie, "Meryl Streep: Surprising Superstar," *McCall's*, March 1983.

Handelman, David, "Winning Streep," *Vogue*, April 1992.

Holter, Rick, interview with Meryl about *The River Wild*, *Dallas Morning News*, October 1994, archived at the Margaret Herrick Library in Los Angeles.

Interview with Arlene Burns.

Interview with Thomas Mack.

Interview with Joseph Mazzello.

Item about *The Firm* excluding Meryl from its cast, *New York*, September 21, 1992.

Kennedy, Dana, "Meryl, Revealed," *More*, December 2002 / January 2003.

Maslin, Janet, "Squeezing the Humor out of Death," *New York Times*, July 31, 1992.

Murphy, Ryan, "The 'Great-Ephemeral-Quality' A-List Is Quite Long in Hollywood, It Appears," *Los Angeles Times*, October 4, 1992.

Price, Michael H., "Meryl Streep Rides Out Skepticism," *Press-Telegram*, October 2, 1994.

Puchko, Kristy, "The Gloriously Queer Afterlife of *Death Becomes Her*," *Vanity Fair*, August 3, 2017.

Schaefer, Stephen, "The Latest Action Hero," *Us*, August 1993.

Intermission: Meryl the Environmentalist

"Apples: U.S. Officially Declares Fruit Safe," *Los Angeles Times*, 1989.

Champlin, Charles, "Just an Ordinary Connecticut Housewife," *Los Angeles Times*, November 6, 1988.

Gordon, Wendy, "Role of a Lifetime: Meryl Streep as Eco-Activist Mom," marias farmcountrykitchen.com, February 28, 2012.

Gunset, George, "Apple Chemical Alar off Market," *Chicago Tribune*, June 3, 1989.

"Ms. Streep Goes to Washington to Stop a Bitter Harvest," *People*, March 20, 1989.

Transcript from 1988 Hollywood Foreign Press Association conference for *A Cry in the Dark*, courtesy of Margaret Herrick Library special collections.

Wasserstein, Wendy, "Streeping Beauty," *Interview*, December 1988.

Chapter 11: Meryl the Romantic

Abramowitz, Rachel, *Is That a Gun in Your Pocket? Women's Experience of Power in Hollywood*, Random House, New York, 2000.

Archerd, Army, "Just for Variety," *Variety*, August 15, 1994.

Brody, Richard, "Clint Eastwood and Pauline Kael," newyorker.com, October 20, 2011.

Commentary from "An Old-Fashioned Love Story: Making *The Bridges of Madison County*," *The Bridges of Madison County*, Warner Home Video, DVD, 2008.

Garey, Juliann, "Meryl Streep," *Us*, October 1994.

Hammond, Pete, "Two-Time Oscar Winner Jane Fonda Back in the Hunt for 'Youth' Three Decades After Her Last Nomination," deadline.com, November 28, 2015.

Levitt, Shelley, "Heart Land," *People*, June 26, 1995.

"Make Her Day," *People*, June 19, 1995.

Meryl Streep interview, *Fresh Air*, NPR, February 6, 2012.

Miller, Mark, and Karen Schoemer, "Streep Shoots the Rapids," *Newsweek*, September 26, 1994.

Pakula, Hannah, "Meryl, Unrehearsed," *More*, October 1999.

Parker, Donna, "Streep Takes 'Bridges' Leap," *Hollywood Reporter*, August 15, 1994.

"Quotes of the Week," *Screen International*, August 1994.

Rich, Frank, "One-Week Stand," *New York Times Magazine*, July 25, 1993.

" 'River' to 'Bridges,' " *Variety*, August 15, 1994.

The River Wild, boxofficemojo.com.

Smith, Liz, "Wild Response for Streep," *Los Angeles Times*, May 23, 1994.

Transcript from 1994 Hollywood Foreign Press Association conference for *The River Wild*, courtesy of Margaret Herrick Library special collections.

Watch What Happens, Bravo, August 9, 2012.

Weinraub, Bernard, "Her Peculiar Career," *New York Times Magazine*, September 18, 1994.

Woulfe, Sharon, "Bart's Voice a Real Character," *Pantagraph*, November 3, 2001.

Intermission: The Ones That Got Away

Archerd, Army, "Just for Variety," *Variety*, June 23, 1989.

Canby, Vincent, "Two New Triumphs Cap a Fine Year for Actresses," *New York Times*, December 12, 1982.

De Vries, Hilary, "Meryl Acts Up," *Los Angeles Times Magazine*, September 9, 1990.

Easton, Nina J., "Meryl's Latest Accent Is a Laugh," *Los Angeles Times*, December 10, 1989.

"Furthermore," *People*, February 18, 1980.

Item about Meryl recording a dub for a potential role in the movie version of *Evita*, *Los Angeles Herald-Examiner*, October 19, 1988.

Item about Meryl saying she would have "died" to star in *Punchline*, *Los Angeles Herald-Examiner*, October 28, 1988.

"Meryl Streep: 'I'm Not Always Happy,' " *Talks*, July 13, 2011.

Schaefer, Stephen, "The Latest Action Hero," *Us*, August 1993.

Smith, Liz, "Streep's Losing Streak," *Los Angeles Times*, May 20, 1991.

Watch What Happens, Bravo, August 9, 2012.

Weinraub, Bernard, "Her Peculiar Career," *New York Times Magazine*, September 18, 1994.

Chapter 12: Mozart Meryl

"Another Soccer Mom," *Press-Telegram*, January 19, 1997.

Bennetts, Leslie, "About Meryl," *Vanity Fair*, January 2010.

The Bridges of Madison County, boxofficemojo.com.

Case, Brian, "Hidden Depths," *Time Out*, February 22 to March 1, 1995.

Corliss, Richard, "When Erotic Heat Turns into Love Light," *Time*, June 5, 1995.

Dawn, Randee, "Meryl Streep," *Hollywood Reporter*, September 1999.

Ebert, Roger, "Music of the Heart," *Chicago Sun-Times*, October 29, 1999.

Eder, Richard, "Thomas Babe's 'Taken in Marriage' at the Public Theater," *New York Times*, February 27, 1979.

Feiwell, Jill, "Streep Plays 'Music' with the Big Boys," *Variety*, October 15, 1999.

Forster, Evan, "Meryl Streep: A Star in Any Language," *Biography Magazine*, September 1998.

Galloway, Stephen, "Streep, Keaton Are Entering 'Marvin's Room,'" *Hollywood Reporter*, March 24, 1995.

Gilbert, Matthew, "Meryl the Mom—In Life and in 'Marvin's Room,'" *Los Angeles Times*, January 2, 1997.

Gritten, David, "In Step with the Team," *Los Angeles Times*, November 8, 1998.

Interview with Carl Franklin.

Interview with Roberta Guaspari.

Interview with Jerry Zaks.

Magee, Audrey, "Tough Exam for Streep in Irish Village School," *Times* (London), September 24, 1993.

"Meryl's Music Opens with $3.7M," *Screen International*, November 5, 1999.

"More Blonde Ambition," *Los Angeles Magazine*, October 1990.

Palmer, Martyn, "Ready, Willing and More Than Able," *Times* (London), January 17, 2000.

"Passionate Parent," *People*, January 27, 1997.

Smith, Liz, "De Niro, Streep in *Before?*," *Los Angeles Times*, August 24, 1992.

Smith, Liz, "Nobody Knows," *Good Housekeeping*, September 1998.

Smith, Liz, "Streep Can't Resist Challenge," *Los Angeles Times*, August 20, 1998.

Weinraub, Bernard, "Her Peculiar Career," *New York Times Magazine*, September 18, 1994.

Chapter 13: Meryl the Wallflower

Brantley, Ben, "Streep Meets Chekhov, up in Central Park," *New York Times*, August 13, 2001.

Brodesser, Claude, "Streep Eyes 'Adaptation,'" *Variety*, September 6, 2000.

Doge, Annie, "Meryl Streep's Former Greenwich Village Townhouse Asks $28.5M," 6sqft.com, September 28, 2016.

Fleming, Michael, "Good as Gold," *Variety*, November 18, 2002.

Goldfarb, Brad, "Facing the Myths with the World's Number One Actor's Actor," *Interview*, December 2002 / January 2003.

Goodridge, Mike, "The Grande Dame of the Cutting Edge," *Screen International*, February 21, 2003.

Green, Jesse, "What, Meryl Worry?," *New York Times*, July 25, 2004.

Interview with Carl Franklin.

Interview with David Hare.

Kennedy, Dana, "Meryl, Revealed," *More*, December 2002 / January 2003.

King, Tom, "Meryl Streep Makes History, Tracks," *Wall Street Journal*, February 14, 2003.

"Mary W. Streep, 86, Artist, Volunteer," newjerseyhills.com, October 4, 2001.

McNamara, Brendan, "Adapt This," *UR Chicago*, January 2003.

Meryl Streep interview, *Fresh Air*, NPR, February 6, 2012.

Perry, Kevin E. G., "The New Yorker's Susan Orlean on Crafting a Story and Being Played by Meryl Streep in Adaptation," www.gq-magazine.co.uk, April 16, 2012.

"Return Engagements," *People*, April 9, 2001.

Schneider, Karen S., "The Great One," *People*, February 3, 2003.

Schneider, Wolf, "A Class Act," *Hollywood Reporter*, June 10, 2004.

Schneider, Wolf, "Power," *Hollywood Reporter*, June 10, 2004.

Shirkani, K. D., "Indies Take Shape," *Variety*, September 24, 1999.

"Trophy Girl," *Us*, December 16, 2002.

White, Lesley, "Her Significant Others," *Sunday Times*, October 31, 2004.

Winters, Laura, "Master Class," *Vogue*, December 2002.

Chapter 14: Meryl the Shape-Shifter

AFI Tribute to Meryl Streep, USA Network, June 21, 2004.

Butler, Isaac, and Dan Kois, *The World Only Spins Forward: The Ascent of Angels in America*, Bloomsbury USA, February 13, 2018.

Chang, Justin, "Meryl Streep, 'The Manchurian Candidate,'" *Variety*, January 3, 2005.

Feeney, Mark, "Hail to the Streep," *Boston Sunday Globe*, July 25, 2004.

Green, Jesse, "What, Meryl Worry?," *New York Times*, July 25, 2004.

Interview with Michael Haley.

Interview with Justin Kirk.

Interview with Mark Livolsi.

Jonathan Demme and the Making of "The Manchurian Candidate," Paramount Pictures, 2004.

Molloy, Joanna, and George Rush, "Lotsa Mileage in These Star Vehicles," *New York Daily News*, December 27, 2002.

"Quote of the Week," *People*, December 22, 2003.

Reuters, "Oscar Politicking Disturbs Streep," *Los Angeles Times*, February 5, 2003.

Schneider, Karen S., "The Great One," *People*, February 3, 2003.

Schneider, Wolf, "A Class Act," *Hollywood Reporter*, June 10, 2004.

White, Lesley, "Her Significant Others," *Sunday Times*, October 31, 2004.

Chapter 15: Meryl the Editrix

"Drama Queen," *Hollywood Reporter*, December 2006.

Fishman, Elana, "10 Years After 'The Devil Wears Prada,' Patricia Field Explains How the Costumes Came Together," racked.com, June 28, 2016.

Fleming, Michael, "Good as Gold," *Variety*, November 18, 2002.

Foreman, Liz, "Streep Has Deal with 'the Devil,'" *Hollywood Reporter*, May 2, 2005.

French, Serena, "The $1 Million Wardrobe of 'The Devil Wears Prada,'" *New York Post*, June 21, 2006.

Grove, Martin A., "Oscar-Worthy 'Devil Wears Prada' Most Enjoyable Film in Long Time: 'The Hollywood Reporter,'" thebookstandard.com, June 28, 2006.

Hasan, Lima, and Katie Hinman, "Anne Hathaway's Ex Raffaello Follieri 'Happy' for Actress, Ready to 'Live My Life' After Prison," abcnews.go.com, June 27, 2012.

Hofler, Robert, "Meryl as Co-star and Coach," *Variety*, April 14, 2008.

Interview with Angel De Angelis.

Interview with Wendy Finerman.

Interview with David Frankel.

Interview with Mark Livolsi.

Interview with Aline Brosh McKenna.

Interview with Zac Posen.

Kaplan, James, "I Chose Family," *Parade,* May 28, 2006.

Kinetz, Erika, "Devil's in the Follow-Up," *New York Times,* November 6, 2005.

Lacher, Irene, "Did She Spill Something?," *Los Angeles Times,* May 28, 2003.

Lamphier, Jason, "Playing *Devil's* Advocate," out.com, undated.

LaSalle, Mick, "Terrorist Attacks, Corporate Control, Election Controversy: Sound Familiar? 'The Manchurian Candidate' Has It All," *San Francisco Chronicle,* July 30, 2004.

The Late Show with Stephen Colbert, CBS, May 24, 2018.

Lieberman, Paul, "Character Building," *Los Angeles Times,* October 23, 2005.

Luscombe, Belinda, "7 Myths About Meryl," *Time,* June 19, 2006.

McKenna, Aline Brosh, *The Devil Wears Prada* screenplay, 20th Century Fox, 2006, and the last iteration script (2005), https://johnaugust.com/Assets/DEVIL _WEARS_PRADA_Full_Script.pdf.

Miller, Julie, "How Meryl Streep Terrified *The Devil Wears Prada*'s Screenwriter," vanityfair.com, June 29, 2016.

Molloy, Joanna, and George Rush, "Wintour Aide's Novel Is Conde Nasty," *New York Daily News,* March 7, 2003.

Schneider, Wolf, "A Class Act," *Hollywood Reporter,* June 10, 2004.

Setoodeh, Ramin, " 'The Devil Wears Prada' Turns 10: Meryl Streep, Anne Hathaway and Emily Blunt Tell All," *Variety,* June 23, 2016.

Silman, Anna, "Remember the Time Anne Hathaway Dated a Con Man?," thecut .com, June 8, 2018.

Silverman, Stephen M., "Raffaello Follieri Sentenced to 4 ¹⁄₂ Years," people.com, October 23, 2008.

"Streep Smarts," *People,* April 24, 2006.

"There's Something About Her," telegraphindia.com, September 18, 2006.

Thompson, Anne, " 'The Devil Wears Prada' at 10: Meryl Streep and More on How Their Risky Project Became a Massive Hit," indiewire.com, July 1, 2016.

Today, NBC, April 6, 2018.

The View, ABC, June 30, 2006.

Weisberger, Lauren, *The Devil Wears Prada,* Doubleday, New York, 2003.

Wickman, Kase, "The Most Iconic 'Devil Wears Prada' Scene Almost Didn't Make It into the Movie," *New York Post,* June 23, 2016.

WWD staff, "Wintour Tales," *Women's Wear Daily,* undated.

Intermission: The *Devil Wears Prada* Career Bump

Jordan, Julie, and Jen Juneau, "Stanley Tucci and Felicity Blunt Welcome Daughter Emilia Giovanna," people.com, June 12, 2018.

Chapter 16: Meryl the Nun

Abramowitz, Rachel, "She Has to Laugh," *Los Angeles Times,* November 30, 2008.
Amiel, Barbara, "The 'Devil' I Know," *Telegraph,* July 2, 2006.
Barbara Walters' 10 Most Fascinating People, ABC, December 12, 2006.
Bennetts, Leslie, "About Meryl," *Vanity Fair,* January 2010.
Corliss, Richard, "The Lions Roar," *Time,* November 12, 2007.
The Devil Wears Prada, boxofficemojo.com.
Fleming, Michael, "She's One Hot 'Mamma,'" *Variety,* January 11, 2007.
Interview with John Patrick Shanley.
Jeffries, Stuart, "A Legend Lightens Up," *Guardian,* July 2, 2008.
Kennedy, Dana, "Meryl, Revealed," *More,* December 2002 / January 2003.
Mamma Mia!, boxofficemojo.com.
"Meet the Acid Queen of New York Fashion," *Guardian,* June 25, 2006.
Meryl Streep interview, *Fresh Air,* NPR, February 6, 2012.
Palmer, Martyn, "Meryl, Up Close," *Good Housekeeping,* August 2008.
Scott, A. O., "In 'The Devil Wears Prada,' Meryl Streep Plays the Terror of the Fashion World," *New York Times,* June 30, 2006.
"10 Most Excellent Things: Mamma Mia!," *Mamma Mia!,* DVD, Universal Pictures, 2018.

Intermission: Viola's Breakthrough

Birnbaum, Debra, "Viola Davis on #MeToo: 'If You're Dedicated to Change, Let It Cost You Something,'" variety.com, February 14, 2018.
Golden Globe Awards, NBC, January 8, 2017.
Interview with John Patrick Shanley.
Macdonald, Moira, "Actress Viola Davis Is No Stranger to 'The Help,'" seattletimes.com, August 8, 2011.
Viola Davis interview, *News & Views,* NPR, December 10, 2008.

Chapter 17: Meryl Masters the Art of French Cooking

Abramowitz, Rachel, "It Only Gets Better," *Los Angeles Times*, September 12, 2009.

Abramowitz, Rachel, "She Has to Laugh," *Los Angeles Times*, November 30, 2008.

Bennetts, Leslie, "About Meryl," *Vanity Fair*, January 2010.

Fernandez, Jay A., "She's Really Cooking," *Hollywood Reporter*, July 7, 2009.

Fleming, Michael, "Streep Eyes U Romance," *Variety*, August 7, 2008.

Fox, Marisa, "Ladies Who Lunch," *Ladies' Home Journal*, August 2019.

Interview with Lake Bell.

Interview with Stephen Goldblatt.

Interview with Larry Mark.

Kit, Borys, "Femme Power Trio to Top Uni Comedy," *Hollywood Reporter*, October 25, 2010.

Meryl Streep interview, Oscars Red Carpet, *Access Hollywood*, 2010.

Meryl Streep interview, Oscars Governors Ball, CNN, 2010.

Pomerantz, Dorothy, "Hollywood's Top-Earning Actresses," forbes.com, July 1, 2009.

Rice, Jerry, "Meryl Streep," *Variety*, December 7, 2009.

Ryan, Beth, "Nancy Meyers: Her 7 Dreamiest, Creamiest Movie Houses," telegraph .co.uk, October 8, 2015.

Schneider, Karen S., "The Great One," *People*, February 3, 2003.

Scott, A. O., "Two for the Stove," *New York Times*, August 6, 2009.

Simmons, Leslie, "Child's Play for Streep in Col's 'Julia,'" *Hollywood Reporter*, November 1, 2007.

Us Weekly staff, "Mamie Gummer Is Engaged!," usmagazine.com, October 19, 2009.

Chapter 18: Meryl the Stateswoman

Abramovitch, Seth, "Meryl Streep Learning Guitar for Diablo Cody Movie," *Hollywood Reporter*, August 8, 2014.

Babington, Charles, "Meryl Streep Stumps for ERA," Associated Press, June 23, 2015.

Carlson, Erin, "Meryl Streep Calls 'Hope Springs' Co-star Tommy Lee Jones '50 Shades of Grumpy,'" hollywoodreporter.com, August 8, 2012.

Child, Ben, "Meryl Streep on Feminist Question: 'I'm a Humanist,'" *Guardian*, October 2, 2015.

Chitwood, Adam, "New Posters for August: Osage County, Labor Day, The Double, Blood Ties, and Delivery Man," collider.com, October 15, 2013.

"Depp, Streep May Join Disney's 'Into the Woods,'" upi.com, April 26, 2013.

Ebert, Roger, "The Iron Lady," *Chicago Sun-Times*, January 11, 2012.

Feinberg, Scott, "Walt Disney's Grandniece Agrees with Meryl Streep: He Was 'Racist,'" hollywoodreporter.com, January 15, 2014.

Fleming, Mike, "Meryl Streep to Play Chief Elder in 'The Giver,'" deadline.com, August 6, 2013.

Ford, Rebecca, "Meryl Streep on Margaret Thatcher's Death: 'To Me She Was a Figure of Awe,'" *Hollywood Reporter*, April 8, 2013.

Freydkin, Donna, "Julia Roberts Lets It All Go in 'August: Osage County,'" *USA Today*, December 25, 2013.

George, Jerry, "Why Meryl Streep Hates Julia Roberts' Guts!," *National Enquirer*, November 26, 2013.

Halberg, Morgan, "Mamie Gummer Is Already Selling Her Charming Chelsea Home," observer.com, July 17, 2017.

Harless, Kailey, and Iona Kirby, "Mom Will Make It Better! Meryl Streep Comforts Daughter Mamie After Her Split from Husband Benjamin," www.dailymail .co.uk, April 2, 2013.

Jimmy Kimmel Live!, ABC, January 13, 2012.

Jimmy Kimmel Live!, ABC, January 15, 2014.

Marcus, Bennett, "Meryl Streep Slams Walt Disney, Celebrates Emma Thompson as a 'Rabid, Man-Eating Feminist,'" vanityfair.com, January 8, 2014.

Marrs, Sarah, "But Why Must It ALWAYS Be Girl Sh*t?," laineygossip.com, September 27, 2013.

"Meryl Streep Attends Parliament for Thatcher Research," independent.co.uk, January 20, 2011.

Meryl Streep interview, *Fresh Air*, NPR, February 6, 2012.

Nerada, Pippa, "Harvey Weinstein's 'Creepy' Obsession with Michelle Williams Revealed," marieclaire.com.au, March 20, 2018.

Pemberton, Max, "The Iron Lady and Margaret Thatcher's Dementia: Why This Despicable Film Makes Voyeurs of Us All," *Telegraph*, January 14, 2012.

Ravitz, Justin, "Mamie Gummer, Husband Benjamin Walker Split," usmagazine .com, March 30, 2013.

Setoodeh, Ramin, "Meryl Streep Blasts Walt Disney at National Board of Review Dinner," variety.com, January 8, 2014.

Siegel, Tatiana, "Meryl Streep to Play Maria Callas in HBO Movie," hollywood reporter.com, June 19, 2014.

Walters, Joanna, "#MeToo a Revolution That Can't Be Stopped, Says Time's Up Co-founder," *Guardian*, October 21, 2018.

Williams, Christian, "Scenes from the Battle of the Sexes," *Washington Post*, December 17, 1982.

Williams, Lauren, "Meryl Streep: Why I Almost Turned Down Oscar-Nominated Role in August: Osage County," metro.co.uk, January 22, 2014.

Intermission: Celebrity Streepers

David Fox, Jesse, "Jennifer Lawrence on Staring at Meryl Streep," vulture.com, January 2, 2013.

E! Live from the Red Carpet: The 2018 Golden Globe Awards, E!, January 7, 2018.

Flint, Hannah, " 'Ocean's 8' Cast Say the Abundance of White Male Film Critics Is 'Unfair,' " uk.movies.yahoo.com, June 15, 2018.

Haas, Brian, "Zoe Kravitz Dishes on 'Big Little Lies' and Working with Meryl 'F**king' Streep!," etonline.com, March 16, 2018.

Palmer, Tamara, "Not That We're Shocked, but Meryl Streep Gave Billy Eichner the Most Incredible Life Advice," bravotv.com, August 10, 2017.

Chapter 19: Meryl the Superhero

Abrams, Rachel, and Jodi Kantor, "Gwyneth Paltrow, Angelina Jolie and Others Say Weinstein Harassed Them," *New York Times*, October 10, 2017.

Ali, Yashar, "Exclusive: Meryl Streep Responds to Rose McGowan's Criticism," huffingtonpost.com, December 19, 2017.

Boot, William, "Exclusive: Sony Hack Reveals Jennifer Lawrence Is Paid Less Than Her Male Co-stars," www.thedailybeast.com, December 12, 2014.

Borchers, Callum, "Meryl Streep Was Right: Donald Trump Did Mock a Disabled Reporter," *Washington Post*, January 9, 2017.

Buckley, Cara, "Meryl Streep, Kate Winslet and Glenn Close Speak Out on Harvey Weinstein," *New York Times*, October 9, 2017.

Carlson, Erin, "Outrageous Sexism in Hollywood Exposed in New Blog," fortune.com, May 8, 2015.

Chi, Paul, "Meryl Streep Is Even Bad at Singing Badly, Says Stephen Frears," vanityfair.com, August 12, 2016.

Cox, Gordon, "Meryl Streep Funds Lab for Women Screenwriters over 40," variety
.com, April 19, 2015.

Farrow, Ronan, "From Aggressive Overtures to Sexual Assault: Harvey Weinstein's
Accusers Tell Their Stories," New Yorker, October 23, 2017.

Gerard, Jeremy, "Meryl Streep Roars (and Sings Lady Liberty) at Human Rights
Gala," deadline.com, February 11, 2017.

Interview with Carl Franklin.

Interview with David Hare.

Kay, Jeremy, "How Spielberg Turned Around 'The Post' in Less Than 10 Months,"
screendaily.com, February 7, 2018.

Kummer, Corby, "Streep vs. Streep," Cue, January 5, 1980.

Lang, Brent, "Patricia Arquette's Comments Draw Praise, Unleash Controversy,"
variety.com, February 23, 2015.

Lawson, Richard, "Meryl Streep's Quest to Become the Queen of August," vanity
fair.com, August 11, 2016.

Linden, Sheri, "Critic's Notebook: Is Meryl Streep Coasting with Roles Like Florence
Foster Jenkins?," hollywoodreporter.com, August 13, 2016.

McClintock, Pamela, "How 'The Post' Pulled Off Possibly the Fastest Shoot 'in the
History of the Film Industry,'" hollywoodreporter.com, February 23, 2018.

"Next Indiana Jones Might be a Woman, Says Steven Spielberg," newshub.co.nz,
September 4, 2018.

Ritman, Alex, "AFM: Meryl Streep, Hugh Grant Drama Sells Wide," hollywood
reporter.com, November 12, 2014.

Rooney, David, "'Into the Woods': Film Review," hollywoodreporter.com, December 17, 2014.

Ryzik, Melena, "Meryl Streep Does a Number on Donald Trump at Public Theater's
Gala," New York Times, June 7, 2016.

Snap Judgment (on Florence Foster Jenkins), NPR, August 1, 2014.

Solotaroff, Paul, "Trump Seriously: On the Trail with the GOP's Tough Guy," Rolling Stone, September 9, 2015.

Epilogue: A Streeping Genius

Abramowitz, Rachel, "She Has to Laugh," Los Angeles Times, November 30, 2008.

Jones, Marcus, "Meryl Streep Says It's Been Hard for Her to Be So Political Under
Trump," buzzfeednews.com, December 12, 2017.

Marcus, Bennett, "Meryl Streep Slams Walt Disney, Celebrates Emma Thompson as a 'Rabid, Man-Eating Feminist,'" vanityfair.com, January 8, 2014.

Osland, Dianne, "Meryl Streep at IU: 'I Thought I Was Too Ugly to Be an Actress,'" indianapolismonthly.com, April 17, 2014.

Transcript from 1988 Hollywood Foreign Press Association conference for *A Cry in the Dark,* courtesy of Margaret Herrick Library special collections.

INDEX

ABOUT THE AUTHOR

ERIN CARLSON is the author of *I'll Have What She's Having: How Nora Ephron's Three Iconic Films Saved the Romantic Comedy* and has covered the entertainment industry for the *Hollywood Reporter* and AP. Her work has appeared in *Glamour, Fortune,* and the *Los Angeles Times,* and she holds a masters in magazine journalism from Northwestern.

ABOUT THE ILLUSTRATOR

JUSTIN TEODORO is a New York City–based artist. Born and raised in Vancouver, British Columbia, Justin moved to NYC and graduated from the Parsons School of Design with a degree in Fashion Studies.

After building a successful career as a womenswear designer, Justin decided to merge his two passions, fashion and art, into a new path as an illustrator and artist. His work has been featured in *Vogue, Harper's Bazaar, Women's Wear Daily, Huffington Post, Glamour,* and *OUT Magazine.* As a creative collaborator and consultant, Justin works with international clients to create graphic imagery and campaigns that are infused with his unique and whimsical sensibility.

You can follow more of Justin's work on his website www.justinteodoro.com and Instagram @justinteodoro.